The Psilocybin Solution

"This book provides a clear and up-to-date picture of what goes on in the brain during the visionary psilocybin experience. The author's intrepid speculations, centering on information as the fundamental stuff of the universe, are clearly signposted. The writing is lucid and a joy to behold, an important contribution."

JEREMY NARBY, ANTHROPOLOGIST AND
AUTHOR OF *THE COSMIC SERPENT*,
INTELLIGENCE IN NATURE, AND
THE PSYCHOTROPIC MIND

"The profound experiences unlocked by the visionary psilocybin-containing mushrooms are more than a recreational holiday for the mind. They are, in fact, the key to understanding that consciousness is not an aspect of reality, it is reality itself."

DENNIS MCKENNA, PH.D, ETHNOPHARMACOLOGIST
AND COAUTHOR OF *THE INVISIBLE LANDSCAPE*

"A worthy successor to Aldous Huxley's *The Doors of Perception*, *The Psilocybin Solution* takes the reader behind the grand curtain of reality with a compelling hypothesis that approaches a unified field theory of human consciousness in an intelligent and interconnected universe."

BILL LINTON, CEO OF PROMEGA

"In this fascinating and provocative book, Simon Powell speculates on the nature of reality. He posits Nature is a deliberate and intelligently behaving system, and he proposes that psilocybin, by altering the neurochemistry of the brain in specific ways, enables novel patterns of information to emerge, allowing the psyche to become a sort of conduit to the Other. If in fact that is what actually happens, then entheogens (psychedelics) are much more important to the human species than has been realized."

DAVID E. NICHOLS, PH.D.,
PRESIDENT AND COFOUNDER OF THE
HEFFTER RESEARCH INSTITUTE

The
Psilocybin
Solution

The Role of
SACRED
MUSHROOMS
in the
QUEST FOR MEANING

SIMON G. POWELL

Park Street Press
Rochester, Vermont • Toronto, Canada

Park Street Press
One Park Street
Rochester, Vermont 05767
www.ParkStPress.com

Text stock is SFI certified

Park Street Press is a division of Inner Traditions International

Library of Congress Cataloging-in-Publication Data

Powell, Simon G.
  The psilocybin solution : the role of sacred mushrooms in the quest for meaning
/ Simon G. Powell.
       p. cm.
  Includes bibliographical references and index.
  Summary: "How psilocybin mushrooms facilitate a direct link to the wisdom of
Nature and the meaning of life"—Provided by publisher.
  ISBN 978-1-59477-405-8 (pbk.) — ISBN 978-1-59477-937-4 (ebook)
  1. Mushrooms, Hallucinogenic. 2. Psilocybin. 3. Shamanism. 4. Mushroom
culture. I. Title.
  BF209.H36P69 2011
  154.4—dc23
                                                                    2011019108

Printed and bound in the United States by Lake Book Manufacturing
The text stock is SFI certified. The Sustainable Forestry Initiative® program
promotes sustainable forest management.

10 9 8 7 6 5 4 3 2 1

Text design by Jon Desautels and layout by Priscilla Baker
This book was typeset in Garmond Premier Pro with Arial used as a display
typeface

To send correspondence to the author of this book, mail a first-class letter to the
author c/o Inner Traditions • Bear & Company, One Park Street, Rochester, VT
05767, and we will forward the communication, or contact the author through his
website at **www.thepsilocybinsolution.com**.

Dedicated to my friend Michael Montebello,
who supported me on the way

My plea to scientists, administrators, and politicians who
may read my words is this: look again at psilocybin, do
not confuse it with the other psychedelics, and realize
that it is a phenomenon unto itself with an enormous
potential for transforming human beings—not simply
transforming the people who take it, but transforming
society in the way that an art movement, a mathematical
understanding, or a scientific breakthrough transforms
society. It holds the possibility of transforming the entire
species simply by virtue of the information that comes
through it.

TERENCE MCKENNA,
THE ARCHAIC REVIVAL

Disclaimer

This book is intended for informational and educational purposes only. The legal situation concerning psychoactive fungi varies from country to country and is subject to unpredictable and sometimes ruthless change. Indeed, many countries forbid the possession of such fungi even if they are to be found growing naturally in the environment. Thus, no clear and concise guidelines can be given here regarding issues of legality. Readers, should they wish to explore the contents of this book in a more direct fashion, must do so entirely at their own risk. Both the author and the publisher can accept no responsibility for the actions of any reader. For the record, the bulk of this book was written and researched at a time when fresh, unprocessed psilocybin fungi were legal to possess and consume in the United Kingdom.

Contents

Foreword

Graham Hancock

The year 2011 marked the fortieth anniversary of the so-called War on Drugs, which was declared by Richard M. Nixon in June 1971. It is appropriate that this misguided, morally bankrupt "war" of harassment against a sizeable minority within society—those adults who choose to alter their own consciousness through the use of drugs—was the initiative of one of the most dishonest, violent, and authoritarian presidents America has ever had the misfortune to elect, a man who stands enthroned by history as the absolute epitome of morally bankrupt leadership. Forty years on, it is our shared misfortune, despite the opprobrium that rightly surrounds Nixon's name, that his "War on Drugs" is still being fought not only in the United States but throughout the world—for where America led in 1971, all other members of the United Nations swiftly followed. Armed bureaucracies were established to police the consciousness of citizens and given powers to break down the doors of drug users in the middle of the night, confiscate their property, send them to jail, humiliate them, and generally ruin their lives. In some countries they can even be executed. All this has been accompanied by years of glib propaganda, paid for with large sums of public money, designed to convince us that drugs have such evil and degrading effects, and are so lacking in any redeemable qualities, that those who use them "deserve" to be persecuted and punished for their "sins."

It is a witch hunt, a moral panic, with nothing rational about it at all.

Indeed the very societies that attempt most vigorously to suppress various drugs, and in which users are subject to the most stringent penalties, have seen a continuous increase in the per capita consumption of these drugs over the past forty years. This is tacitly admitted by the huge armed bureaucracies of the drug war that every year demand more and more public money to fund their suppressive activities; if the suppression were working, one would expect their budgets to go down, not up.

Worse—and we may all see the effects—the criminalization of drug use has empowered and enriched a global criminal underworld by guaranteeing that it is the only source of supply of these drugs. We have, in effect, delivered that large minority within our societies that feels the need to experience altered states of consciousness into the hands of the very worst mobsters and sleazeballs on the planet. Those who wish to buy drugs have no choice but to approach and associate with violent and greedy criminals. And because the proceeds from illegal drug sales are so enormous, we are all caught up in the inevitable consequences of turf wars and murders among the gangs and cartels competing in this blackest of black markets.

It should be completely obvious to our governments, after forty years of dismal failure to suppress illegal drug use, that their policies in this area do not work and will never work. It should be completely obvious, a simple logical step, to realize that by decriminalizing drug use and making the supply of all drugs available to those adults who wish to use them through legal and properly regulated channels we could, at a stroke, put out of business the immense criminal enterprise that presently flourishes on the supply of illegal drugs.

It should be obvious, but somehow it is not.

Instead the powers that be continue to pursue the same harsh and cruel policies to which they have been wedded since 1971, ever seeking to strengthen and reinforce them rather than to replace them with something better. Indeed the only "change" that the drug warriors have consistently sought across the decades has been to demand ever more money, ever more surveillance technology, ever more arms, and ever more draconian legislative powers to break into homes, confiscate property, and deprive otherwise law-abiding citizens of liberty. In the process we have seen our once free and upstanding societies, which used to respect individual choice, conscience, and adult responsibility above all else, slide remorselessly down the slippery slope that leads to the police state. And all this is being done in our name, with our money, by our own governments, to "save us from ourselves"!

In such a climate riddled with propaganda and disinformation, overshadowed by fear and suspicion, where users of illegal drugs are vigorously persecuted by public agencies, it is very difficult, and takes courage, to speak out about the possibly beneficial, mind-expanding, eye-opening, and consciousness-enhancing effects of certain illegal drugs. That, however, is precisely what Simon G. Powell has done in *The Psilocybin Solution,* where he makes the case for nothing less than the systematic, targeted use of psilocybin and other natural psychedelics to explore the fundamental mysteries of our own existence.

Psilocybin, Powell believes, has the power to open our consciousness to the communications of "the Other," which he ultimately defines as the vast, guiding intelligence that underlies all of Nature and that has harnessed the entire universe to its cause—"a sentient and intentional agency made of information whose presence and teachings await us." And he adds: "When one has encountered the Other through the visionary effects of a strong dose of psilocybin mushrooms it becomes quite evident that, whatever the Other's ultimate intent, consciousness is an essential part of the plan."

There's a widespread assumption that the brain makes consciousness the way a factory makes cars. But there's no proof that this is actually how things work. The brain could equally well be a receiver, or transceiver, that manifests consciousness on the physical plane. We simply do not know how these few pounds of jelly inside our skulls allow us to appreciate a sunset or a symphony, or experience love or joy. It's the greatest mystery of science.

Into this mystery Powell steps with the radical suggestion that everything is information and that all the information accumulated by the universe in the fourteen billion years since the big bang is best understood as a sort of gigantic computation intentionally designed to result, somewhere, sometime, in the evolution of consciousness—just as it has done on earth. Most proponents of intelligent design focus on the apparent irreducible complexity of specific organs or organisms—a losing proposition, since evolutionary theory explains complexity quite well without having to call for a designer. But Powell focuses much more plausibly on the grand context in which evolution unfolds. That context, he contends, can only be the work of an intelligence of a far higher order than our own that wilfully endowed the universe with precursor conditions and laws of physics capable of nurturing the eventual evolution of consciousness.

These are provocative and powerful ideas that contribute to a growing debate in science and philosophy about the mysterious nature of reality. And while Powell's thesis may be controversial, he is surely right that the targeted use of psilocybin and related entheogens offers our best hope for solving the mystery. These substances must be demythologized as the folk devils of the war on drugs and welcomed as valuable allies in our search for meaning in the universe. In precisely those areas of inquiry where science and all its instruments fail us we are fortunate indeed that "the sacred mushroom now beckons."

Graham Hancock, born in Edinburgh, Scotland, is a British writer and journalist. His books, including *Fingerprints of the Gods, The Sign and The Seal,* and *Heaven's Mirror,* have sold more than five million copies worldwide and have been translated into twenty-seven languages. His public lectures, radio, and television appearances have allowed his ideas to reach a vast audience, identifying him as an unconventional thinker who raises controversial questions about humanity's past.

Preface

This book has passed through many hands and been subject to many revisions. To be sure, it has been a very long and laborious struggle to reach this stage. Now that the book has finally been accepted for publication, I should say a few brief words about its admittedly unusual content. Essentially, I present the reader with a series of bold ideas and concepts concerning the nature of the user-friendly Universe in which we find ourselves. In particular, I explore the significance of consciousness within the Universe, for consciousness is the very core of our being. And it is precisely the very core of our being that psychoactive fungi can so dramatically illuminate. This may explain why such fungi were more often than not venerated and deified by those historical cultures that employed them.

I have tried, to the best of my abilities, to make sense of my own personal experiences with one particular psychoactive fungus native to Great Britain (at a time, I might add, when possession of this mushroom in its fresh state was completely legal). These experiences involved dramatic changes in consciousness and the acquisition of what seemed to be a new kind of knowledge. The experiences were generally so profound as to make it difficult to integrate them into more traditional modes of thought. And yet it is undoubtedly this assimilation of what would appear to be higher knowledge that is so crucial if these kinds of experience are to have a lasting, positive effect. Hence my writing of this book. However, it would be ludicrous for me to suggest that I have written the "truth," for truth is something that must be experienced personally. At heart, then, this book consists of a series of provisional hypotheses about the meaning of life, which have been formulated in the wake of certain extraordinary states of mind. The experiences themselves were real and were thus "true," whereas, of course, my interpretation of them might well be in error.

One thing of which I am wholly convinced and that I should make clear at the outset is that the ingestion of traditionally deified plants and fungi can, in the long run, afford a benign change in our understanding and conception of Nature. It is evident that at the current time our relationship with the natural world is so alienated and so out of balance that only radical means may prevent global catastrophe. In this sense the sacred mushroom is, at least potentially, a very powerful eco-psychological catalyst able to heal our relations with the rest of the web of life. Of this, no one should be fearful.

SIMON G. POWELL
LONDON

A Question of Life and Death

It might be a decidedly curious way to begin a book, but humor me and ask yourself the following question: Who or what killed Einstein? What entity or force ended the life of perhaps the greatest mind of our era, that scientist whose name is synonymous with intelligence? Well, it was clearly not a butler who did it, nor, as far as we know, was it an assassin belonging to some sinister governmental agency. To put it bluntly, it was *the reality process* that killed the great Einstein.

Although this deceptively simple answer may seem reminiscent of a wry Woody Allen joke, what I mean to convey is that all of us, regardless of age, sex, race, or creed, are born out of, and are destined to die within, a massive ongoing process consisting not only of the evolution of life on Earth but of the evolution of the Universe as a whole. It is this relentless and all-encompassing process within which we are all so intimately embedded that we term *reality*. We might also refer to this process as *Nature*. Thus, another obvious way of answering my peculiar question is to say that natural causes killed Einstein. This means, in the final analysis, that Nature birthed Einstein, gave him seventy-six years of existence, and then summarily dissolved him.

Call it Nature or call it reality, either way they are but small words for an immense process that flows inexorably onward. Whatever one's preferred term, it most certainly is a process, a word whose Latin roots mean "to advance" or "move forward," and there can be little doubt that reality is, at heart, a singularly vast process that has been running nonstop for some fourteen or so billion years. Not bad. Pretty impressive, in fact.

So what? you might ask. Well, one of the prime functions of this book is to explore and hopefully elucidate the ultimate point of this creative but fatal reality we find ourselves in. To put it bluntly once more, are we biologically woven into a pointless accident, or is reality somehow directed? This is quite some question, perhaps the most profound we can ask in our short earthly sojourn, and one we know to have crossed Einstein's astute mind. Consider, for example, a famous remark attributed to Einstein in which he claimed that the most incomprehensible thing about our Universe is its comprehensibility. What he meant to convey by this rather sublime assertion (of which there are many paraphrased versions) is that it is truly astonishing that Nature makes sense, whatever part of it we care to study. Law and order are everywhere, whether in the domain of physics, chemistry, biology, or cosmology. Moreover, Nature has somehow conspired, through a process of organic evolution, to build biological brains endowed with minds capable of comprehending physical, chemical, biological, and cosmological phenomena. Why? Why exactly should Nature be that way? Why should the Universe be endowed with the creative capacity to construct millions of spiral galaxies and millions of delicate spiral seashells, as well as the human brain with its ability to perceive and understand those things? Could reality have been otherwise?

Whatever the case, should we believe the reality process to be essentially a mindless accident that just happens to be blessed with extraordinary powers of creativity, then we might conceive ourselves to be hapless mortal prisoners entrapped in the process. Or, if we instead believe reality to be purposeful and meaningful in some way, then we might consider ourselves fortunate functional components of the process. Whatever you may have read, let me assure you that this issue has most definitely not been settled. It is neither completely obvious that the Universe is a purely accidental affair nor is it clear that the Universe is purposeful (or at least one can say that the jury is still out). Neither science nor religion—arguably the two dominant strands of thinking that tend to confront the fundamental nature of reality—has absolutely conclusive evidence at hand.

But if we look to science for clues—because science has enjoyed more evident practical success than religion—then clearly over the past three hundred or so years since the time of Newton and the development of classical physics, science has made great headway in elucidating how reality works; not why it works, but how. Because the process of reality is so obligingly comprehensible, science has enjoyed a dialogue with Nature in which operating principles have been ascertained by means of scientific experimentation. In this way, scientists like physicists, chemists, biologists, and cosmologists have acquired a wealth of information concerning the subatomic, chemical, biological, and astronomical aspects of reality and have subsequently built elaborate models detailing them. However, how one *interprets* the language of Nature, how one translates the data collated by science into a theory about the ultimate nature of reality, is a subjective affair very much up for debate. Thus, our big opening question awaits a satisfactory answer, and Einstein's killer remains very much on the loose.

At heart, if we wish to know what, if anything, the reality process is really up to, we can do little more than assess all the relevant information revealed by science and all the intuitive wisdom accrued through personal experience, and then attempt to form a viable theoretical overview. Absolute truths, it would seem, are all but inaccessible, and thus the true nature of Einstein's creator and killer might forever remain a mystery. But, whatever we believe about the reality process, we are, willy-nilly, most definitely all "in it together" whether we like it or not, and it is for this terrifying or wonderful reason that I have taken it upon myself to explore by any means necessary just what it is exactly that is driving reality, whether the driver is blind or has vision.

Before I reveal to you my particular mode of investigation, let us briefly review what most of the science community believe to be the essential meaning of existence. As it is, current scientific thought definitely veers toward a purposeless and mechanistic account of the

Universe, an account that is, with all due respect, depressing and devoid of spirit. Although our scientific knowledge of the world reveals its microscopic and macroscopic complexity and highlights the universal mathematical precision of things like physical law, this knowledge has in effect reduced the Universe to a kind of pointless mechanism devoid of high intelligence apart from our own. Everything from a cell to an orchid to the emergence of our species is generally reduced to a set of *merelys*. Indeed, the more successful a scientist is in reducing whatever facet of Nature he or she is working on to "merely this" or "merely that," the more warmly is that scientist's work received. To argue otherwise by, say, suggesting that Nature is purposeful in some way, is to ostracize oneself from mainstream science. Certainly it is the case that nobody will win a Nobel Prize for planting purpose in Nature, despite the uplifting appeal that such an intentional theory of reality would undoubtedly carry.

But is it valid to build a new and overtly optimistic theory concerning the ultimate nature of reality solely because our current theories are not uplifting enough? Obviously not. A new theory like this would represent nothing more than whim, a psychological artifice formulated solely because the consensus truth about reality is perceived to be too gloomy and too unpalatable to swallow. Indeed, to enthusiastically infer, say, that conscious existence has some kind of special purpose in the reality process, that consciousness is somehow at the center of an intentional Universe, smacks of the prescientific beliefs confined to the pages of history books, to a time when supernatural thinking governed human minds. This kind of anthropocentric religious ideology has now been all but crushed by rational scientific thought, which firmly places our kind on a mere satellite circling a mere star among billions. We are no more than the product of evolution, one particular species out of countless millions, whose only real claim to fame is our big brains with their ability to think and direct complex behavior.

Over a few centuries, in particular from the seminal publication of Charles Darwin's *The Origin of Species* in 1859 (which can be cited as a definitive turning point in our concepts of humankind's place in

Nature), the ideological pendulum has swung 180 degrees, from a position in which humanity was the crowning glory of creation to a position in which we are but speckish organic bystanders in an essentially pointless universal exercise of physics and DNA-orchestrated biochemistry. Life is accidental, mostly hard, and then you die—a tough fact best swallowed, perhaps, with a large brandy.

To revert to the more ancient view in which life, and in particular human consciousness, is considered to be somehow significant therefore seems completely out of the question, a futile move serving only to stir up false hope in a Universe that basically "just don't give a damn." This is especially so if our sole motivation is a dislike of current scientific reasoning. Only if a grand optimistic view of existence were driven primarily by direct conscious experience could it possibly hope to possess validity. And not just wishy-washy conscious experience either. The experience, if it were to bear upon notions of the ultimate nature of reality, would have to be remarkably compelling and potentially accessible to all. It would have to provide *incontrovertible evidence* that we have some significant role to play in the reality process. But could a direct conscious experience really afford a deep insight into our big question?

Well, if we keep in mind that science proceeds through verifiable experimentation in which information is gained through conscious experience and that we depend upon such experience to build our models of reality, then it would indeed appear to be a possibility. In other words, new forms of conscious experience might well offer us a solution to the most perplexing questions that the Universe presents us with. Which brings me to the central fact permeating this book, namely that *conscious experience is entirely mutable.* And herein lies hope for a new optimistic theory concerning the significance of human consciousness within the reality process.

The mutability of consciousness: What does such a concept imply? First of all, we should consider the fact that consciousness, whatever it is exactly, is the "stuff" that mediates all science and, for that matter, all types of reasoning and all of our theories about the world. Whatever a person's view on the meaning of existence, it is through conscious experience that all views are formed. Consciousness can therefore be understood as the very ground of our being, the "X factor" that makes us what we are. In order to become fully engaged in the important point I am here trying to express, consider the following simple thought experiment.

Imagine, if you will, that all scientists wore identical spectacles and that these spectacles determined the perceptual view of the things being scrutinized by the scientists. All the data amassed by these scientists would be related in some intimate way to the effects of their spectacles, since all their perceptions will have passed through the self-same lenses. Now, it isn't pushing credulity too far to suggest that the scientists would do well at some point—possibly over their morning coffee break, or perhaps at a stage when their theories are proving to be inadequate—to reflect on the characteristics of their shared state of "bespectacledness." In other words, it would be quite a breakthrough for these scientists to suddenly cease their traditional research in order to focus on the nature of the factor mediating their research, namely, their glasses. What they would soon come to realize is that their glasses represent a subject worthy of analysis because they are, in a real sense, the closest thing to them.

This imaginary situation is not unlike the real world, only this time it is our consciousness, or rather our *state of consciousness,* as opposed to glasses, through which we gain knowledge and experience. For simplicity's sake, we can call this "normal consciousness," a kind of shared lens through which science and scientific interpretation proceeds. Thus, it is quite legitimate to reflect on this "lens of normal consciousness" and ask whether, perhaps, it could be altered or be enhanced. In short, one might well wonder if it is possible to improve on the lens of normal consciousness and attain a state of mind in which the essence of Nature is more clearly discernible.

Although one cannot escape these rather odd facts about consciousness, science has had little to say about it, preferring to place the human mind safely outside of the theoretical picture of reality. Put simply, the phenomenon of human consciousness is a scientifically slippery and vexing anomaly that is in stark contrast to the more empirically approachable phenomena of, say, stars and molecules. Yet since we are conscious beings whose minds literally interface with the external world, then until we understand the nature of the "mind-stuff" carried by our brains, we will not be able to fully comprehend the nature of the reality process. This must be so because, as we have just established, consciousness is itself as much a part of reality as are the things perceived by consciousness, such as the aforementioned stars and molecules. Indeed, if we were not conscious beings, we would not be in a position to seek explanations about the nature of reality in the first place. It is only because we are conscious and because we stand in a mindful relationship to the reality process that we feel compelled to account for our existence. Our conscious minds long for knowledge about the Universe so that we might understand both our place within the totality of existence and the natural forces that led to our being here. Hence the enterprise of science (which means "to know").

Now, as I will show throughout this book, consciousness is mutable because it is mediated by chemistry, which is to say that mutable or transformable chemical processes underlie consciousness. In effect, this means that our normal ways of thinking and feeling are constrained by the brain's chemical hardware (or wetware, as it is sometimes called in neuromantic circles). It is therefore conceivable that certain aspects of the world remain hidden because of the limitations of our everyday type of consciousness. Thus, if we truly wish to grapple with the ultimate questions concerning the nature of our existence, then it is surely worthwhile to seek out new forms of perception, forms, for instance, in which all of perceived reality is grasped at once, holistically as it were, and not in the piecemeal fashion of science, which, it must be said, tends to focus on isolated parts of the world.

Historically speaking, altered forms of consciousness in which the whole sense of reality is immediately discerned and felt in a kind of joyous flash of insight are the sole domain of mystics, those persons who claim, rather controversially and often with alarming vigor, to have directly experienced "ultimate truths." Many mystics and religious visionaries have employed various techniques with which to foster their insights—like fasting, yoga, meditation, perceptual isolation, and so forth—and these disciplines are known to alter brain chemistry. This again testifies to the fact that the normal human brain is somehow constrained in its mindful activity and that the chemical system that does the constraining can be overcome. For most of us, such esoteric endeavors, regardless of whether they do actually yield valid knowledge, are perhaps a little beyond our normal way of life, and we might therefore wish to stick with less suspect nonmystical science for answers to the big questions about reality.

However, there is another, more immediate route to transcendental knowledge, as it is termed in philosophy. This route involves *the deliberate ingestion of naturally occurring entheogenic (sacred) plant and fungal alkaloids in order to access information inaccessible to the normal mind.* Traditionally, this little-documented enterprise is engaged in by shamans, or native healers, who often employ entheogenic flora to gain transcendental knowledge, which they utilize for the benefit of their culture (note that the term *entheogenic,* which I use throughout this book, means the "generation of the divine within").

To this day, aboriginal shamans in places like Amazonia and Mexico still utilize the powerful effects of indigenous entheogenic plants and fungi to fulfill their shamanic healing role within their native culture. So strong can the revelational effects of such plants and fungi be upon the human psyche that they generally come to be deified. Earth's entheogens become a sacred link to divinity, almost as if they represent an organic modem connected directly to the realm of the gods. This was what luminary Aldous Huxley was alluding to some sixty years ago in his cult classic *The Doors of Perception,* in which he poetically describes the fantastic perceptual enhancement that accompanied his ingestion of mescaline, an entheogenic alkaloid derived from the peyote cactus.

It is precisely because entheogenic plants and fungi facilitate states of consciousness in which Nature is perceived in a radically new way that makes them useful epistemological tools (epistemology is the study of knowledge). But, more than this, these kinds of illuminating changes in consciousness *also offer us a way to understand consciousness itself,* since one can analyze the subtle chemical changes accompanying the altered state of mind and then attempt to use such data to comprehend how normal consciousness works. Thus, the virtue of investigating the effects of entheogenic substances is twofold.

First, through their dramatic action within the brain we might come to perceive Nature in an enhanced way. Second, we might come to understand more about the underlying chemistry that is bound up with normal conscious processes, that is, the modus operandi of entheogenic substances reveals the delicate chemical mechanisms that govern consciousness and our perceptions of reality. If, through the use of entheogens, we can enhance our understanding of the interface between the mind and the "world out there," then we shall know more clearly what consciousness is, how it is formed, and how it can come to experience transcendence. And if the transcendental information accessed in the altered state of consciousness has any truth value—and native shamans all testify to this—then we will be one step closer to an overall conception of what is driving reality. Only then might we apprehend Einstein's creator and killer, for then we would have begun to establish its ultimate nature. At least it sounds promising.

It is my contention throughout this book that naturally occurring entheogenic plants and fungi are indeed the key to solving the twin mysteries of consciousness and reality. Once ingested, entheogens are intimately involved with the bridge between consciousness and the world around us. The numinous experience that entheogenic agents can induce, no matter how bizarre it might appear in the context of the mundane world and no matter what brain mechanism underlies it, is a real thing; it exists, potentially at any rate. As we shall see, the archetypal tale of transcendence reported by entheogen-using shamans results from direct and verifiable experience.

It is on the basis of such verifiable experience that this book rests. The apparent capacity of the human mind to transcend "normal" reality demands investigation, for it must surely be a tenable step toward reclaiming significance for the existence of human consciousness in the Universe. However, if such an enterprise is spurious and built of no more than ephemeral imagination, then it will only point to the fact that the human imagination under certain chemical circumstances is extraordinarily creative. But it is my belief that entheogenic agents unleash a form of consciousness better able to grapple with the ultimate questions about the reality process than our normal frames of awareness, that they truly offer us a glimpse of some great meaning hitherto the sole domain of the shaman and the mystic, a meaning only alluded to in the conventional religions of the world.

As I see it, if we are genuinely interested in the function of the Universe and the function of human consciousness within it, then we are obliged to follow all and any paths of inquiry. I would suggest that the untrammeled path laid out by entheogenic plants and fungi is, perhaps, the most viable route to evidence that indicates that human consciousness is central to reality. If, instead, this unusual path should prove to lead nowhere, then we may have to accept that human life and human consciousness are devoid of any real purpose, a view proffered, it must be said, by all manner of "experts." This book can therefore be read as an alternative, user-friendly guide to the nature of reality, the implications of which herald all manner of good news. Very good news indeed.

So stand by for a controversial tale of a recently rediscovered entheogenic substance native to most parts of the Earth's Temperate Zone. And brace yourself for the astonishing insights into mind and Nature that this substance provokes. Fasten your seat belts, because if I have done my job correctly, you are poised for a roller coaster ride into the very heart of the mystery of existence. As the chapters unfold we will gradually climb up to a peak, from which point we will be propelled through exhilarating vistas in which the significance of consciousness is breathtakingly apparent. By the end of the book, I hope to have shown, beyond any reasonable doubt, that the reality process is essentially *smart* through and through and that we conscious beings have a privileged role to play in its intentional unfolding. I assure you that this will become crystal clear as the chapters progress.

ONE

Sacred Ground

On May 13, 1957, the well-read pages of *Life* magazine carried a ground-breaking article that was to profoundly alter the West's attitude toward the wilder side of the natural world. Here was the first-ever personal account written by a Westerner describing the extraordinary psychological effects induced by a mushroom deified and ritually worshipped by native Mexicans. Consumption of the sacred Mexican mushroom allowed one to contact the gods, experience profound visions, and gain mystical knowledge. Or at least these were the most extravagant of the native Mexican beliefs about the mushroom that were reported by anthropologists during the first half of the twentieth century.

In pre-Columbian times the mysterious mushroom had been known by the Aztecs as "God's Flesh," testifying to its divine potency. Such veneration ensured the mushroom a cult status among native Mexicans, despite the violent cultural upheavals wrought by the Spanish Conquest in the sixteenth century. Thus, although the once-mighty Aztec culture was eventually destroyed, the sacred mushroom continued to be used in and around Mexico throughout the Spanish occupation. Yet despite the legendary effects of this peculiar species of fungus, it wasn't until the middle of the twentieth century that an outside investigator finally consumed the mushroom and hence verified its alleged spiritual potential.

Transmitted solely by word of mouth from the time of the Spanish Conquest, detailed knowledge of the revered mushroom had lain principally in the hands of jealously guarding shamans or native healers, who were loath to disclose their botanical secrets to outsiders. They feared, perhaps justifiably, that the sacred mushroom's supernatural power would be diminished or be used profanely should the untrustworthy white folk gain full admittance into its living mystery. Therefore the 1957 *Life* article in which the secret of the mushroom was openly exposed dramatically symbolized the West's bypassing of this long-standing cultural security system. The sacred mushroom had been forcibly plucked from its localized shamanic niche and was now being presented to the Western world in the form of mass-circulated print, with color photographs and specimen drawings to boot.

Despite exposure to the prying eyes of the West, the status of the Mexican mushroom remained as lofty and as tantalizingly ethereal as ever, more so even since the Western psyche was just as stunned and awed by its transcendental visionary effects as were local Mexicans. In the following decades a psychedelic mushroom cloud of fascination would slowly expand and loom beyond Mexico, eventually extending its magical influence as far away as Europe, but at this initial stage in its sudden growth, the strange mushroom remained a purely Mexican phenomenon.

On the front cover of that auspicious edition of *Life* magazine, the simple headline read "The Discovery of Mushrooms That Cause Strange Visions," a rather unusual claim from such a traditionally conservative magazine. The article was included as part of *Life* magazine's series of *Great Adventures* and was written by R. Gordon Wasson, vice-president of a Wall Street banking firm, who, with the aid of his wife, Valentina, had spent some thirty years of part-time research creating a new scientific discipline— ethnomycology, the study of the cultural and historical use of fungi.

Ethnomycology is clearly specialized and seemingly remote from the affairs of modern culture. It was only through the dedicated efforts of the Wassons—who learned of the sacred Mexican mushrooms, sought to find them, and experienced them firsthand—that psilocybin (the as-yet unnamed active constituent of the mushroom, pronounced silla-SIGH-bin) came to the attention of the West. Once the sacred Mexican mushrooms were discovered, ethnomycological science suddenly acquired a distinctly mystical edge, allowing it to breach the domains of religion and psychology. It also provided a new impetus to humankind's enduring quest to access transcendental knowledge, and there can be no doubt that Wasson's discovery and vivid description of the effects of psilocybin were crucial in generating the subsequent cultural wave of psychedelic experimentation that soon followed in the 1960s. Moreover, as we shall eventually see, the mushroom also reveals itself as the key to unveiling the secrets of consciousness and the hidden riches of Nature. Theophany, mind, and reality: these three most profound of topics are all met in some way through use of the mushroom. But, before we jump into the deep end, who, pray, was this Wasson fellow, this financier-cum-adventurer? And how had he come to penetrate the Earth's secret psychedelic dimension? Who was he to bring news of sacred fungi to the attention of the Western world?

In effect, Wasson's *Life* article was timed to coincide with the release of his magnum opus two-volume book *Mushrooms, Russia and History*, cowritten with his wife, Valentina. This work fully reveals the extent of Wasson's long-standing interest in the cultural use of fungi and how he finally came to be at the door of perception marked *psilocybin*.

With only 512 handcrafted copies luxuriously bound and printed, *Mushrooms, Russia and History* stands as a rare piece of art. Indeed, by the late 1970s its value had reached some $2,500, making it the most valuable book in existence at that time whose author was still alive. It is a highly polished book, written in a lively style that reflects the love of ethnomycology borne by the Wassons. It represents the distilled wisdom drawn from their extensive studies into the role that various species of mushroom played in different cultures, and it culminates in their discovery of the sacred mushroom ceremonies still being conducted in Mexico, a discovery important enough to warrant the further account in the more accessible pages of *Life* magazine.

A Trail Begins

The event that originally launched the Wassons on their mushroom crusade was simple, almost trivial, yet it was enough to provoke them into a three-decade-long bout of invaluable research. The Wassons married in 1927, and one day during their honeymoon they decided to take a casual stroll in the Catskill Mountains of New York. At some stage, Valentina, who was Russian by birth, stopped to pick wild mushrooms, delighting in such a fortuitous find. Her husband, on the other hand, being true to his Anglo-Saxon heritage, was appalled at his wife's avid interest in lethal fungal abominations, especially since she planned to cook and eat them later. After all, were not all fungal growths poisonous toadstools to be avoided like the plague? With growing dismay, Gordon Wasson imagined himself waking up the next morning with a corpse instead of a wife.

This pronounced and deep-rooted difference in attitude between the two of them over the culinary virtues of fungi led them to suspect a cultural rift, that there were mycophobic peoples (sensible mushroom haters like the Anglo-Saxons) and mycophilic peoples (reckless mushroom aficionados like the Russians). Furthermore, the Wassons reasoned that there must be a historical reason for these diametrically opposed traditions, due not to something like food availability, but rather to cultural and psychological factors. Thus began the Wassons' academic quest to explore this strange cultural anomaly. From the start both figured that religion somehow played a causal role.

Their intuition proved correct. Research soon unearthed the Siberian cultural history of the *Amanita muscaria* mushroom, also known as fly agaric, that extraordinary bright red and white-spotted autumnal fungus found throughout the Northern Hemisphere and often charmingly depicted in the illustrations adorning the pages of children's books. Indeed, it has been suggested that Lewis Carroll was influenced by knowledge of the Siberian use of the fly agaric and used the information to great effect in his book *Alice's Adventures in Wonderland,* in which, you might recall, Alice nibbles on a mushroom that subsequently alters her size.

As we shall see, compared with the psilocybin mushroom, the fly agaric's psychoactivity rates a poor second, though it is potentially entheogenic due to the presence of an alkaloid named muscimol. Despite muscimol's entheogenic inferiority to psilocybin, the cultural role and use of the fly agaric mushroom among Siberian shamans is beyond dispute, and the Wassons uncovered a wealth of literature testifying to this fact. The fly agaric mushroom proved to be a link to primitive religion just as the Wassons had originally foreseen, and it soon became clear to them that psychoactive fungi were no small feature of cultural history.

Echoes of a Shamanic Beat

Since the time of Tsar Peter the Great (1672–1725), the Kamchatka Peninsula, the easternmost part of Russian Siberia, was visited by travelers, political exiles, explorers, fur traders, and anthropologists. All were to bear witness to the nomadic reindeer herders who ritually ingested fly agaric mushrooms (their only intoxicant) in order to obtain contact with the spiritual dimension. The word *shaman* itself derives from the Siberian Tungus *saman,* which means "diviner," "magician," "doctor," "creator of ecstasy," "the mediator between the human world and the supernatural world."

The Siberian fly agaric user would sun-dry the mushrooms and later ingest them either alone or mixed with milk or water. If taken alone, the mushroom would first be moistened in the mouths of women, who would produce a kind of pellet for the shaman to swallow.

The effects of consuming this mushroom included convulsions, delirium, visual hallucinations, perceptual distortions of size, feelings of superhuman strength, and a perceived contact with a numinous dimension, this last effect being the most important for the practicing shaman, whose predominant function was to access the spiritual realm to attain supramundane knowledge for the good health of his or her tribe.

The most bizarre aspect of this shamanic tradition, however, was the habit of urine drinking. Somehow, the Siberians discovered that the active ingredient of the mushroom passed through the body without being metabolized and that drinking fly-agaric-spiked urine could prolong intoxication. Possibly the Siberians learned of this odd fact by observing reindeer, which not only reputedly eat the fly agaric themselves with much gusto, but also have an equal passion for human urine, so much so that Siberian reindeer herders considered it dangerous to pee out in the open!

The rather disturbing and unpalatable practice of drinking psychoactive urine attained great significance in Wasson's later work in the 1960s, as urine drinking is mentioned in the Rig-Veda, the ancient religious scripture of India. Written in Sanskrit and derived from the oral traditions of the Indo-Europeans who migrated down into the Indus Valley some three and a half thousand years ago, the Rig-Veda eventually went on to influence the development of Hinduism.

Of the one thousand holy hymns in the Rig-Veda, more than one hundred are dedicated solely to the divine plant *Soma* and its spectacular psychological effects. Because urine drinking is clearly alluded to in these hymns deifying Soma, Wasson came to the conclusion that the fly agaric mushroom was the sacred Soma worshipped by the ancient Indo-Europeans. Indeed, in parts of India, followers of the Vedic tradition still perform a religious ceremony in which Soma is ingested, only they now utilize an inactive surrogate species of plant. Wasson's identification of Soma was, at the time he made the claim, one of only a handful of serious attempts to explore and name the legendary Soma plant. To this day his identification is considered plausible by many Vedic scholars.

Mushroom Lore

The shamanic use of fly agaric mushrooms by primitive Siberians seemed to date far back in history, as various legends spoke of its mythical origins. For instance, a Koryak legend tells of a hero named Big Raven who was able to attain immense strength by eating spirits given to him by the god Vahiyinin—the god of existence. By spitting upon the earth, Vahiyinin caused the necessary spirits to grow, these being fly agaric mushrooms with their ability to provide supernatural strength and wisdom.

The Wassons theorized that it was this archaic shamanic practice of fly agaric ingestion, so well reflected in legend and mythology, that eventually led to the mycophobic pre-Christian taboos against eating mushrooms, which were still evidently shared by most of the peoples living around the shores of the North Sea. In other words, because the fly agaric mushroom was used mainly by shamans in a ritual context, cultural injunctions and taboos would conceivably have evolved to stop others wantonly utilizing its strange power. Or, it is just as likely that through migrations and invasions, misinformation spread regarding the true nature of the mushroom's effects. Through such typical cultural mechanisms as these, the psychoactive fly agaric mushroom gradually came to attain a mythical status, guaranteeing it cultural immortality as it progressed as the stuff of legend from generation to generation.

The shamanic use of fly agaric diffused out from Russia, and while some peoples gradually came to eschew the mushroom, others embraced its effects. Not only did the Aryan people who migrated down into the Indus Valley thirty-five hundred years ago bring with them their religious cult of Soma, later still, approximately 1000 B.C., we find artistic representations of mushrooms on Swedish, Norwegian, and Danish Bronze Age objects. On bronze artifacts like razors are mushroom motifs (generally stylized cross-sectional views of a mushroom) that depict the mushroom in a way that suggests that it was an object of worship. Because the fly agaric mushroom abounds in Scandinavia, these motifs are thought to represent a fly-agaric-worshipping cult similar to those of Siberia.

Apart from Siberian folklore, many European folktales testify to the enigma of the fly agaric mushroom, providing an echo of the distant cultural interconnections of the past. Stories arising from the region once known as Yugoslavia take the mushroom's supernatural origin back to the time of pre-Christian Nature gods. A legend relates that Votan, chief of all the gods and a potent magician and healer, was riding his magical horse through the countryside when demons suddenly appeared and started chasing him. As he fled, his horse galloped so fast that flecks of bloodied foam flew from its mouth. Wherever this bloody foam fell, fly agarics sprang up.

Hungarians once called the fly agaric *boland gamba* or the "mad mushroom." Austrians and Germans used to speak of the "fool's mushroom" and were wont to respond to peculiar behavior with the phrase "have you eaten crazy mushrooms?"

The Wassons also analyzed the vast array of words used to describe mushrooms in different cultures and the latent metaphors that these words conveyed; words like *toadstool,* for instance, which links the toad to the mushroom, the toad being a creature much maligned in myth and folklore. The Wassons also conjectured that the *fly* in *fly agaric* was not a reference to its supposed insecticidal effect; rather, the common insect used to be associated with demonic power (Beelzebub is "Lord of the Flies") and was thus fearfully associated with the mysterious mushroom.

In short, the Wassons uncovered a vast cultural diffusion of mushroom lore indicative of a common origin. The psychoactive fly agaric mushroom seemed most likely to be the instigator. Wasson later summed up his views in the following way in his book *Soma: Divine Mushroom of Immortality.*

> Death will come if the layman presumes to eat the forbidden fruit, the Fruit of Knowledge, the Divine Mushroom of Immortality that the . . . poets of the Rig-Veda celebrated. The fear of this "death" has lived on as an emotional residue, long after the shaman and his religion have faded from memory, and here is the explanation for the mycophobia that has prevailed throughout northern Europe, in the Germanic and Celtic worlds.[1]

At this point the Wassons might well have ended their mycological investigations, an interesting enough climax since they had left the fungal world and ventured into the domain of primitive religion. The plot, however, was going to thicken as the fly agaric became overshadowed by the far more powerful figure of the psilocybin mushroom, a mushroom whose living mystery Wasson would eventually confront within the inner sanctums of his soul.

Intimations of a Sacred Mexican Mushroom

In 1952 an acquaintance of the Wassons, the noted poet and historical writer Robert Graves, wrote a crucial letter informing them of a supposed secret mushroom cult still in existence in Mexico. Graves included in his letter a clipping from a Canadian pharmaceutical journal that discussed finds made by Richard Evans Schultes years earlier. It transpired that Schultes, one of the world's leading ethnobotanists attached to Harvard, had, in 1938, identified a species of *Panaeoleus* mushroom as being the sacred sacrament allegedly employed by Mexican Indians. At that time, only this one entheogenic species had been identified by Schultes, and although a few European people had observed a native Mexican mushroom ceremony, no outsiders had been permitted to partake of the mushroom itself. This is significant, for without actually personally experiencing the psilocybin mushroom, one can only guess at its effects, and therefore the early anthropological observations passed by without much interest.

Once the Wassons learned of these intriguing facts, armed as they were with detailed knowledge of fly agaric mushroom history and lore, it was only natural for them to heed Graves's investigational indications and focus their attention upon Mexico. If mushroom ceremonies were still being practiced, it would be testimony to the shamanic use of fungi not limited to the pages of history.

Through associates, the Wassons were soon in avid correspondence with one Eunice Pike, an American linguistic student and Bible translator (in other words, a missionary) who had been living among Mazatec Indians in Huautla, Mexico, for more than fifteen years. Having become familiar with the native customs and beliefs about certain sacred mushrooms, she was only too willing to share her knowledge with the Wassons.

Pike informed the Wassons by letter that one Indian boy had referred to the mushroom as a gift from Jesus, no less than the blood of Christ. The Indians also said that while it helped "good people," it killed "bad people" or made them crazy. Furthermore, the Indians were sure that Jesus spoke to them while in the "bemushroomed" state.

Everyone whom Pike asked agreed that they were seeing into heaven itself through the mushroom.

As well as highlighting the ongoing integration of the Christian faith into native Indian culture, the Indians' claims indicated that the mushroom was highly powerful in its psychological effect, able to induce a radical alteration of consciousness still relatively new to Western science. It was also clear that the normal procedure was for a shaman to eat the mushroom on behalf of another, usually in order to heal, this being the classic social function of the shaman found in most of the world's native cultures.

Pike ended her informative and tantalizing letter by wishing that the natives would consult the Bible instead of resorting to consumption of the strange mushroom, a remark natural enough to anyone concerned with preaching the Bible and unfamiliar with the psychological territory accessed through psilocybin. But still, is it not odd that someone so obviously religiously inclined, as this woman was, should not have detected something of spiritual importance in the Indians' claims? If so many of them readily attested to the virtues of the sacred mushrooms, why did she not try them for herself? After all, she mentions no harmful effects apart from the dangers of possessing a "bad heart."

What is the nature of this fear that would prevent a single open-minded experiment with such fungi? How can one claim to be fully religious and not take the testimonies of shamans seriously? This was an anomaly that was to continually crop up in the relations between the Western psyche and the mushroom. Psilocybin would come to generate absolute awe or absolute rejection in those who confronted it, this being indicative that something significant is at work in the actual experience. If there was nothing of real interest to be gained from visionary substances, if the experiences were purely limited personal fantasies, then there would be no stimulational force with which to generate enduring fascination. However, as I will show, many have claimed that psilocybin does offer great knowledge about our existence, that it can yield soulful insights into the nature of reality. This is why the psilocybin mushroom experience has remained such an abstruse phenomenon and why opinions are so divided.

Sensing in Pike's letter that there was indeed some great revelational discovery to be made, the Wassons decided to travel as soon as possible to Huautla, and in 1953 they did so. There could be no mistaking the aroma of the ethnomycological Holy Grail as they neared its living presence. As an aside, they also realized that to judge from Pike's description, the mushroom being used by these Indians was not the *Panaeoleus* species previously identified by Schultes. This was further reason for prompt scholarly investigation.

Getting Warmer

By August 1953 the Wassons had managed to enlist the help of a Mexican *curandero,* or shaman, and this was an achievement in itself, as the Indians were reluctant to discuss the mushroom with outsiders. Under the pretense of wanting supernaturally inspired news of their son, the Wassons were permitted to take part in a mushroom rite during which the shaman would ingest sacred mushrooms in order to gain the requested information. Unfortunately the shaman was the only person allowed to consume the fungus, and the Wassons were forced to remain uninitiated.

The shaman, under the effects of psilocybin, made three specific predictions concerning the Wassons' son, which, at the time, he (Wasson) politely humored, as he had no real inkling into psilocybin's latent ability to produce feats of clairvoyance. His interest was, after all, still predominately academic, and any kind of supernatural utterances were to be taken with a large pinch of salt. As it later transpired, all three of the shaman's predictions were borne out, and Wasson was at a loss to explain this. Was it coincidence? Or was it a genuine case of the paranormal? Whatever it was, the mysterious mushrooms demanded closer scrutiny, for they seemed to promise much more of interest. Wasson was being drawn ever nearer, as his lifelong adventure drew to an epic climax.

A fully detailed witness account of this mushroom ceremony was to be the culminating chapter of *Mushrooms, Russia and History,* though just as the book was going to press in June of 1955 a new breakthrough was made. In fact, it was the ultimate breakthrough and became the highlight of R. Gordon Wasson's scholarly career. It also generated another chapter in his book and the seminal piece for *Life* magazine. The middle-aged New York banker-turned-ethnomycologist became the first Westerner on record to deliberately consume sacred Mexican mushrooms and behold their entheogenic glory. Wasson had sought, and finally accessed, one of the most remarkable experiences to be had upon this Earth. Thanks to his lifelong persistent efforts, humanity's exploration of Nature and of the limits of conscious experience became suddenly enhanced as psilocybin made its extraordinary psychedelic presence felt. Indeed, for our purposes, it is rather apt that our man Wasson was provided with an informative and illuminating experience at that time—almost an earthly calling card in fact—as only a few months earlier Nature had consumed the great Einstein. At least it was apt in a relative kind of way for anyone interested in the subtle-yet-never-malicious force of such a wily killer/creator as Nature.

The Mystery Explodes into *Life*

In telling of his experiences in *Life* magazine, Wasson comes across as a kind of Prometheus figure, bringing the world news of a hitherto secret gift of the gods. Among dreamy 1950s Technicolor photographs and numerous advertisements for miracle filter cigarettes and various brands of alcohol, Wasson's article shines like some otherworldly beacon signaling the awesome visionary power latent within the Mexican mushroom. We can only guess at the amazement that this article must have evoked in the psyche of a reader soaked in 1950s thinking and values. This was the decade of Cadillacs, rock 'n' roll, television, and electronic gadgetry, a decade in which the postwar generation could live happily upon the bountiful fruits of consumerism. Having recently conquered both Everest and the secret of the atom, humankind seemed truly on the ascent. Unlimited atomic energy and unlimited material growth were in the cards. Nature had been tamed and set to work for our own ends.

Of course, what no one realized at this time was the devastating effect upon the environment that an unchecked material culture could wreak. As yet unconceived in holistic organismic terms, the natural environment was a place to take the kids on the weekend, not the grounds for concern, let alone the grounds for a bizarre shamanic consummation. And, after all, weren't shamans just primitive witch doctors who spouted all sorts of unsophisticated nonsense? It must therefore have been with some surprise that *Life's* readers found themselves being informed about visionary fungi, a facet of the environment still wild and untamed and one that spoke of a very different kind of reality from that of the American dream.

Deep in the south of Mexico in a small village in Oaxaca, Wasson recounted to the readers of *Life* how he had once more gained the confidence of a local shaman, a woman named Maria Sabina, under whose guidance he was allowed to ingest sacred mushrooms. Judging from the photographs included in his account, the house where the ceremony took place was small and sparsely furnished, with various Christian icons on display. The paucity of modern furnishings, however, was in stark contrast to the luxuriousness of the visionary experience that followed the ingestion of the mushrooms, the surroundings all but melting into insignificance.

At 10:30 p.m. Wasson received six pairs of mushrooms from Maria Sabina as she commenced the auspicious rite. At long last he held the elusive mystery in his trembling hands. Tangible and open to physical analysis, the fungi were no native myth or figment of the imagination. But what of their legendary effect? All theory and hearsay became vanquished as Wasson swallowed his destiny.

Like all good empiricists Wasson determined to remain objectively aloof and ward off any major psychological effects so that he could study more clearly the nature of the revered shift in consciousness engendered by the mushroom. As noble as such efforts are, however, they generally prove futile in the face of potent entheogens, as one is forced to wholly succumb to the emergent global alteration in mentation.

As Wasson lay in the dark confines of the hut, the power latent within the mushroom gradually made itself known to him. Visions unfolded before his eyes, visions so intense and so profound that they breached the ineffable realms of religious mysticism. They began as vividly colored art motifs of an angular nature, as found on textiles and carpets. Then the visions evolved into resplendent palaces and gardens laid over with precious stones. At one point, Wasson perceived a great mythological beast drawing a regal chariot. Still later it seemed as if his spirit had broken free from the constraints of his body and lay suspended in midair, viewing vast mountains rising to the Heavens. Wasson confessed that the sights were so sharp and clear as to be more real than anything that he had previously seen with his eyes, somewhat akin to archetypes and the Platonic realm of Ideas.

In *Mushrooms, Russia and History,* Wasson's description of his visionary experiences is more explicit than in the *Life* piece. What had started out as a unique work of ethnomycology, touching on ancient Siberian shamanism, had now transformed into a personal testimony of the mystical experience. Coming from a man normally concerned with the world of finance, this is a truly remarkable turn of events, even more so since he was not overtly religious. It was also the case that any of Wasson's residual mycophobia had now been utterly obliterated, as the incontrovertible truth of psilocybin-induced shamanic ecstasy seized his soul. The sense of awe, the sense that he had been witness to an event of staggering cultural significance radiates from these more detailed accounts, and the book subsequently ends as a veritable mystical treatise.

At one point during the mushroom ceremony Wasson thought

the visions themselves were about to be transcended, and dark gates reaching upward beyond sight were about to part, and we were to find ourselves in the presence of the Ultimate. We seemed to be flying at the dark gates as a swallow at a dazzling lighthouse, and the gates were to part and admit us. But they did not open, and with a thud we fell back, gasping.[2]

Although the visions lasted only a minute or so by watch, Wasson noted that he experienced them as having an aeonic duration, as though he had passed out of the confines of normal time. He was also certain that the visions originated from either the unconscious or from an inherited source of racial memory, concepts borrowed from the work of Carl Jung, with which Wasson was obviously familiar. He readily conceded that the intense visionary episodes arose within him, yet they did not recall anything previously seen with his own eyes. He wondered if maybe the mushroom visions were a subconscious transmutation of things read, seen, and imagined, so much transmuted that they appeared to be new and unfamiliar. Or, mused Wasson, did the mushroom allow one to penetrate some new realm of the psyche?

I assume here that Wasson was referring to something more than a personal unconscious and more like an organized field of intelligence or a transcendental sentience of some sort, interpreted by native shamans as a Great Spirit or God. Wasson failed to elaborate on this matter, pre-ferring to stick to more acceptable ideas, and he ventured no further than Jungian territory in his enthusiastic speculation.

Wasson was also struck by the fact that the dazzling visionary mate-rial engendered by the mushroom must reside somewhere within the mind, in a kind of latent state, until the mushroom's psychoactive con-stituents stirred them into activity. But how was it possible, he won-dered, that we could be carrying around an inventory of wonders deep within us, wonders that the mushroom could unleash so spectacularly? Perhaps, he suggested, some creative faculty of the brain was stimulated by the mushroom and this capacity for creative thought was somehow linked to the perception of the divine.

The visionary effects of the mushroom, so clearly related to the experiences of religious mystics, suggested to Wasson that these kinds of fungi might be connected in some significant way to the very origins of the religious impulse, an idea he first introduced in the *Life* piece and one that he would constantly return to for the rest of his life. Wasson asks us if perhaps the idea of a deity arose after our distant ancestors first consumed psychoactive mushrooms, surely a compelling scenario if we are pushed to explain the origins of religion in natural terms. He was later to help coin the contemporary word *entheogen* to refer to these sorts of plants and fungi, a word that, although devised to mean "becoming divine within," is more often considered to mean "generating the divine within."

Readers of the *Life* article were also informed as to what the Mexican Indians themselves had to say about the mushroom. The Indians claimed that the fungi "carry you there where God is."[3] Always the mushroom was referred to with awe and reverence. It was not some common drug like alcohol to be taken at the drop of a hat in order to drown one's sorrows or deaden oneself to reality. On the contrary, native shamans used the fungus for oracular reasons to cure and prophesize. Wasson was intimately familiar with the Indians' sacred traditions, and he was at pains to portray this cultural phenomenon to his readers in the respectful light it deserved. No Indian ate the mushroom frivolously for excitement; rather, they spoke of their use as "muy delicado," that is, perilous.

A deeply inspired man, Wasson was not only the first Westerner to document the psilocybin experience; he was also the first to attempt to account for the mysterious effects in reasonable psychological terms, and his tentative speculations remain valid. It is remarkable to think that had he not had such a profoundly spiritual experience, or had his mind not been able to cope with the onslaught of a visionary dialogue, then the Mexican mushroom might well have remained a buried phenomenon to this day. Fortunately for us, this was not so, and the entheogenic mystery is very much alive and "unleashed." Indeed, given the current world situation in which relentless material consumption is rapidly destroying the biosphere and our value systems are devoid of any vivifying spiritual dimension, the sacred mushroom experience is now more relevant than ever before.

Regarding Wasson's brave attempts to provide a reasonable explanation for his experiences, I will deal with what is currently known about "the neuropsychological how" of psilocybin in later chapters. For now it is enough to recognize that the mushroom had proved itself to be the psychological analogue of physical fire, its effects able to innervate and enliven the very soul of *Homo sapiens*.

To simply dismiss Wasson's visionary encounter as no more than the drug-induced fantasy of a middle-aged man is to miss the point completely. The significance of the entheogenic experience for psychological science alone is enough to warrant our attention since psilocybin is clearly able to galvanize highly constructive systems of thought and emotion into action—that much can be said at the absolute least. Any substance able to evoke an organized flow of symbolic information seemingly issuing from somewhere outside of one's sense of self, or ego, has got to be worth studying, especially if the experience appears more real than real. And as far as the actual experience of sacred transcendence is concerned, if we are truly interested in such things, if we are truly concerned with perceiving our existence in a way that is beyond the confines of a culturally conditioned secular perspective, then we should surely have cause to investigate the mushroom's visionary potential. Whereas the most limited explanation for this psychological phenomenon in terms of, say, creative imagination on an unprecedented scale, is still immensely important and fascinating, the more radical and speculative scenarios—which seem compelling when one has personally tasted exhilarating states of mind—offer an even greater and more brilliant conceptual view of reality.

It is here, in the personal impact of the psilocybin experience upon one's perceptions of reality, that the importance of Wasson's work resides, for he was able to verbalize his entheogenic experiences in a way that captured their remarkable character. Wasson had shown how sacred realms of experience were not dependent on churches or on the blessings of popes and priests, but could be accessed through the consumption of entheogenic fungi. Wasson had effectively laid such a natural option at the feet of the modern world.

At the end of his seminal account, Wasson discusses the accessibility of the mushroom experience to large numbers people whose psychological disposition might not be in the same league as traditional visionaries like, for example, the poet William Blake. If Wasson was able to briefly become a visionary through eating a simple mushroom, no doubt others would want to follow suit. This inevitable social consequence of his tale was to become manifest in the next decade to a degree that he could never have anticipated, for his news of visionary fungi was instrumental in attracting the West's interest toward entheogens. As Blake had written, once the doors of perception are opened, the infinite beauty of reality can be discerned. Whether he had planned it or not, Wasson, like his contemporary Aldous Huxley, now had his foot firmly wedged between those perceptual doors.

As yet unnamed, its chemical structure still unknown, psilocybin thus began its gradual infiltration of the modern technological world, flowing for the first time in and out of the nervous systems of Westerners, facilitating a spectacular kind of cerebral information processing in which the blazing divinity of Nature was potentially discernible. The world would never be the same again as intellectuals, artists, and spiritual seekers with the aid of the psilocybin mushroom began scratching away at the restricted surface of normal everyday awareness. Such intrepid peering beyond the confines of routine perception seemed to reveal much, much more in the way of reality, allowing access to information of the most stimulating and enchanting kind, as if the mushroom was able to offer up all of Nature's best-kept secrets.

Despite the widespread interest generated by his *Life* piece, Wasson later chose, perhaps wisely, to distance himself from the 1960s psychedelic hippie culture, revolving as it was around synthetic LSD. Instead, he concerned himself with investigating the role of the fly agaric mushroom in ancient Indo-European Soma cults. He also went on to make invaluable contributions to our knowledge of the use of psilocybin mushrooms by the Aztec and Mayan civilizations of ancient Mesoamerica, and we shall now step briefly back in time to view these historical entheogenic traditions before bringing the history of psilocybin fully up to date.

TWO

An Ancient Form of Communion

The discovery of the shamanic use of psilocybin among contemporary Mexican Indians was indicative of a sacred tradition that, although almost buried, had its roots firmly set in the glories of past civilizations. In particular, the mighty Aztec empire had been familiar with the mushroom, and the various documents written by Spanish conquistadors almost five hundred years ago, which mention mushroom use by the Aztecs, can be reanalyzed according to what we now know of the actual entheogenic experience. Psilocybin emerges as no mere incidental feature of the natural world, restricted to secretive and isolated use; rather, its ritual role as a potent sacrament was overtly established within the very fabric of ancient Mesoamerican society. Until, that is, it came under the merciless gaze of the Catholic Spanish conquistadors.

The Aztecs were an immensely powerful civilization whose cultural achievements are ranked by some in the same league as those of ancient Egypt and Babylonia. Religious ideology permeated all aspects of Aztec society, driving them to conquest and expansion and giving rise to their infamous bloody human sacrifices on a scale that cannot fail to shock.

Located in the Central Valley of Mexico, the Aztec capital Tenochtitlán (now Mexico City) reached its peak of power and magnificence immediately prior to the arrival of Hernán Cortés and his gold-rushing Spanish army in 1519. With the advent of the Spanish conquest, all aspects of Aztec religion, including the use of the psilocybin mushroom, were systematically wiped out, condemned as devilish heresy.

To the invading Spanish clergy, the Aztecs' claim that certain mushrooms (some two dozen or so psilocybin-containing species are indigenous to Mexico) were *teonanácatl,* or "God's Flesh," was to admit to some blasphemous unholy communion. In the Roman Catholicism touted by the marauding conquistadors, communion with the divine was not based on personally revealed knowledge or gnosis. Absolutely not. Rather it was the case that "inside" information concerning the divine was considered acceptable only if one was connected to a formally established religious hierarchy within which one accepted, without question, its most cherished doctrines.

In other words, the organized drive of Catholicism that descended upon the Aztec nation derived its power structure through force-feeding religious dogma to its adherents. To openly question this dogma, or to criticize it, could and did mean death five hundred years ago. One is therefore hard-pressed to conceive of a more heretical act than that of the Aztecs' consumption of supposedly divine mushrooms. The Spanish Catholic clergy, eager to spread their faith, would have been utterly appalled at the concept of eating some foul and unsightly fungus in order to facilitate divine communion. As we shall see, this negative reaction was clearly reflected in the lively written Spanish accounts of Aztec customs. To be sure, the intense disgust generated within the orthodox religious minds of the Spanish priests echoes the hatred meted out to women accused of being satanic witches in medieval Europe, as they too were found guilty of possessing heretical botanical knowledge. Whereas the Aztecs employed psilocybin mushrooms to induce numinous states of consciousness, the witches of the Middle Ages achieved similar states of mind by utilizing plants like henbane and belladonna. Historically speaking, the spiritual use of plants and fungi tends to generate the same blunt response in the male psyche of any monotheistic culture—namely, unremitting persecution. The Aztec religion succumbed to just such a fate.

The Catholic Constabulary Take Note

The Aztecs' use of psilocybin is clearly revealed in many of the records made by Spanish chroniclers at the time of the conquest, who diligently recorded their own observations and translated Aztec historical documents as well. For instance, during the coronation of Montezuma the second in 1502, we learn that teonanácatl was consumed during the celebrations. Many war captives were slaughtered to honor the new king, their hearts torn out and offered to the gods. After the grisly sacrifices, the celebrants were bathed in blood and then given raw psilocybin mushrooms to eat.

Perhaps it was this kind of terrible juxtaposition that helped the finger of heresy point toward the mushroom. After all, a mass bloody sacrifice followed by some strange ritual fungal inebriation is a hellish concept to the West, yet it was bound with the Aztecs' desire to supplicate their pantheon of gods. Blood spilled in the name of religion whether through war or sacrifice is, unfortunately, a kind of pious tradition that highlights the immense power of the religious impulse over the human mind and soul. The gods of the Aztecs were deemed real, and they had to be worshipped and placated.

At any rate, the Aztecs utilized psilocybin in their religious rituals and engaged in various other rites that would have appeared horrendously alien to the invading Spanish, who were unlikely to react in the manner of refined social anthropologists. The excessive sacrifices together with the ingestion of psychoactive mushrooms must have sorely confused the Spanish invaders. To be sure, while they were at once amazed at the glorious wealth and regality of the Aztec cities that they encountered, they were less enthusiastic about the underlying psychological forces that had led to the physical magnificence set in stone.

Further accounts from the occupying Spanish clergy reveal the Aztecs' use of psilocybin. The following testimonies—which paint a sometimes vivid picture of Aztec tradition—are detailed in Wasson's *The Wondrous Mushroom*. For example, Diego Durán, a sixteenth-century Dominican friar translating a document in Nahuatl (the language spoken by the Aztecs), writes of the coronation of Tizoc in 1481:

> And all the lords and grandees of the provinces rose and, to solemnize further the festivities, they all ate of some woodland mushrooms, which they say make you lose your senses, and thus they sallied forth all primed for the dance.[1]

On the aforementioned coronation of Montezuma, Durán tells us:

> The sacrifice finished and the steps of the temple and patio bathed in human blood, they all went to eat raw mushrooms; on which food they all went out of their minds, worse than if they had drunk much wine; so drunk and senseless were they that many killed themselves by their own hand, and, with the force of those mushrooms, they would see visions and have revelations of the future, the Devil speaking to them in that drunken state.[2]

Because of his own personal experiences with psilocybin, and in light of historical research that clearly showed the Aztecs' reverence for teonanácatl, our mushroom expert Wasson came to the conclusion that Durán had imposed his own views on the matter in order to further demonize the mushroom practice. Which is to say that to identify the Devil at the heart of the psilocybin experience was an interpretation peculiar to the psyche of this sixteenth-century friar. With his particular theological training he would have had no choice but to sniff the sulphurous traces of the Devil in the Aztecs' unusual entheogenic rites. Durán's perception of psilocybin-inspired suicides within the Nahuatl texts is therefore more likely to be the result of bias and exaggerated translation than actual fact. Today's tabloid press would doubtless be impressed by Durán's sensational rhetoric.

Another friar, the Franciscan Bernardino de Sahagún, also left us an account of native mushroom use. In the *Florentine Codex* he writes of a merchant's celebration.

At the very first, mushrooms had been served. They ate them at a time when, they said, the shell trumpets were blown. They ate no more food; they only drank chocolate during the night. And they ate the mushrooms with honey. When the mushrooms took effect on them, then they danced, then they wept. But some while still in command of their senses entered and sat there by the house on their seats; they danced no more, but only sat there nodding.[3]

On the face of it, this would seem to be a less prejudiced portrayal of psilocybin use, though in the following report, also by Sahagún, he soon slides into the familiar tabloidlike sensationalist mode while describing mushroom use.

It is called *teonanácatl*. It grows on the plains, in the grass. The head is small and round, the stem long and slender. It is bitter and burns; it burns the throat. It makes one besotted; it deranges one, troubles one. . . . He who eats many of them sees many things which make him afraid, or make him laugh. He flees, hangs himself, hurls himself from a cliff, cries out, takes fright.[4]

Such scare stories are echoed by the rumors that surrounded LSD use in the 1960s. People were supposedly hurling themselves from high-rise apartments and foolishly attempting to stop highway traffic by the power of thought alone. In actuality, of all the millions of doses of LSD taken in the 1960s, there were only a handful of deaths through misadventure resulting from LSD's effects. It appears that any psychedelic substance with a powerful mystique seems to instill fear in those who are unfamiliar with its effects and who are easily threatened by the unknown. Moreover, fear often precedes persecution and the spreading of inaccurate information, which is why it is so important to have an unconditional flow of informed, hysteria-free knowledge regarding the psychological action of visionary plants and fungi. One hopes, then, that we live in more enlightened times. The fact remains, however, that the Aztec use of psychoactive agents, which included the use of other entheogens like the morning glory plant (whose seeds contain LSD-related compounds), proved to be so abhorrent to the Spanish that they sought to drive all such practices to extinction.

That they were successful in forcibly burying the mushroom is made clear by the academic events in the early part of the last century, as it was erroneously believed that there never were any psychoactive mushrooms to be found in Mexico in the first place. It was assumed by scholars that a mistake had been made by the obviously dim-witted Spanish historians, and that dried peyote cactus buttons (containing the entheogenic alkaloid mescaline) were the legendary teonanácatl. This botanical conjecture, or blunder as it was, went completely unchallenged by the academic fraternity when it was presented in 1915, and it remained unchallenged until a species of psychoactive mushroom still being used in Huautla was identified in 1938.

Perhaps, then, we should conclude that mycophobia is not merely a cultural phenomenon, but a remorseless genetic trait. This is an idea that Wasson would certainly have appreciated, as he was to come across much in the way of scholarly disregard for psilocybin's religious role within ancient Mesoamerican culture. It is only since Wasson's work has come to be acknowledged that historians have begun to realize that psychedelic agents like the Mexican mushroom have the power to move people, that their tremendous psychological impact was significant in shaping the belief systems of those cultures that used them. The point that Wasson was continually at pains to make was that one should be wary of underestimating the cultural and historical role of entheogenic flora, although, of course, he came to this conclusion by way of his own personal psychedelic experiences. Alas, such personal insights are not shared by most other Mesoamerican scholars.

Illuminating Flowers

One of the most remarkable pieces of evidence testifying to the exalted status conferred upon the psilocybin mushroom by the Aztecs is in the form of an early sixteenth-century statue of the god Xochipilli, or the "Prince of Flowers." The significance of this magnificent piece of art was first recognized by Wasson, and thereafter the real message that it conveyed became glaringly apparent.

The statue represents a cross-legged male figure—the god Xochipilli—caught up in an ecstatic trance. There can be no mistake. The very essence of ecstasy has been captured in stone. The arms, legs, and base of this stone-carved ecstatic prince carry stylized engravings of flowers, and on each of the four sides of the base of the statue are carved mushroom motifs. These mushroom motifs also appear upon the subject so enraptured.

Until these carvings came under the attentive gaze of Wasson, they had never been botanically identified. Wasson realized that the stylized flowers were the key to deciphering the true meaning of the Aztec statue and, moreover, the very meaning of "flowers" in classic Aztec literature. As soon as Wasson intimated the statue's full raison d'être, he immediately contacted noted ethnobotanist Richard Evans Schultes at Harvard's Botanical Museum, who was the obvious man to consult regarding a botanical analysis of the motifs.

Schultes was subsequently confident enough to identify the carved "flowers" as *Nicotiana tabacum,* the common tobacco plant considered sacred by almost all native American cultures; *Turbina corymbosa,* a species of morning glory whose psychoactive seeds are known to have been employed by Mesoamerican cultures; and *Heimia salicifolia,* also a psychoactive species. Wasson noted that these species were representative of the Aztecs' most revered plants, hence there were no depictions of less-esteemed plants such as those employed by the Aztecs to make maize beer.

Wasson believed that previous ignorance of the statue's true nature reflected the aforementioned widespread failing of historians to acknowledge the important role that psilocybin mushrooms and other sacred flora played in Mesoamerican history. In *The Wondrous Mushroom,* Wasson writes: "Our statue of Xochipilli serves us as a touchstone, as a cultural Rosetta Stone, bypassing the friars encumbered with their theological preconceptions, speaking to us directly with the voice of the pre-Conquest Aztecs."[5]

It appears then that the Spanish clergy were ultimately unsuccessful in silencing the claims made by their subdued and conquered subjects; messages in stone speak far louder than words. Xochipilli provides rock-hard testimony for the Aztecs' sacred bond with the natural environment and its array of potent botanical resources. What exactly the Aztecs experienced through psilocybin remains debatable, although we can be sure that their visions were vivid and convincing enough for them to regard the mushroom as a link to divine realms of being, no less than the manifestation of God's Flesh on the Earth.

Wasson also went on to study pre-Conquest Aztec poetry written in the native Nahuatl language. When this poetry first became accessible to the West, it had been noted that "flowers" were referred to often. Peculiarly often in fact. Moreover, the oft-mentioned "flowers" were seldom, if ever, distinguished from one another. Like the statue of Xochipilli, Wasson realized that the "flowers" referred to visionary agents, most notably the psilocybin mushroom.

For instance, the poetry speaks of "the flowers that inebriate," "the joyous flowers," "the flowers without roots," "the precious flowers," and so on. Careful study shows that Nahuatl poetry is teeming with embellished references to "flowers." This only makes sense if we accept that the Aztecs worshipped the mushroom and other psychedelic agents because of their transcendental psychological effects and set their praises to poetry. As in the sculpting of the "Prince of Flowers," the Aztec poets who wrote of "flowers" were producing their art from direct experience, their works channeling their deific respect.

As a final testimony to the Aztecs' use of psilocybin, mushroom motifs are also found in pre-Conquest codices (these codices are the pictorial records of the Aztecs themselves and not those made by Spanish historians), in particular within the pages of the Vienna Codex, a historical document rich in pictographic information, including a section on ancient myths, aptly named the "Origin of Things." One page of this codex depicts the famous Mesoamerican god Quetzalcoatl being tutored in the use of mushrooms. There is no ambiguity in the depictions—an entire page clearly portrays ritual mushroom use.

Psychedelic Temples

Prior to the Aztecs' rise to dominance and before the time of the Toltecs' reign, the religious core of pre-Columbian Mesoamerica was the prosperous city of Teotihuacán, located in the Valley of Mexico, near modern-day Mexico City. The city dates from 150 B.C. to 750 A.D., but little is known about the Teotihuacáns, although Aztec legends equate this location with the birthplace of their deities. Its very name was given by the Aztecs who had discovered it six hundred years after its mysterious collapse and means "Place of the Gods" in Nahuatl.

Due to the immense scale of Teotihuacán's religious architecture, which includes the spectacular Pyramids of the Sun and Moon and highly sophisticated wall paintings rife with ornate serpent motifs, it can be reasonably assumed that it was the center of an important religious cult. The overt presence of serpent motifs on the architecture is a strong indication of religious worship, since the pantheon of almost all Mesoamerican cultures includes mythical serpentine entities, such as the feathered serpent god Quetzalcoatl. Elaborately stylized serpents were used both to represent gods and to symbolize divine power penetrating the mundane world. Their fearsome presence on and around temples signified that the temple was a sacred place to be guarded from profane intrusion.

Of most concern here are the style and content of the numerous mural paintings that adorn most of Teotihuacán's temples and shrines. In these murals we once more find depictions of various flowers, one of which is the morning glory (either *Turbina corymbosa* or *Ipomoea violacea*). As stated, the seeds of this plant species contain LSD-related compounds known to have been used by the Aztecs for religious communion. It is therefore reasonable to assume that the templegoers at Teotihuacáan knew of, and thus utilized, the psychedelic effect of the morning glory.

Whether mushrooms are depicted in the temple murals is a somewhat contentious issue. While Wasson affirmed this and pointed out what he considered to be mushroom symbols, these same motifs have been identified by other Mesoamerican scholars as representing the water lily. Although various related African species of water lily are thought to be psychoactive, it has not been firmly established whether the New World variety are equally as potent. Either way, Wasson conjectured that the various temples of Teotihuacan, decorated as they are with depictions of psychedelic plants (the morning glory at least), were sacred sites where the ritual ingestion of entheogens took place.

Secret Psychedelic Legacies

The concept that indigenous visionary agents have been ritually consumed by ancient cultures in order to induce theophany and religious solidarity should come as no surprise. In ancient Greece the classic Eleusinian Mystery cult echoes the inferred scenario occurring at Teotihuacán. Mystery rites took place each year at Eleusis, near Athens, centered on the drinking of some secret potion that granted a transcendental vision to initiates. The entire sacred ceremony was held within the guarded confines of a hallowed temple. Recent theories have proposed that this Eleusinian drink was made from barley exposed to ergot. This would mean that it contained entheogenic substances because ergot, a tiny plant fungus that grows on wheat and barley, contains a number of LSD-related compounds. Although this psychedelic scenario has not been confirmed and remains merely an engaging hypothesis (ergot is also potentially toxic), the point is that the potion was almost certain to have contained some form of psychedelic alkaloid with the capacity to engender the type of mystical experience attested to in Greek historical literature. Wasson assumed that Teotihuacán was a Mesoamerican equivalent to Eleusis, that is, that both were sacred places where visionary agents were ritually administered.

Clearly the morning glory plant was utilized for its psychoactive effect by the Teotihuacáns (assuming of course that they did not just like the look of it), as the various murals testify, and it follows that psilocybin mushrooms would also have been ingested had their properties been known at the time.

The Birth of the Religious Impulse

Claims that infer that psychoactive plants and fungi played a major role in ancient religion might be considered to belittle religion in some way, as though one were reducing everything to "damnable drugs." Nothing is further from the truth. Far from reducing the religion, the religion becomes firmly entwined with the unequivocal numinous effects of vision-inducing fungi and plant species. That is the strength and force of such environmental resources. Visionary plants and fungi cannot fail to have a dramatic impact. Anyone like Wasson who has made the sacred connection within his psyche through the action of natural entheogens knows of their profoundly spiritual impact.

Ultimately one comes to suspect, like Wasson, that the very historical source of humankind's religious impulse lies in our ancestors' primeval encounters with raw entheogenic species like the psilocybin mushroom, which are effective without the need for elaborate preparation. This scenario does not lessen religion; it empowers it, giving it an unstoppable impetus created through the effect of visionary alkaloids in opening up the boundless capacities of the human mind. God becomes connected to a *state of consciousness,* an inwardly felt presence mysteriously welling up from the depths of the psyche and not from some abstract dogma. However, religious dogma might well allude to the experience and indeed testify to the reality of entheogen-induced theophany. Yet once a detailed knowledge of the plant or fungus in question is lost in the hazy mists of time, then any lingering memory of its original entheogenic power will be no more than words, an echo of a once-living mystery.

The greatest reason to embrace an entheogen-based explanation for the rise of the religious impulse, however, is that it is couched in wholly naturalistic terms, therefore lending itself to scientific study. If a man claims to have had a life-changing theophany, then that is one thing. But if he bears in his hand the very method whereby he attained such an experience, then you are obliged, if you wish to determine the man's claims, to explore and verify the means. In more ways than one, psychedelic plants and fungi must be taken seriously in terms of their role in the development of religious ideology. As intimated, their historical influence can never be overestimated.

Mushrooms and the Maya

Psilocybin mushroom use has also been associated with the Maya, whose spectacular Mesoamerican civilization dates back almost four thousand years and whose Classic period held sway from A.D. 250 to 900. At the turn of the last century, Guatemalan "mushroom stones" came to the attention of archaeologists. These Mayan relics, of which hundreds have been found, some dating as far back as 1000 B.C., were initially considered to be phallic representations, though the current consensus is that the mushroom stones reflect a Mayan religious mushroom cult.

To bolster support for this theory, it has been noted that some of the stone mushrooms are carved emerging from human figures with trance-like facial expressions. Others are linked to kneeling female figures at a *metate,* a kind of work surface upon which plant items are crushed. When Wasson first explored mushroom use in Huautla in the 1950s, metates were still sometimes used to grind mushrooms so that an entheogenic infusion could be made. Still other mushroom stones exhibit "toad" effigies at their base, and this creature has always been mysteriously linked with psychoactive fungi the world over, perhaps because of knowledge that certain toads exude psychoactive alkaloids from their parotid glands. (Incidentally, this odd "toady" fact might account for the fairy story *The Frog Prince,* as magical events happen after a frog has been "kissed.")

Is there any other evidence that the Maya employed psilocybin mushrooms in their religion? A look at Mayan codices might shed light on this matter, yet our not-so-delightful conquering Spanish priests made that almost impossible with their blundering haste to burn everything that stood in their theological way, including virtually all Mayan scriptures. As an example of this hooliganism, consider the fact that in 1562, one Diego de Landa, a hardened Spanish priest of some frightening zeal, seized thousands of Mayan "idols" and books, and burned all and sundry as though they were worthless. Among the treasures destroyed were twenty-seven roles and signs of hieroglyphics, invaluable sources of knowledge about the Mayan civilization. According to Robert J. Sharer in *The Ancient Maya,* Landa commented: "We found a large number of books in these characters and, as they contained nothing in which there were not to be seen superstition and lies of the devil, we burned them all, which they regretted to an amazing degree, and which caused them much affliction."[6]

Such a foolish and insensitive act has left the world with only a handful of Mayan codices with which to assess Mayan customs and beliefs. Within two of these remaining works, the *Popul Vuh* and the *Annals of Cakchiquels,* are references to psychoactive fungi, but there is no indication of the extent of their role within Mayan belief systems. In the so-called Books of Chilam Balam there is mention of trance-like states, though no mention of entheogenic plants. Again, in many Mayan relief carvings, which seem to possess a psychedelic air about them, are found scenes depicting visionary ecstasy, although plants are not explicitly shown. Some scholars have therefore rejected the notion that the Maya employed natural psychedelic agents in their religious rituals (despite the existence of the many mushroom stones) and have opted instead for the alternative view that the Maya, unlike the martial psilocybin-using Aztecs who were to follow, were of a radically different nature and temperament. However, recently discovered Mayan mural paintings have depicted fearsome-looking battle scenes, so it is not absolutely certain that these two cultures were entirely different.

If we look more closely at the actual similarity in religious belief between the Maya and Aztecs, a common historical thread connecting the two cultures can be discerned. Both peoples divided the cosmos into upper worlds and lower worlds with their respective gods. Both believed in the cyclical destruction and regeneration of the Earth, and both followed a ritual 260-day calendar. Bearing in mind these cultural similarities, it has been reasonably suggested that the Maya also utilized the mushroom as well as other psychedelic agents and that this practice influenced the nature of ancient Mesoamerican cosmology (it is even feasible that the Aztecs *adopted* psilocybin mushroom use from the Maya—by way of a succession of mushroom-using cultures).

It has also recently come to light, as many Mayan vases and pieces of pottery attest, that the classical Mayan elite used enemas. The objects that depict scenes of enema use date from the first millennium A.D. The daunting practice of administering enemas has been well documented in South American native peoples. In particular, it has been established that the Incas introduced psychoactive infusions into the body via enema, using bulbed syringes made from local rubber sap. Apparently, the use of an enema to introduce drug compounds into the body is almost as effective with regard to speed of action as is the method of intravenous injection. Its effectiveness with entheogens occurs because the colon is the receptive site of the enema and this is where absorption by the bloodstream occurs. A number of scholars have therefore claimed that entheogenic brews were involved in these Mayan enema rites, and thus psilocybin might well have been employed in this manner.

We should also be aware that much Mayan artwork is given over to portrayals of "vision serpents" manifesting themselves before entranced members of the Mayan nobility. As I stated earlier, to the Mayan psyche, serpents represented the entry of divine forces into normal reality, and to depict fantastically decorated serpents hovering above an enraptured individual signified a communion with the gods. Such individuals are often shown holding a special receptacle. This object is believed to either hold blood from a bloodletting rite or an entheogenic brew, both alternatives offering an effective avenue for attaining a desired visionary state of consciousness (blood loss can apparently lead to an altered state of consciousness—although I am not convinced it would be an enhanced altered state).

Taking into account all of this data, particularly the hundreds of elaborately carved mushroom stones so far uncovered, many historians are compelled to accept that the Maya utilized entheogenic flora including psilocybin mushrooms, and that the visionary realms made accessible by these plants and fungi influenced the development of the Mayan cosmological and religious outlook on reality.

Some Colombian Treasures Also Ring a Bell

Psilocybin mushroom use has also been inferred in pre-Hispanic Colombia due to the discovery of hundreds of beautiful gold objects belonging to the Sinú culture, dated to approximately A.D. 1200. These are decorative anthropomorphic works of art that characteristically carry two bell-shaped forms atop the head and were originally referred to by historians as "telephone-bell gods" (the shapes in question look like the bells found on old-fashioned telephones). Some of these bell-shaped forms are tipped with a small peak, while others are soldered onto the main body of the anthropomorphic figure by a thin "stem." Harvard's ethnobotanical expert Richard Evans Schultes has suggested that the bell shapes are representations of psilocybin mushrooms, which would seem reasonable since several species of psilocybin mushroom are known to flourish in Colombia, some of which possess thin stems and caps topped with a small peaked tip, or umbo.

It is also worth noting that these mushroom objects are often adorned with toad effigies, as is the case with many Mayan mushroom stones. Schultes sees this as further evidence that these objects were made in veneration of entheogenic agents, because, as you will recall, certain toads, including South American species, secrete psychoactive substances from their parotid glands. The evidence is strong then that the historical use of psilocybin fungi and other entheogens extended well beyond Mexico and Guatemala, and that wherever they were employed they were deified and incorporated into works of art.

Viewed in the historical light of the Aztec and the Mayan empires, and to a lesser extent in pre-Hispanic Colombian culture, the psilocybin mushroom emerges as the conductor of a sacred legacy. These once-powerful native peoples knew its worth as an entheogen, a naturally occurring device for communicating with the spiritual domain. This is the botanical Holy Grail that Wasson had long quested for and eventually found half-buried in a remote Mexican village. An unlikely Grail knight, Wasson nonetheless recovered the power of the psilocybin mushroom from more than four hundred years of subjugation and presented it to the modern world. Once unleashed, the psilocybin mushroom helped initiate a tremendous cultural change, only to fade once more into a period of obscurity. Before its departure, however, psilocybin had managed to inch its way into the very heart of the West's academic establishment, where it left a profound impact upon all who encountered it. We now return to the wake set by Wasson's fortuitous discovery.

THREE

Psilocybin Flows in and out of the Western Mind

Wasson's *Life* story sits like a glowing spiritual ember in the tinder-dry secularity of America's 1950s culture. The United States, caught up in a burgeoning but banal materialistic dream, could not fail to be ignited by such a soul-stirring otherworldly tale. A few years earlier Aldous Huxley had written *The Doors of Perception,* which detailed the entheogenic effects of mescaline. Both accounts were seminal in terms of their slow-fuse cultural impact. Each captured the psychedelic zeitgeist that was about to erupt upon the world stage, and Wasson and Huxley emerged as the founders of a cultural movement that would eventually blossom into the "psychedelic sixties," with its colorful burst of artistic creativity and mind expansion.

However, psilocybin, although initially sparking the psychedelic fire, soon left the scene of the divine crime, once more to fade underground into its mysterious place of origin. By the mid-1960s, its synthetic rival, d-lysergic acid diethylamide, also known as LSD and acid, a substance whose structure and psychoactivity are distinct from psilocybin, had taken over as the prime mover, demonstrating the popular appeal of laboratory-produced pills and tabs.

Easily manufactured, packaged, sold, and swallowed, pills are what the public came to expect, and even demand, in a technological consumer age, and therefore mass-produced LSD was quick to fill the ever-growing market for psychedelics. More significant, the synthesis of substances like LSD allowed the power of production to lie in our hands and not the Earth's. In this way, the natural and "earthy" shamanic aspect of entheogenic species was lost. Which is to say that the potential of entheogenic plants and fungi to forge an informative relationship between our species and Nature was not fully realized. Thus from our discerning vantage point this side of the third millennium, we can look back to the dreams and quixotic idealism of the 1960s and understand that without a holistic appreciation of the biosphere and without an insight into the traditional historical usage of psychedelics, a realistic new world vision in which our species reconnects with the bigger picture was unlikely to take a firm cultural hold.

What this boils down to is the concept of naturalness and the intimation that Nature is more informative than we may imagine. In particular, I would argue that the realization that entheogenic plants and fungi are part of the Earth's ecology inevitably affects the significance and import of the entheogenic experience. This means that the concept of naturalness acts as an important *context* for the entheogenic experience, should that experience derive from a natural plant or fungus.

It was precisely this natural biospherical/environmental context that was sorely lacking in the early wave of popular interest in psychedelics. Without acknowledging the botanical environment as the original supply line for the entheogenic agents that started the psychedelic sixties rolling, the acid gurus, despite their vocal enthusiasm for a positive psychedelic world revolution, were still stuck with themselves, caught in a sort of anthropocentric loop, and thereby isolated from an intimate union with the rest of the biosphere. As I will show, the biospherical connection to the entheogenic experience represents the newest phase of psychedelic history, an interesting turn of events full of profound implications for our species.

Unsurprisingly then, although the psychedelic pioneers of the early 1960s were originally turned on by the psilocybin experience—most notably the members of Harvard University's psychology faculty—they soon became completely embroiled in LSD and the media, and never really picked up on the grounded shamanic pulse of the mushroom. Perhaps this is why Wasson remained highly aloof of the whole hippie counterculture. He quietly pursued his academic research into ancient mushroom use, while other researchers, like Richard Evans Schultes, continued to meticulously document visionary plant use among fast-dwindling native peoples. Indeed, the diligent work of both these scholars has provided us with an invaluable legacy of academic material on native psychedelic shamanism.

Bugged by the CIA

Before recounting Harvard's brief scientific flirtation with psilocybin, I should like to alert the reader to a rather sinister twist to the events that led up to the isolation and naming of psilocybin in 1958. In particular, one of Wasson's trips to Mexico unfortunately carried a countercurrent to psilocybin's holy mystique. Just when you thought it was safe to proclaim a spiritual renaissance of sorts, who should arrive on the scene but the CIA. These disturbing mischief-makers, who so profane history with their presence, will seemingly do anything to maintain a grim state of affairs in which the dour "we was miserable in our day" archetype is nourished.

In his book *The Search for the "Manchurian Candidate,"* John Marks tells us of the CIA's covert involvement with our hero Wasson. In its relentless and arguably psychotic search for ever-more effective weaponry, the CIA had, by the 1950s, initiated a massive twenty-five-million-dollar, long-term program called MKULTRA. True to its suspicious-sounding name, Project MKULTRA involved finding chemical and biological materials for use in "mind kontrol" and other psychological unpleasantries. Despite the morally questionable nature of such an unsavory federal project, its dogmatic pursuit meant that it was soon to pick up on rumors of sacred Mexican mushrooms.

After learning of Wasson's 1955 experiences with the mushroom, an unscrupulous chemist named James Moore immediately began to work undercover for the conspirational agency. Presumably dollars changed hands surreptitiously. At any rate, in 1956 Moore craftily wrote to Wasson informing him that he knew of a foundation willing to finance another Mexican trip in order that he and Wasson bring back some of the legendary mushrooms. Moore innocently claimed that, as a chemist, he simply wanted to study the chemical structure of the mushroom's active constituents. The foundation was the CIA-backed Geschwickter Fund for Medical Research, and they were offering a two-thousand-dollar grant. Would Wasson be interested?

Understandably Wasson took the bait, and so it came to pass that the CIA's secret quest for the sacred mushroom became Subproject 58 of the MKULTRA program, possibly representing the most crass approach to psilocybin to date. It was as if the CIA were lobbing stones at angels.

Fittingly, it transpired that the double-dealing Moore was well out of his comfort zone in Mexico and loathed the entire episode. Wasson later recalled that Moore had absolutely no empathy for what was going on. Whereas Wasson was sensitive to the customs of the native Mexican Indians and respectful of their cultural beliefs about the mushroom, Moore was there merely as a CIA pawn.

Once again, all those who were in Wasson's party took part in a mushroom ceremony hosted by the shaman Maria Sabina, though it was Moore alone who had a bad experience. Despite this, Moore was still able to bring back some of the fungi to the United States in the hope of isolating the active ingredient. Thankfully, however, he was beaten in his pharmaceutical pursuit by Roger Heim, an eminent French mycologist and coworker of Wasson, who managed to grow a supply of the mushroom from spore prints that he had taken in Mexico. Heim sent his newly cultivated samples to Albert Hofmann of Sandoz Laboratories in Switzerland, and it was Hofmann, a highly distinguished chemist who had originally synthesized LSD, who, in 1958, first isolated and then named the entheogenic alkaloid within the mushroom. Psilocybin was thus officially born, a name devoid of the weaponry connotations the CIA would invariably have conferred on the substance had they successfully isolated it first.

Having failed in his allotted task, Moore was not terminated but later applied directly to Sandoz for a supply of psilocybin, as the CIA still maintained their clumsy interest in using this compound as an agent for mind control. Indeed, the CIA soon began to covertly test psilocybin on unsuspecting American prisoners, probably not the best of subjects when it comes to being in possession of a stable, healthy psyche. As the prisoners reported some rather bizarre experiences, it became clear that psilocybin could not enter the CIA's arsenal—it was just too darn unpredictable. Thankfully, the CIA then turned their belligerent attentions elsewhere.

The Psychedelic Infiltration of Harvard

After Hofmann began to synthesize psilocybin from extracts of the mushroom, the door was open for properly conducted scientific investigation to commence. Apart from the rather dismal CIA attempt, it was 1960 that marked the beginning of the brief affair between the scientist and the mushroom. This occurred at no less a place than the psychology department of Harvard University, that bastion of academic respectability.

What happens when professional psychologists come up against the phenomenal power of psilocybin? One of two things generally results. Either they experience the substance personally and divine its profound implications for humanity in terms of knowledge acquisition, psychotherapy, self-knowledge, and personal growth, or they refuse to take it and instead interpret psychotomimetic (literally psychosis-mimicking) symptoms in those who do take it. A rather sharp division therefore occurs, as it did at Harvard. On the one side stood the infamous and lanky figure of Dr. Timothy Leary, heading a scholarly band of psychedelic intronauts, while on the other side stood members of the unimpressed "establishment," who tolerated systematic experimentation for only a few years.

If one pinpoints Leary as the man of the moment at the start of that turbulent decade, able to seize the media and galvanize the American youth into rebellion, then we can zoom in on the actual experience that launched his prolific psychedelic career. It was, of course, a mushroom experience.

Dr. Leary Gets Turned On

For forty-year-old Leary it began, as ever, in Mexico. Already an established and respected psychologist at Harvard, Leary spent the summer of 1960 with some friends at the Mexican resort town of Cuernavaca. During his stay, an anthropologist associate at the University of Mexico, who had come across references to sacred mushrooms while studying the Aztecs, suggested that Leary try some.

At noon one Saturday Leary gulped down six obnoxious-tasting local Mexican mushrooms, which had been obtained with much more ease than those consumed by Wasson five years earlier. Through this strange lunch, Leary's fate was effectively sealed. As he later wrote in his autobiography, while the psilocybin coursed its way through his "virgin" Irish bloodstream, he enjoyed the most awe-inspiring religious experience of his life.

Leary was convinced that in just four hours under the influence of psilocybin he had learned more about the mind and the brain than in the fifteen years that he'd been a professional psychologist. This gives good measure to the strength and psychological impact of his first psilocybinetic encounter. Under the right conditions the mushroom is able to restructure one's culturally determined concepts about reality and proffer an entirely different set of beliefs with which to navigate oneself through life.

Being a keen and responsive practitioner of psychological science, alert to new fields of discovery, Leary immediately requested funds to set up a research program into psilocybin. In no time at all the Harvard Psilocybin Project was initiated, commencing at the end of 1960, when a handy batch of psilocybin arrived from Sandoz. Already the natural mushroom had been replaced with jars of precisely dosed pills, thereby subtly altering the context of the psilocybin experience. How different might the implications of psilocybin have been at Harvard had the scientists had to go out into the wilds to pick their research material by hand . . .

One of the most impressive projects undertaken was the systematic study of 175 subjects given psilocybin in which the experimental emphasis was on providing a relaxed and supportive setting. This important notion of set and setting—the subject's mental and physical environment prior to taking the psilocybin—can never be stressed enough, as they are crucial factors in determining the subsequent psychedelic experience. Leary and his coworkers had already established these facts among themselves prior to their official experimentation, and they were at pains to point out how set and setting played a key role in whether the psilocybin experience proved well or ill. It is possible that had someone without Leary's temperament and intimate knowledge of psilocybin organized the experiments instead, then more negative experiences would have been reported.

As it was, most of the subjects reported a pleasant or ecstatic experience, that the psilocybin experience had changed their lives for the better. No psychological casualties were reported even though stronger doses had been used than in previous experimentation. There was no evidence for psychological or physical addiction, although 90% wished to repeat the experience. No hangovers were reported and presumably no one awoke the morning after to rooms strewn with empty bottles and cans. In a six-month follow-up study, none of the subjects had developed enduring psychotic or neurotic symptoms. The experiment was a success in demonstrating that under favorable conditions, ordinary people were able to have an inwardly enriching experience with psilocybin. Things on the psychedelic front were looking good. The Earth's special mushroom, albeit in pill form, was showing promise.

These findings were eclipsed however by the legendary Good Friday Experiment of 1962, surely one of the most radical and far-reaching psychological studies ever undertaken. In their general approach to research and the collection of data, psychologists, particularly up until the 1950s and 1960s, had always had a rather special affinity for rats, more often than not placing them in specially constructed boxes where behavioral phenomena like classical conditioning (you remember Pavlov's dog salivating to the sound of a bell) could readily be observed. Go into any academic psychology department and you will likely find and smell a rat or three, so beloved are these furry rodents by the ardent psychologist. Rats are cheap, easily maintained, and behave in a remarkably reliable way (like small machines) in their reactions to the manipulating advances of experimental psychologists. Explanations about human behavior can then be extrapolated (so they say) from the results of these rattish experiments on the reasonable but limited assumption that all mammalian brains run on similar principles.

Such ratomorphism, as the writer and philosopher Arthur Koestler cynically termed it, used to dominate psychological science, and topics like mind and consciousness were banished from the scientific arena like some forbidden fruit unfit for empirical consumption, even though, of course, the science of psychology is itself mediated through the stuff of consciousness. Today things are fortunately beginning to change, and a kind of philosophical psychological approach to mind and consciousness is emerging, a topic I will later explore in much detail.

Back in 1962 the Good Friday Experiment was as far removed from rats as is possible, stretching empirical science to its limits. It was the type of experiment that our controversial psilocybin demanded, and its results remain significant.

A Divine Invasion Upsets the Status Quo

A psychology student named Walter Pahnke, working for his doctorate, arranged the experiment with the help of Leary and other members of the Harvard Psilocybin Project. It was an attempt to capture the psilocybin-induced mystical experience in quantitative measures through questionnaires. Although questionnaire studies fall foul of a number of methodological criticisms, it is the only viable scientific approach to measuring the reported subjective effects of drugs. It is not enough for someone to claim that psilocybin is a wonderful substance that elicits transcendental feelings of awe. Rather, one must obtain objective measures if one wants to bring entheogens under the analytical eye of science; if, that is, one is a scientist who believes science offers the best approach to psilocybin—a moot point to be sure. If you've tried the stuff yourself and you've traveled to those divine realms, then you are one who *knows*. Leary knew, as did the other members of the project, but though they had tasted superconsciousness, they were still caught in the unenviable position of trying to document the psilocybin experience with the relatively cumbersome tools provided by the science of that era. Understandably perhaps, Leary was soon to don a kaftan, abandon academia, and hijack the media instead. Yet the Good Friday Experiment, or "Miracle of Marsh Chapel" as it became known, still stands out as the classic psychology experiment of that pre-LSD period.

Five rooms in the basement of Boston University chapel were reserved for Pahnke and the psilocybin project team. Twenty subjects, all theology students and therefore at home in the chapel building, took part in the study, which employed a double-blind methodological approach. This meant that half of them received psilocybin while the other half received a mildly psychoactive placebo. No one knew who got what, not even the experimenters, though it soon became clear who had been given the mushroom pills.

Leary later recalled that the ten psilocybin subjects began to act rather unconventionally. Some began to wander around the chapel murmuring prayer. One lay on the floor, some lounged on benches, while another began playing strange music on the chapel organ. The most intense effects, however, were occurring in the depths of the subjects' psyches, and an analysis of the subsequent 147-item psychological questionnaires completed by the subjects soon revealed what had taken place.

The questionnaires were designed to probe various aspects of the psilocybin experience. Parts of the subjects' reports were then rated by naive markers, who had to compare this psilocybin phenomenology (phenomenology is the study of direct conscious experience) with mystical phenomenology taken from various religious scriptures, without knowing which was which.

Incredibly, the results showed that the psilocybin group had mystical religious experiences indistinguishable from those reported in religious literature. This was a decidedly controversial finding. A naturally occurring substance, although in pill form thanks to Sandoz, had been shown to be capable of generating a full-blown mystical experience within the religiously ripe minds of theology students. The implications were enormous, and, as we shall see, many a storm was to brew over the validity of chemically induced theophany. Traditionally cherished beliefs about mystical enlightenment and the religious impulse were being threatened by, of all things, a drug, and this was guaranteed to cause uproar and dissent among those members of the priestly elite who serve to police communion with the divine.

Despite the beginnings of heated controversy, Pahnke's thesis on psilocybin was uneasily approved, though he was not allowed to continue his line of work and his requests for further government funds were denied. Something was obviously amiss. Psilocybin—this wild alchemical product of Nature—was becoming a threat to long-established power structures both in academia and in the realm of traditional religious beliefs about divine communion. Psilocybin's wild and ebullient energy, dormant for so long, was once more on the loose, this time flowing though the very heart of the Western establishment.

In one sense, it was as if the Good Friday study could be viewed as the last experiment that the scientist keen on ascertaining the nature of consciousness and reality needed to perform. The message seemed clear. Humanity could transcend its secular level of being and raise itself to a new order, an idealistic dream shared by many early Western psychedelic explorers. Psilocybin could be carefully used as a source of knowledge and wisdom, allowing people glimpses of a transcendental reality that is a mere perceptual step away.

As it was, the lofty psychedelic dream shared by so many at the time never quite materialized, although I would argue that this was mainly due to the lack of an explanatory framework for the psilocybin experience, and not because the idealism of the dream was untenable. Indeed, at this early stage in psychedelic research, almost nothing was known of psilocybin's mechanism of action, and apart from Jung's notion of the collective unconscious, there were little in the way of speculative psychological theories able to capture the full import and impact of the psilocybin experience in a nonreductive way. In a real sense, language let the scientists down, or at least the lack of descriptive terminology and lack of conceptual sophistication meant that psychedelic phenomenology remained an abstruse anomaly. And anomalies, even if they might contain the essence of some new ways of understanding the nature of reality, are more often than not deliberately buried out of sight, or at least the conceptually uncomfortable data are all too easily lost somewhere at the back of the scientific community's filing cabinet. Such a fate did indeed meet the psychedelic experience, and by the late 1960s almost all of the world's known psychedelic substances had been deemed a dangerous social threat and were promptly declared illegal. Scientific research into psychedelics was thereby halted.

However, this was not a big and final end to the matter, and today scientists are once again gradually returning to experimentation with psilocybin—often with a view to elucidating psilocybin's therapeutic potential. It is also the case that psilocybin mushroom use by the public is now more widespread than ever, particularly in Europe. Indeed, various specialized spore samples and grow kits can now be purchased in many countries—although it is still unclear how the law will react to this novel situation. Given recent scientific reports on the relatively benign nature of psilocybin (which I discuss in more detail at the end of this book), one hopes that good sense will prevail and that the mushroom's decidedly spiritual influence will continue to be integrated within our Western culture.

Update: Just How Good Was That Friday?

As further evidence of psilocybin's vivid effect upon those fortunate theology students, and so that I can build support for my enthusiastic contention that the psilocybin mushroom represents a kind of medicinal soul food with which to reconceive the nature of reality, I now recount a follow-up study of sixteen of the twenty original subjects of the Good Friday Experiment. This was undertaken by Rick Doblin, president of the Multidisciplinary Association for Psychedelic Studies (MAPS), in the late 1980s when, by this time, many of the subjects were practicing ministers.

Doblin administered the same questionnaire used in the original experiment and found that there was still a significant difference between the two groups as to the reported effects of the experience. After twenty-five years, the psilocybin group's characterization of their mystical experiences had actually strengthened (or matured). Also, whereas the control subjects who had received the placebo could barely remember the day in question, the psilocybin group still had clear memories of that eventful day. For instance, Reverend K. B. remembered:

It left me with a completely unquestioned certainty that there is an environment bigger than the one I am conscious of. I have my own interpretation of what that is, but it went from a theoretical proposition to an experiential one.[1]

Reverend Y. M. recalled:

I closed my eyes and the visuals were back . . . and it was as if I was in an ocean of bands, streams of color, streaming past me. The colors were brilliant and I could swim down any one of those colors.[2]

More from Reverend K. B., who is more specific:

With my eyes closed I had an unusually vivid scene of the procession going by [from the Passion of Christ]. A scene quite apart from any imagining or anything on my part . . . kind of like watching a movie or something, it was apart from me but very vivid.[3]

And further:

I've remained convinced that my ability to perceive things was artificially changed, but the perceptions I had were as real as anything else.[4]

That this minister viewed psilocybin as an artificial catalyst is to be forgiven. Careful consideration reveals that psilocybin is a legitimate natural product of Nature, an unusual piece of biospherical fabric to be sure but no more artificial than the oxygen we breathe or the plants that we eat. Rarer perhaps, and not absolutely essential, yet certainly not artificial.

The Reverend K. B.'s description of the visionary experience as a kind of movie issuing from somewhere outside of one's sense of self is one of psilocybin's hallmark effects and could not be put more clearly. This is the overwhelming impression gained while in the visionary state that arises with eyes closed. One is confronted with a powerful communicatory flow of organized symbolic information that compels one to infer an intelligent presence of some kind as the issuer of the information. Although after such a profound experience one might question the grounds for inferring an "Other," during the visionary episode itself one might well be utterly overwhelmed by a sense of intentional communication, leaving no room for doubt.

In a way, these animated superdreamscapes, charged as they are with striking metaphorical imagery, are akin to those vivid dreams we sometimes experience during sleep and that leave us momentarily in awe as we later recall them before they invariably fade away. However, during psilocybin-induced visions one is still very much conscious—more conscious and attentive in fact than normal—so that the visionary scenes are not forgotten, or at least their overall message, impact, and urgency are not forgotten.

Remarking on the sense of eternity that often accompanies the effects of psilocybin, Reverend S. J. remembers:

All of a sudden I felt sort of drawn out into infinity. . . . I felt that I was caught up in the vastness of Creation. . . . I did experience that . . . classic kind of blending. . . . The main thing about it was a sense of timelessness.[5]

Again, these quite simple reminiscences show that psilocybin carries epistemological value, as it seems to elicit a special kind of knowledge not ordinarily available but that is of immeasurable value to us in terms of spirit and soul. Even the most dogged skeptic must concede that, at the very least, psilocybin taps deep realms of the unconscious or imagination, revealing a hitherto unknown and unrealized creative potential.

My claim is that a form of "higher intelligence" and wisdom is indeed accessed through the mushroom. Whether this "higher intelligence" stems from some unconscious psychological realm, that is, that deep within the psyche lie vast fields of highly organized information that are "released" into personal consciousness during the entheogenic state, or that one actually gets to communicate with a sentient presence—the transcendental Other as we can call it—is open to question, although both suggestions may be linked in some way.

For the time being, whatever we suspect underlies the visionary state, we can see that the psilocybin experience is a compelling area of study, since consciousness and perceived reality, the very ground of our lives, have the potential to exfoliate like some new, exotic flower. Our everyday awareness is seen to be constrained and bounded, as if we were, for most of the time, subroutine prisoners in some vast, Matrix-like computation that surges ever onward. Psilocybin temporarily dissolves these constraints, conferring on the experiencer an increased cognitive freedom, facilitating new directions of thought that are not normally available. The inner world becomes subject to pictographic myth, while the outer world reveals itself as the living structure of some divine being, even the most mundane objects suddenly acquiring a holy aura. This is the latent promise of the mushroom: to reveal psychological realms that can enrich our collective existence as living, breathing hominid creatures knitted together within the Earth's evolving biosphere. Natural entheogenic agents like the psilocybin mushroom enable a particular type of knowledge to come to an individual, a type of knowledge that science and philosophy can barely approach, but which nonetheless bears heavily on our innermost nature.

The Good Friday Experiment took science as close as it is likely to get to mysticism, apart from analyzing the actual brain during the mystical state. Yet even that high-tech approach would dodge the main issue, which is the experience itself and what it tells us about consciousness and reality. One has a choice regarding strategies. One can try to map the brain to the nth degree in the laboratory or one can simply plunge into a direct confrontational experience. The mushroomic Miracle of Marsh Chapel indicates the latter endeavor as being the most attractive, rewarding, and adventurous option befitting the human spirit. At least to start with . . .

Objectivity forces me to disclose a mild downside to the aforementioned study. Doblin's long-term follow-up showed that most of the psilocybin subjects reported some negative aspects to their experiences that were somewhat downplayed at the time of the original experiment. In other words, their inner worlds were not constantly flooded by divine light but rather there was a mixture of positive and negative aspects to the experience. Actually, psychological unease of one kind or another is somewhat inevitable if one engages with the mushroom. One sees oneself clearly without the superficial trappings of a contrived image and personality. The mushroom somehow amplifies the subconscious and the unconscious, forcing one to confront bad habits and neuroses. One is also made aware of any problematic relationships with friends, family, and associates. Nothing remains hidden to the mushroom, and this will often lead to a psychological "shake-up" to persons hitherto blind to self-knowledge. After all, the tenet "know thyself" is bound up in some way with all spiritual disciplines, suggesting that one must come fully to terms with oneself before one can begin to inwardly develop one's state of consciousness. Psilocybin and other entheogens would seem to highlight this timeless truth to such an extent that further psychedelic experimentation will prove to be of negative value unless one has dealt adequately with one's state of self-knowledge. The more balanced and healthily resolved one's inner world, the more rewarding will the mushroom experience be.

Another negative and unpublicized fact about Pahnke's original experiment was that one of the psilocybin subjects had to have a shot of chlorpromazine (an antipsychosis drug) to combat some unwelcome symptoms. It seems that the student took the words to a sermon about the Christian need to spread the word rather too literally, a struggle ensuing as he tried to leave the chapel. I would point out that such impractical messianic zeal can be countered by administering some self-control rather than chlorpromazine, though we must bear in mind that these theology students were essentially naive to psilocybin's psychological effects. The more prepared one is to receive psilocybin in terms of an awareness of its scope of effect, the more likely will the ensuing experience be wholly positive and trouble free.

Despite the unearthed downsides, at the end of his follow-up study, Doblin concluded that: "All psilocybin subjects participating in the long-term follow-up, but none of the controls, still considered their original experience to have had genuinely mystical elements and to have made a uniquely valuable contribution to their spiritual lives."[6]

And there you have it, straight from the mouths of practicing ministers. Psilocybin doth work, and it doth work well. Human consciousness is positively mutable and reality is up for reinterpretation. Amen.

Leary Begins to Spread the Good News

During the early days of the psilocybin project, Leary actually got to meet Wasson. Although both had received the sacred mushroom vision and had come to value the experience as highly significant, their attitudes toward its use were glaringly opposed. According to Leary, Wasson tried to come across as the authority on mushrooms, more interested in his own experiences than those of Leary and his associates. Wasson was also vehemently against the current trend of widespread psilocybin use, informing Leary that disclosing the secret of the mushroom to the modern world had destroyed its power. Indeed, he would later write of his abject remorse at publicizing the Mexican sacred mushroom ceremonies.

Leary, however, was soon to prove Wasson wrong on the potency of the mushroom. Psilocybin cannot fail to empower those who explore its magical effects, and, having taken it over fifty times within the first year of the Harvard project, Leary was by this time a much-inspired man on the verge of attempting world revolution.

With his constant supply of mushroom pills, the heavily armed Leary soon began extending his influence to various contemporary American poets, writers, and artists, in particular, luminaries like Jack Kerouac, Neal Cassady, Allen Ginsberg, William S. Burroughs, and Dizzy Gillespie, to name but a few. Leary began to realize that while many were enthralled by the experience, others were overtly disinterested. Youth emerged as a salient factor in attitudes toward psilocybin, and this led Leary to propose that the older that people were, the more fear they would have toward the visionary experience.

I would surmise that this fear was the same fear that led the Spanish friars to denounce the Aztecs' mushroom use as devil worship. Such fear also led to the fervent witch-burning policies undertaken by medieval inquisitors. Once a person has a rigidly established psychological model of reality, then any tearing asunder of that model, any kind of incompatible data that threaten its existence, produces a negative and often violent reaction. An open-minded approach to psilocybin is therefore essential if it is to have a beneficial effect. One must tread slowly and carefully and familiarize oneself with the new territory since pitfalls lie in wait of the unwary and hasty explorer. The experience must then be somehow integrated into life in a way that minimizes social disharmony.

The year 1962 saw the ominous arrival of LSD at Harvard, and the entire cultural psychedelic momentum was to change. Leary was so struck by this new synthetic alternative to psilocybin that LSD fast became the focus of attention, and the mushroom faded almost into obscurity. Leary claimed that LSD was superior in effect to psilocybin, and his high priest standing at this time meant that others were only too keen to follow his recommendations. Conversely, the late Terence McKenna argued that natural psilocybin is a far more visionary substance and ranked its worth above synthetic LSD (McKenna also popularized the term *Other* to refer to the intelligible presence accessed through psilocybin). McKenna held a more contemporary organic view that linked the mushroom with the natural homeostatic systems of the biosphere. As mentioned, in the 1960s there were little in the way of holistic theories about the biosphere, and ethnobotanical investigations of plant-using shamans had yet to gather much publicity.

At the same time that LSD flooded Harvard, opposition to psychedelic experimentation began in earnest, partly due to the omnipresent influence of the CIA, which still wanted a monopoly on psychedelic drugs, and partly because of the alarming growth in popular experimentation with LSD, which was still legal and fast becoming available everywhere. In 1963 Leary was forced to resign from Harvard, and so he duly took his LSD interests out into the big experimental arena of mainstream culture, where he found himself to be quite adept in the role of psychedelic revolutionary. It is unfortunate that his clarion call, "Turn on, tune in, drop out," was only two-thirds commendable. Drop out? This kind of negative turn of phrase could only serve to condemn Leary. (Why not "learn" or "listen carefully"?) Still, the pop psychedelic insurgency instigated by Leary ensured that the "swinging" 1960s got under way, and despite the mass drop-out by the youth populous, the resulting counterculture was to spawn a wealth of innervating art, literature, and music.

Leary's anarchic adventures went on to include the formation of the League for Spiritual Discovery (yes, that's LSD), major court cases, his brief role as the most dangerous man in America, incarceration, a dramatic jailbreak, and his kidnapping by the Black Panthers in the early 1970s. Interested readers can read of Leary's enthralling escapades elsewhere, in particular, within the pages of his autobiography, *Flashbacks,* or in a lively book by Jay Stevens called *Storming Heaven: LSD and the American Dream.*

Unbeknown to virtually anyone at this time, mushrooms containing psilocybin were to be found growing throughout Europe and North America, and not just in Mexico. The Earth itself, a far more efficient and ubiquitous supplier of entheogens than the lab technicians at Sandoz, was secretly churning out millions of psilocybin mushrooms across its biospherical surface, an extraordinary fact that did not reach public attention until the late 1960s and early 1970s (since then it has been speculated that prehistoric Europeans knew about psilocybin and that its use influenced the dreamy spiral icons carved on rocks in places like Ireland. Interested readers should consult Paul Devereux's book *The Long Trip* for more information on this incipient subject).

Attempts to Dam the Flow of Psilocybin

At this point in our journey I should like to examine the main objections that were often leveled against the use of psilocybin when it first became available in the wake of Wasson's discovery. Such objections were expressed precisely and clearly by various writers and social commentators, most notably the writer and philosopher Arthur Koestler, whom I briefly mentioned earlier. Koestler, who had written numerous acclaimed books on science, philosophy, and the paranormal, tried psilocybin on at least two occasions at the start of the 1960s. Leary, a fan of Koestler's work, had written to him about psilocybin's miraculous properties and had invited him to come out to Harvard to try it for himself.

As it happened, Koestler's first encounter with psilocybin occurred at the psychology department of the University of Michigan, which, unfortunately, was another hotbed for covert CIA experimentation and therefore not the best of places in which to start one's entheogenic journeying. His second taste occurred at Leary's apartment, as Leary had originally intended. Both encounters convinced Koestler that psilocybin was basically worthless, an opinion dramatically at odds with Leary and most others who had tried it.

On March 12, 1961, the British newspaper the *Sunday Telegraph* published a polemic article by Koestler in which he denounced the psilocybin experience. Entitled "Return Trip to Nirvana," this account described Koestler's personal psychedelic experiences and concluded in no uncertain terms that psilocybin had nothing whatsoever to offer humanity. He wrote: "Chemically induced hallucinations, delusions and raptures may be frightening or wonderfully gratifying; in either case they are in the nature of confidence tricks played on one's own nervous system."[7]

He offered even harsher words about his second trip at Leary's apartment. When an American writer and acquaintance talked of "cosmic awareness," "expanding consciousness," and "Zen Enlightenment," Koestler thought this "downright obscene, more so than four-lettered words."[8] Clearly, here was a man a trifle irritated by the blossoming psychedelic culture. Koestler was no hip hippie.

Koestler went on to argue that psilocybin gave rise to "pressure-cooker mysticism" and no more. Discussing Huxley's pro-psychedelic observation that many mystics and religious visionaries employed various physiology-changing techniques like breathing exercises and fasting to facilitate altered states of awareness, Koestler countered with a parable about mountain climbing, claiming that the view obtained when one has slogged for hours on foot up the mountain is far superior to the view obtained at the end of a cable-car journey. In other words, the laborious toil undertaken by the fasting, self-flagellating, cave-dwelling ascetic leads to a qualitatively different revelation than the armchair mystic who merely pops down a handful of Sandoz pills.

This is the classic philosophical objection laid against the potential transcendental effects of substances like psilocybin. It is too easy. Where is the relentless sweat and toil? Where are the physical scars of the tortuous journey that preceded the mystical illumination? How can one possibly have access to realms of spiritual ecstasy without undergoing years of suffering? Are we to admit that any Tom, Dick, or Leary can achieve transcendence without experiencing untold pain, misery, and self-mortification?

Koestler, at least, was convinced that there were no shortcuts to the divine, and he stated this clearly to Leary and in the newspaper article. Significantly, he admitted to Leary that he was in the wrong state of mind when he tried psilocybin at Leary's apartment, that he had been awoken to painful memories of being a political prisoner during the war. Similarly, on the night before his first unpleasant brush with the drug, he'd had disturbing dreams that lingered on long enough to pervade the psychedelic state. In fact, Leary himself had second thoughts in inviting Koestler to try psilocybin, as he came across as being too controlled and rational. Although these considerations go a long way in explaining Koestler's negative encounters, the criticisms he raised still stand strong, and the advocate for the continued investigation of psilocybin must perforce respond to the allegations.

I can offer two lines of defence to parry Koestler's objections. First, it is almost certain that Koestler did not dwell upon the fact that psilocybin is a natural part of the environment and not an unnatural synthetic product. Had he actually gone out and picked psilocybin mushrooms for himself perhaps his experiences might have been more rewarding, because the actual act of mushroom collection leaves an indelible earthly mark upon the memory. This fact of psilocybin's naturalness, which I consistently remark on, deserves a still more detailed examination, and this is a good opportunity to begin doing so. I will return to answering Koestler's criticisms after this brief diversion.

Food for Thought

As we shall see in much more detail later, psilocybin is believed to cause its effects by acting upon nerve cells, or neurons, within the brain. In particular, it acts on those neurons that utilize a substance called serotonin. Serotonin is a chemical messenger, or neurotransmitter, that allows individual neurons to communicate with one another to transmit and process information. Now, the various compounds employed by brains to process information have evolved over millions of years, and they are determined by the chemicals available in the environment, in particular, from the raw materials available in food. Serotonin has emerged as a key neurotransmitter, or chemical messenger, because it can be produced relatively simply from raw materials. You cannot just have any old chemical compound acting as a neurotransmitter; it has to have arisen through evolution under the deterministic constraints set by the laws of chemistry and the further constraints set by the availability of food.

Hence, serotonin is bound up with the chemistry of the environment. If the chemical constituency of the natural environment was radically different, Nature would have been forced to evolve completely different neurotransmitters that reflect to the constraints set by that environment. In this sense, we are indeed what we eat, and the notion that consensus reality is a popular serotonergic hallucination yields a formidably uncanny wisdom. Our minds, our very consciousnesses, depend upon the hardware of the brain, which in turn depends on chemical structure, which further depends on diet. Natural psilocybin mushrooms can enter one's diet, and the new chemicals subsequently operating within the brain will alter awareness so that our common hardwired "serotonergic reality" shifts, as it were, to a rare "mushroom-wired psilocybinetic reality."

Having said this much it should now be absolutely clear that the psilocybin mushroom experience is wholly natural, and that it arises out of an environmentally driven alteration in brain chemistry in as much as the psilocybin mushroom is part of the environment. There is nothing artificial about this process at all. Just as we can selectively pick wheat to make bread for our physical well-being, so too can we selectively pick and consume natural psilocybin mushrooms for our spiritual well-being. Both wheat and mushroom are legitimate natural expressions of the interwoven biospherical system within which we are embedded. I think it unlikely that Koestler considered these environmental facts before making his negative judgments.

The second line of defence against Koestler's classic objections is that it is not certain that technological short-cuts—as he called them—are necessarily bad. Is not the Earth viewed from space satellites beautiful? Viewed thus, is it really any less beautiful than if we were to build a really large ladder and clamber up to get the same view? Should we abandon all labor-saving technology and make things as hard as possible for humanity?

I think not. Huxley's vision in *The Doors of Perception* of a mass-marketed psychedelic that enlightens the world cannot be faulted on its technological methodology. If technology, pharmaceutical or otherwise, can hasten some form of improved psychological condition, then the only thing stopping this is a sense of distrust and guilt, arguably instilled more often than not by dogmatic religion. Indeed, Leary surmised that Koestler's mountaintop parable arose from a deep-seated Catholic guilt, a guilt that arises all too easily in the face of pleasure, ecstasy, and the bounds of human freedom.

Having defended the idea of humanity-saving technology, I would once more remind the critical reader that psilocybin is not a technological product anyway (at least not in the traditional sense). Koestler perceived it so because his psilocybin came in the form of a Sandoz pill, the perfect symbol of a modern technological fix. This is in direct contrast to the overtly organic symbolism of the wild mushroom.

When Koestler left Leary's company to return to New York, it was wryly noted that he did not walk back but got a plane. Leary concluded that to ignore psilocybin as a psychological tool would be akin to rejecting the microscope because it made seeing too easy, a good analogy since both tools uncover the hidden riches of Nature.

I think it safe to conclude that Koestler's negative attitude stemmed principally from his painful store of POW memories and the unresolved conflicts lying in the depths of his psyche. In particular, I would suggest, as did Leary, that Koestler's Catholic guilt played a large part in his rejection of the mushroom.

This same type of traditional religious guilt, which seems to have plagued humans from time immemorial and which easily transforms into an oppressive drive against other people's freedom, was also displayed, among others, by the French poet Baudelaire. Like other nineteenth-century poets and writers, such as Byron, Shelley, Balzac, De Quincey, and Samuel Taylor Coleridge (who reputedly wrote *Kubla Khan* after an opium reverie), Baudelaire once used "trendy" psychoactive plant products like opium and cannabis for creative purposes. Yet he later came to utterly despise them, as if they were the root of all that is evil and misleading, no less than the most cunning of the Devil's tools for thwarting humankind from reaching God.

The point is missed, almost deliberately it seems. Psychoactive plant substances are not inherently evil; rather they can become destructive if used in excess or for the wrong reasons, much as any benign substance can become harmful if used beyond moderation. Had Koestler been in the possession of the right frame of mind and received the ultimate gift of the psilocybin mushroom, that is, had he perceived a direct communion with the transcendental Other and realized that this was a wholly natural phenomenon, then perhaps he would have embraced psilocybin's cultural healing potential.

It seems, then, that if the potentially spiritual effects of the mushroom are likened to a stream, the stream can "hit" the wrong human mind, or at least the wrong state of mind, causing the stream to be blocked. Where it cannot flow on and blossom, psilocybin's numinous potential will remain unrealized. God's Flesh is clearly not for everyone. This fact must perforce be considered at length before any kind of nontrivial investigation commence.

The Mushroom as Medicine

In his noted book *The Ghost in the Machine,* written in 1967, Koestler had a wonderful opportunity to praise the virtues of entheogenic agents. Among other things, the book is concerned with humankind's violent, paranoid, destructive streak and how this evil can be overcome. After documenting the awful historical effects of our "schizophysiology," as he terms it, Koestler argues that our only hope for survival is to develop techniques that supplant biological evolution. He reminds us of all the ways we have tampered with Nature—like birth control, disease prevention, and artificial environment creation—in order to simulate and control the process of evolution for our own adaptive advantage. So, asks Koestler, can we not invent a remedy for the human tendency toward destruction?

Unable to ignore Aldous Huxley's popular advocacy of psychedelics as cultural healing agents, Koestler opposes that kind of solution, claiming that it is fundamentally wrong and naive to expect drugs to confer free gifts upon the mind. In other words, Koestler asserts that drugs cannot put into the mind something that is not already there. He argues that the "psycho-pharmacist" cannot add to the faculties of the brain, at best we can only eliminate obstructions that might impede the brain's proper functioning.

Koestler finally envisages a "mental stabilizer" or hormone that can integrate the psyche. He even goes as far as fearing that his readers will be disgusted by the idea of relying upon salvation through molecular chemistry rather than spiritual rebirth. This is an astonishing claim, even the more so since he refuses to advocate natural entheogenic substances as his "mental stabilizer."

Contrary to Koestler's beliefs, Nature and the evolutionary process have not let the human race down; rather, we have been blind to Nature's subtle ecological solutions. Nature works in mysterious ways, one of which is the production of plants and fungi possessing vital shamanic power through which the web of life, which includes human culture, can continue to function healthily.

Although it might sound somewhat archaic to seek curative help from plants and fungi in our modern era, we should keep in mind that shamanism is perhaps the oldest form of religious psychotherapy and that the knowledge gained by visionary shamans was used precisely to help heal the tribe. There is no reason to assume that such psychedelic shamanism is now impotent or irrelevant, especially if we consider the interconnectedness of the biosphere. In ecological terms, the shamanic ingestion of plants and fungi is an entirely natural process that—when we take into account the ecological system of shaman, tribe, and plant—is essentially homeostatic in that one part of the environment acts upon another to restore balance and health; in this case certain plants and fungi yield aid through their psychological effects and the higher knowledge that they convey. This "eco-psychotherapy," as we may call it, highlights just how much we are connected to the rest of life's web and how the solutions to our problems are often to be found growing around us (including, of course, potential botanical cures for cancer and AIDS still to be discovered in what is left of the Earth's great rain forests).

Entheogenic species of plant and fungus still offer us a wealth of psychotherapeutic power if we choose to look their way, not to mention the information they reveal about the chemical mutability of human consciousness and the possible transformation of our models of reality.

Like most philosophers, Koestler seemed far removed from the natural botanical world, but with the advent of ecological awareness movements and a renewed interest in all things Green and environmentally friendly, our deep connection to the rest of Nature looms ever more apparent and a Green cultural ethos is already establishing itself. By radical means, Nature itself may yet cure our destructive streak.

Support for the Mushroom Grows

Another well-known writer at the time of psilocybin's first wave of Western use was the revered author and poet Robert Graves, who also wrote publicly of his mushroom experience. Actually, Graves had been intrigued by mushrooms ever since he had licked a species of fly agaric as a young boy and had consequently experienced burning sensations on his tongue. Perhaps the incident was a symbolic biospherical kiss of sorts, or at least a taste of things to come. At any rate, as the reader will recall, it was Graves who originally notified Wasson of the secret mushroom ceremonies still extant in Mexico. It comes as no surprise then that Graves eventually went on to write speculative articles on entheogenic mushroom use in ancient Greece (his speculations remain contentious) after he tried the sacrament in Wasson's New York apartment in 1960.

Graves was, it transpires, understandably apprehensive about his first brush with psilocybin, especially worried that he might perceive "demons" behind his closed eyes. Being the author of the acclaimed *The White Goddess,* a book about a historical cult of goddess worship, was no guarantee that Gaia's mushroom would shower him with grace (Gaia was originally the name of the Greek Earth goddess).

As it was, Graves need not have worried. Unable to write during his rapture, he passively let the experience overwhelm him. Afterward he was to write that he had seen a "mountain-top Eden" and experienced the "bliss of innocence" and "the knowledge of good and evil."[9] He had even felt capable of solving any problem in the world, as if he had access to all of the world's knowledge.

Graves went on to predict that a once-sacred substance entrusted to an elite few would soon be sought by "jaded sensation seekers," although they would likely be dissatisfied with psilocybin, as it was not a "drug" as such because it failed to stupefy like alcohol. He ended his descriptive account with the following warning, which still rings true today:

> Good and evil alternate in most people's hearts. Few are habitually at peace with themselves; and whoever prepares to eat hallucinogenic mushrooms should take as careful stock of his mental and moral well-being as initiates took before attending the Eleusinian Mysteries. . . . This peculiar virtue of *psilocybin,* the power to enhance personal reality, turns "Know Thyself!" into a practical precept; and may commend it as the sacramental food of some new religion.[10]

Fine and prescient words indeed, once more indicative that psilocybin should be approached cautiously and with a "good heart." Graves's remark about "jaded sensation seekers" is almost identical to Wasson's emerging dismay at the hoards of "oddballs," "thrill seekers," and "riff-raff" who were already descending in droves upon Mexico in search of divine mushrooms. However, this type of popular reaction to a new phenomenon was surely inevitable. Although it was to cause abject consternation among the psilocybin elite, to deny the mushroom outright to the masses is an impractical, short-sighted reaction to basic human nature. I would argue that knowledge of psilocybin's spiritual power is best laid open to all who might wish to seek it out. If this be considered by some as casting pearls before swine, then so be it. The point is that the end will justify the means, this end being, hopefully, a culture transformed with a revitalized veneration for the natural systems of the Earth and a deeper insight into the transcendental aspects of the reality process. The eco-destructive age in which we live surely demands a cure along these lines.

Moksha-Medicine Grows on the Verge of Paradise

Aldous Huxley explicitly summed up the early mood of optimism surrounding psychedelics in a speech he delivered to psychologists in 1961, and somewhat more implicitly in his Utopian novel *Island,* published in 1962. In the speech Huxley predicted that psychological science would inevitably be confronted with more and more data on the visionary experience induced by substances like psilocybin. Although these experiences might be valueless—no more significant than a trip to the movies—it might be the case that if the visionary experience were cooperated with, if some deep meaning were ascertained and acted on, then this could be crucial in changing the lot of humanity. Huxley conjectured that psychedelics encouraged a state of mind in which reality is perceived in a non-utilitarian manner and that the visionary experience could lead to a change in behavior for the good. If so, this would reinforce the maxim of eminent psychologist William James that a spiritual or mystical experience be judged pragmatically through its consequences upon the life of the experiencer. If the psychedelic visionary state can enrich one's life, then, by definition, it is for the good.

In *Island,* which was Huxley's final novel, his fictional Edenic islanders use "moksha-medicine," an entheogenic mushroom, as part of their religious rites. Indeed, the mushroom supports the islanders' paradise. This invented mushroom was almost certainly based upon the psilocybin mushroom, as Huxley had tried psilocybin on a number of occasions.

The issues raised in his earlier work *The Doors of Perception* are discussed by his islanders, in particular, whether the effects of moksha-medicine are illusory or real. Through one particular piece of fictional dialogue we are asked to consider the idea that perhaps the brain *transmits* consciousness rather than produces it. In other words, perhaps moksha-medicine allows a larger volume of what Huxley refers to as Mind at Large (Mind with a big "M") to enter one's individual mind (mind with a small "m"). Later, I will have much to say on this deceptively simple remark, as it bears heavily upon the whole notion of the stuff of consciousness.

As the islanders who champion moksha-medicine assert, even the bottom line places value on the experiences engendered by their mushroom, for if there is no objective content at all in the experience, it is still life-enriching and provides a "blessed transformation."

At one point in the story, the archetypal skeptic and disbelieving character Murugan receives the following rejoinder.

> You've been told that we are just a set of self-indulgent dope-takers wallowing in illusion and false *samadhis*. Listen, Murugan—forget all the bad language that's been pumped into you. Forget it at least to the point of making a single experiment. Take four hundred milligrams of *moksha*-medicine and find out for yourself what it does, what it can tell you about your own nature, about this strange world you've got to live in, learn in, suffer in, and finally die in. Yes, even you will have to die one day—maybe fifty years from now, maybe tomorrow. Who knows? But it's going to happen, and one's a fool if one doesn't prepare for it.[11]

Arguably the greatest, most eloquent, and most passionate spokesperson for the intelligent use of psychedelics during the 1950s and early 1960s, Aldous Huxley was unaware that his beloved moksha-medicinal fungi were, even as he wrote *Island,* spreading their mycelial networks throughout the wild unfarmed soil of most of the planet's Temperate Zone, their presence stretching across vast tracts of unspoiled land. In the autumn months, this secret underground arrangement was yielding countless psilocybin mushrooms, and Huxley never lived to discover this most astonishing of truths. All but forgotten by the mid-1960s, the psilocybin mushroom would eventually rise and fruit again.

Investigating the Earth's Alchemical Skin

Mexico and South America are the areas most associated with ritual entheogenic plant use. Apart from utilizing over twenty species of psilocybin mushroom, native Mexicans are also known to have employed the peyote cactus, the morning glory plant, and various species of datura, all of which contain potent visionary substances. The appeal of these plants, like the appeal of the mushroom, is that they support a channel of communication between the shaman and the spiritual domain. As we have seen, this unusual state of affairs arises not from hearsay or dogma, but from the mind-expanding effect of these plants on the human psyche, an effect equally reported by Westerners who might not necessarily be as spiritually inclined as native shamans.

In South America, aboriginal Amazonians still prepare a highly innervating psychedelic concoction called *ayahuasca,* made principally from an indigenous species of *Banisteriopsis* jungle vine, along with various other plant ingredients. This same potion is also taken as a sacramental tea by members of the União do Vegetal, an officially sanctioned church found throughout Brazil. The active principles in these potions are the substances harmine and dimethyltryptamine (DMT for short), the latter being a close structural relative of psilocybin. Shamans claim that ayahuasca facilitates communion with mythological beings as well as the souls of their ancestors. Similarly, species of *Virola* tree—the resin of which also contains DMT—are used to prepare entheogenic snuffs in Amazonian Colombia, which are taken to free the soul so that it may travel in the spiritual dimension.

These rich shamanic traditions highlight the ultimate way in which the natural environment can inspire an individual, as an intimate link is forged between the human psyche and the transcendental dimension of reality. Once such an emotionally charged shamanic connection has been so established and is reinforced through ritual use of a particular visionary plant, the process will generally cultivate an enduring sense of spirituality as well as a religious cosmology, as is the case surrounding the use of ayahuasca.

It is not surprising then that the profound psychedelic effect of these indigenous plants becomes firmly integrated into native culture, the shamanic knowledge so acquired reaffirming the culture's identity and the people's beliefs about the nature of reality. Furthermore, and perhaps of most importance, these plant species aid the practice of healing, whether mental, social, or purely physical. In native societies without a health service or subjugation to pharmaceutical conglomerates, the curative role of the shaman becomes an essential feature of daily life, with natural plant allies being very much a tool of the healing trade.

This kind of spiritual relationship between *Homo sapiens* and Nature is relatively rare, compared with, say, our close relational links to environmental resources like wood, grain, oil, or gas, yet the natural entheogenic link leaves all others behind in terms of its impact on one's sense of being. Whereas most of the relational ties that weave us into the living fabric of the biosphere are purely utilitarian in material terms, the resource provided by entheogenic plants operates at a different level, offering us spiritual nourishment, which, although seemingly intangible, can still have a cultural role to play, as witnessed by the important role of the shaman or native healer within aboriginal societies.

Of course, we might object here and assert that we have no need for shamans or entheogens in our technological culture, that we should leave these ostensibly marginal phenomena to those academic anthropologists and ethnobotanists whose vocation it is to gather information on such matters. Indeed, over the past thirty or so years a wealth of research articles have appeared that describe, in quite exacting botanical detail, how various entheogenic concoctions are prepared by the native cultures who still use them. However, it is almost unheard of for the witnessing ethnobotanists or anthropologists to actually experience the visionary brew for themselves. All the surrounding paraphernalia associated with the alchemical preparation might well be attested to right up to the actual implements employed to administer it, yet the principal substance of interest remains exempt from inquiry. This missing factor is what is actually driving the researchers' interests, namely, the resulting psychological effect of the preparation. After all, if the eventual experience generated by the sacrament were not in any way notable, there would be no shamanic legacy to study.

We can see then that although science might be commended for documenting what is, after all, a fast-disappearing aspect of aboriginal culture, the most important ingredient—the experience—is generally not witnessed. Perhaps this is because ethnobotanists feel there is no scientific banner under which one could reasonably and legitimately go ahead and sample the entheogen in question. But there is. It's called phenomenology—the study of immediate experience and its implications for the allied science of psychology. To actually personally partake of shamanic substances is to glean an insight into the psychological forces that they set in motion. With an inside view, we might understand more clearly the role of the entheogenic experience within the belief systems of native cultures. More to the point, we might gain valuable insights into the mutable potential of consciousness, thereby allowing us to make intellectual ground in otherwise intractable areas of human inquiry.

The Blind Eye of Science

The inadequacy of science in the study of entheogens is doubtless bound with the compartmentalization of science into separate disciplines. While it is rare for a scientist in any particular field to stray into another discipline, it can be argued that cross-boundary studies may be fruitful in initiating new insights and broader theories. In the case of entheogenic compounds, if we wish to properly understand the entire complex of the entheogenic experience—whether the experience of a native shaman or the experience of a Western experimenter—then a marriage must perforce be made between psychology, phenomenology, anthropology, and ethnobotany (and even metaphysics) since the subject area can embrace all these fields. If we bear in mind that disciplines like ethnobotany are relatively new anyway, the new discipline that I am envisaging is a distinct possibility. Waxing lyrical, I would call such an enterprise neo-shamanic phenomenology. At least it has an impressive ring to it.

But perhaps we assume that we already know all there is to know about the psychological modus operandi involved in the action of a classic entheogen like psilocybin? Perhaps a complete and satisfactory explanation of the visionary heights of the psilocybin experience has already been delivered by mainstream psychological science, reduced to a handy set of *merelys*? Alas (or thankfully), this is not the case. Not only are substances like psilocybin relatively new to the West, but also empirical psychological research was effectively curtailed for decades. The Harvard Psilocybin Project merely scratched the surface of the mushroom phenomenon, yet that in itself was enough to cause consternation to the scientific elite. Not to mince words, but psychedelic plants and fungi intimidate the scientific community, not just because of the multifarious disciplines potentially involved but also because their effects are just too controversial to handle. Heads turn away. Cold shoulders are shrugged.

Despite the dangers posed by the use of psychedelic substances—like their capacity to induce intense psychological terror (the so-called "bad trip")—native cultures have managed to "tame" them through a learned appreciation of their scope of effect. Furthermore, these cultures have acquired a wealth of edifying knowledge along the way. Hence, it is my belief that entheogenic flora and fungi have yet to make their full impact on the Western psyche. The knowledge to be gained from their use relating to our conceptions of reality and our theories about consciousness will prove to be of great value not only on an individual level but on the collective level also. These are reasonable claims since we undoubtedly base our value systems and mass cultural behaviors on our tacit beliefs about the Earth, life, and our role in the whole caboodle. The alluring possibility with the psilocybin experience is that after initiation one can come to view life in a radically different light. One learns what shamans have always known, that Nature is somehow imbued with intelligence, or at least the characteristics of intelligence. The biosphere, or Gaia, suddenly appears to be *really* alive, with visionary plants and fungi acting as a kind of interface between the wisdom of Nature and the human mind. In this way, an experienced and receptive individual can access transcendental information loaded with cultural and personal significance.

Given their uplifting and profoundly informative properties, psilocybin fungi can be viewed as a potentially symbiotic partner with our species. The symbiosis involves the new range of conception and perception galvanized into operation through the mushroom's effects and, in return, our propagation of the species or at least action on our part that serves the biosphere's overall interests in some way. In any case, psilocybin fungi, like other naturally occurring entheogens, are very much with us and here to stay. As far as we know, more people are familiar with the mushroom today than at any other time in history. Indeed, its use has continued to grow in popularity since the 1970s, when books first appeared detailing the various species that could be located in Europe and North America.

Notwithstanding the saturation of the entire globe in fungicides, restricted access to wilderness areas, or other madcap responses to the presence of psilocybin fungi, we have a choice as to whether to investigate the Earth's alchemical skin further or to turn our backs for fear of the unknown. If we do decide to pick up the "entheogenic gauntlet," we might well be rewarded with a cascade of novel insights into the deepest mysteries of being along with a vastly improved relationship with the rest of Nature. Official science can play a role in this noble venture as can independent research at the behest of no authority other than one's own.

An Inner Revolution Awaits

With various species of psilocybin mushroom growing throughout most wild places of the world (more than one hundred species are now known to flourish across the globe), and bearing in mind their illuminating properties, with which more and more people are becoming familiar, one suspects that some innervating cultural alchemy is at hand. As we shall see in more detail later, paradigms—conceptual belief systems—crumble and are rebuilt in the wake of the psilocybin experience. This kind of paradigm shifting is not simply an event that transpires after ingestion of the mushroom; rather, the process can continue long after the original experience, almost as if some process of long-term digestive refinement was taking place. By this I mean that if we reflect on the experience in terms of how, say, the mushroom works chemically, then we gain exceptional knowledge about the underlying chemistry of the brain and the potential parameters of consciousness. And if we reflect on the self-knowledge that the mushroom affords, our inner lives may duly be improved. The very real possibility of perceptual enhancement is also at stake, potentially raising our dialogue with Nature to new levels never imagined by conventional science and philosophy.

It is through these new conceptual tools, or new improved lenses, to borrow from an earlier metaphor, that old paradigms will perforce be challenged. If these old paradigms cannot deal with the psychedelic experience, then they must either be adapted or be confined to the past. It is in this way that psilocybin and its effects can become integrated into our culture.

Psychedelic Science: Round Two

By now, the reader might assume that mainstream science only skirts around the issues we are most concerned with, that the only extant psychedelic research revolves around ethnobotany. Indeed, with America's illegalization of LSD in 1966 and with the subsequent illegalization of almost all psychedelic drugs (Europe followed suit), human-based studies stopped dead. Everything on the experimental front went into cold storage. You could almost hear the bolts and locks sliding into place. Consciousness alteration had become a hostage to politics.

However, after all these years the locks have been surreptitiously picked and the politics of consciousness challenged. To be sure, a new kind of psychedelic research is gradually becoming apparent. This time around the scientists involved do not throw wild parties, nor do they exhort young people to "turn on, tune in, and drop out." Dressed in traditional lab coats and sensible shoes, the second generation of psychedelic scientists have got their empirical act together. Human-based psychedelic science is now returning to the academic fold, only with far less publicity than fifty years ago and with a lot more caution and circumspection. This time around, science is taking it step by careful step.

Leading the resurgence are two American organizations: The Multidisciplinary Association for Psychedelic Studies (MAPS), which I briefly mentioned in the last chapter, and the Heffter Research Institute (HRI). Founded in 1986, MAPS actively funds psychedelic research (as well as medical cannabis research) and helps scientists draw up their research protocols, a tough job when you have to approach notoriously conservative governmental agencies for permission to do your study. The HRI is a slightly younger organization, inaugurated in 1993 and named after Arthur Heffter, who, at the end of the nineteenth century, became the first scientist to isolate and systematically study a psychedelic compound from a plant—in this case mescaline from the peyote cactus. Of particular interest is a 2006 psilocybin study by the Johns Hopkins University of Medicine that was partly funded by the HRI. Researchers looked at the effects of psilocybin in healthy volunteers and found that when administered in comfortable and supportive conditions psilocybin potentiated life-affirming mystical experiences in the majority of the subjects. While this is nothing new, it is at least refreshing. The study also made headlines in many magazines and Internet video reports.

Apart from studying the effects of psychedelics upon healthy people, the main thrust of both MAPS and the HRI is finding a therapeutic use for these substances. This is a practical agenda that appears to be more acceptable to the various officiating bodies that control the availability of psychedelic agents to science. In reality, I believe that both organizations are acutely aware of the role that entheogens can play in the study of consciousness in and of itself. They are, perhaps wisely, less vocal about this "other" agenda. Despite wishes to the contrary, politics and science invariably mix, and this is the main reason why the therapeutic application of entheogens gets priority funding. Perhaps we are witness to paradigm shifting by stealth.

One recent study of note involved giving psilocybin to patients suffering from advanced-stage cancer. This was done to ascertain if psilocybin could, somewhat ironically perhaps, alleviate feelings of anxiety. Although the study was tentative and only involved a dozen terminal-cancer patients, the results were encouraging and showed that, according to some scales, anxiety was indeed reduced. This suggests that psilocybin can allow one to come to terms with troubling processes beyond one's control, to let go as it were to that which must perforce be left behind, and thereby find some kind of peace and acceptance. I have seen a poignant video clip of Pam Sakuda, one of the subjects involved in the study, and was deeply moved by her account of how the psilocybin experience helped her deal with the terrible ordeal of having a terminal illness. I was even more moved when I did an Internet search about her and learned she had died a few years after the study. It seemed that her psilocybin experience enabled her to speak bravely about what she was going though at the time.

Similar tentative studies have been conducted in which psilocybin was administered to patients suffering from obsessive-compulsive disorder (OCD). All those in the study showed decreases in their OCD symptoms while under the influence of psilocybin, with an improvement in their condition generally lasting more than 24 hours. As of 2011, psilocybin investigations are also under way under the auspices of the Beckley Foundation, a charitable trust based in Oxford in the United Kingdom. They are currently setting up studies to investigate psilocybin's role in memory recall, particularly the recall of repressed memories, which can be useful in psychotherapy, along with studies that will determine whether psilocybin can be used to successfully treat addiction to drugs like nicotine and alcohol. This latter study will prove interesting. For if psilocybin can, through sheer spiritual force, help people kick their addiction to booze and tobacco, then millions of people will likely be up for treatment and thus millions of spiritual experiences might be in the making. Who knows? Maybe we will be witness to an alchemical plot of global proportions in which various psychoactive substances are mingling, catalyzing one another's production, and even vying for cultural supremacy.

The Medical Use of Ibogaine

Another psychedelic drug presently receiving much scientific scrutiny over its possible medical utilization is ibogaine, an alkaloid derived from the West African plant *Tabernanthe iboga*. The plant is employed in situ by members of the Bwiti cult, a religious society found in Gabon and the Congo, who use it in much the same way psilocybin mushrooms and ayahuasca are traditionally used. The aim is to free the soul to connect with God and the ancestors. Here is a typical report from a native African user: "I wanted to know God—to know things of the dead and the land beyond. . . . I walked or flew over a long, multicolored road or over many rivers which led me to my ancestors, who then took me to the great gods."[1]

Ironically, perhaps, scientists have now established that the psychological effects of ibogaine can be used to break hard drug addiction. In the mid-1980s, Howard Lotsof, an ex-junkie cured through his experiences with ibogaine, formed a company to promote the medical use of ibogaine. So assured was he of ibogaine's capacity to break drug addiction, that Lotsof patented ibogaine treatments in the mid-1980s. Apparently, it is the unusually intense and personally significant visionary effects of ibogaine that can break the curse of hard drug addiction. Lotsof describes the visions induced by ibogaine in patients he has treated as being like movie clips: "The presentation of visual material is rapid. Some patients have described it as a movie run at high speed.

Others describe it as a slide show, each slide containing a motion picture of a specific event or circumstance in the viewer's life."[2]

Once more, we see the capacity of entheogens to instigate dramatic visionary experiences within the human psyche. Lotsof refers to these movie-clip visions as having Freudian and Jungian connotations, as if they could convey deep and significant meaning to the experiencer, and he infers that it is this process that lies at the heart of ibogaine's efficacy in breaking patterns of addiction. Lotsof believes that ibogaine is able to make patients reevaluate their lives and see the mistakes that they may have made and that may have led them into uncontrollable bouts of drug-taking. After treatment with a single dose of ibogaine, the majority of patients remain free from chemical dependence for three to six months, which indicates that ibogaine therapy needs to be ongoing and, if possible, be accompanied by other treatments. Interestingly, a recent BBC television documentary named *Tribe* showed intrepid explorer Bruce Parry taking part in a lengthy and sometimes harrowing Iboga religious ritual in Gabon. Parry reported that the Iboga plant allowed him to view his life from the perspective of those to whom he had caused emotional pain. After the Iboga rite was completed, Parry felt truly reborn.

Dimethyltryptamine

A leading figure in the second wave of psychedelic research is Dr. Rick Strassman, a psychiatrist who carried out some remarkable studies at the University of New Mexico in the mid-1990s. A look at his groundbreaking research reveals the spirit of a scientist determined to break through political bureaucracy in order to advance the frontiers of knowledge and add to the pharmaceutical armory of the practicing psychiatrist.

Strassman's work has centered on the prototypical entheogen dimethyltryptamine (DMT). Recall that DMT is a naturally occurring substance employed for millennia in the botanical potions and snuffs utilized by native Amazonian shamans. Classed as an ultra-short-acting hallucinogen, DMT, when administered intravenously to humans (as

opposed to the drinking of an ayahuasca brew), causes fantastic alterations in consciousness and yet is completely inactive within thirty minutes (the effects of ayahuasca can last for hours). If DMT is smoked, the
experience is even shorter, sometimes lasting less than five minutes.

Because DMT is believed, strangely enough, to occur naturally in
the human brain (trace amounts have been found in blood, urine, and
spinal fluid, and precursor enzymes for it have been found in brain tissue), it was apparent to Strassman that an understanding of its action
might shed some light on the development and possible treatment of
endogenous hallucinatory conditions like schizophrenia. It is in this
way that clinical science comes to make antipsychotic drugs, substances
that can block pathological forms of thought. Once you understand the
neurochemical events that accompany abnormal states of mind, then
you are in a position to develop drugs to treat such conditions.

Despite his purely clinical leanings, Strassman was also interested
in using DMT to explore the ever-more-popular brain/mind issue. This
murky area of science—which we shall be returning to in later chapters—
is concerned with how the physiochemical brain (the unsightly mass of
gray jellylike stuff in our skulls) is related to the nonphysical mind with
all its attendant thoughts, ideas, fears, beliefs, and so on. What exactly
is the connection? Strassman argues that because psychedelic drugs alter
consciousness, they should be able to tell us something about how consciousness is formed in the normal brain. In other words, since psychedelics alter higher cognitive functions connected with what it is to be a
conscious human being, then they can essentially be employed as probes
to study the mind/brain interface. This is, of course, exactly the point I
outlined in the prologue of this book.

It took Strassman two long years to secure permission to carry out
DMT studies with humans (experienced psychedelic users were utilized,
as this was deemed more ethical). Indeed, this magnitude of effort probably explains the current lack of human-based hallucinogen research. A
look at Strassman's struggle reveals the horrendous bureaucratic forces (a
kind of lingering cultural symptom of the 1960s) that face the potential
psychedelic researcher. Strassman had to get permission from all sorts

of official bodies, such as the formidable Drug Enforcement Agency (DEA) and the Food and Drug Administration (FDA), not to mention the numerous ethical bodies that serve to monitor human-based experimentation.

Two years of uphill struggle and Strassman finally acquired all the necessary permission to perform a DMT study. The remarkable results were subsequently published in reputable but specialized scientific journals, a bit like planting the seeds of a new paradigm underground. Perhaps the most interesting finding concerned the subjects' reports on what the (intravenously injected) DMT experience was like. As with psilocybin, the effects of DMT warrant our attention if we are interested in the latent potential of human consciousness to transcend "normal" reality. In Strassman's own words:

> Several aspects of DMT's effects are interesting. The rapidity of onset is quite remarkable; nearly instantaneous when given intravenously. Also the short duration is remarkable; people are quite over the inebriation within 20 to 25 minutes. Many people describe an "intelligence" within the DMT state, which is either just "felt" or "sensed" and sometimes actually "seen" with the mind's eye. People often lose insight into their participation in a drug study for several minutes, forgetting how they got into the mental state they find themselves so suddenly thrust into.[3]

As with its close structural relative psilocybin (molecules of these two compounds are only a few atoms different from one another), subjects reported that the DMT experience felt more real than normal reality. Indeed, it is presumably this novel reality encountered through DMT, especially with regard to the perceived contact with an "intelligent Other," that has led to the use of DMT-containing plants by Amazonian shamans. As already noted, shamans consistently claim that their DMT-containing concoctions put them in direct contact with a transcendental dimension infused with intentionality. What makes this even more intriguing is that Western DMT users report similar experiences. Consider this lucid report from author Daniel Pinchbeck, author of *Breaking Open the Head*.

> I had the sense of floating through a fractal tapestry, a curving and unfolding plane of synthetic, plastic, fantastic whiteness and gleaming colors in endless vibrant hues. This extradimensional realm I had pitched into was made, I felt certain, of data, of quantum equations, visible shamanic harmonics, and the self-weaving fabric of extradimensional superconsciousness. . . . There was, in that place, rushing toward me, an overwhelming force of knowledge and sentience. I knew it was impossible that my mind, on any level, had created what I was seeing. This was no mental projection. This was not a structure within the brain that the drug had somehow tapped into. It was a non-human reality existing at a deeper level than the physical world.[4]

Clearly the chemistry of the brain is indubitably bound with consciousness. Both are mutable. Moreover, certain realms of consciousness can be generated in which, as Pinchbeck forcibly attests, a seemingly autonomous intelligence is apprehended. If ever there was a "hard" approach to spirituality, this is it.

Although the study of mystical experiences and neurochemistry might seem like compelling science, the fact of the matter is that most scientists exercise great caution when it comes to explaining, in scientific terms, something as precious and as guarded as the mystical experience. Those who tend to police communion with the divine, like religious leaders for instance, are quick to react when scientists attempt to reduce an epiphany to neurochemical events occurring in the brain. Indeed, recall the reaction to Walter Pahnke's findings in the 1960s at Harvard. Many religious authorities felt their toes being stepped on, and Pahnke was refused further funding. Yet science, with its inevitable expanding interest in the nature of human consciousness, is surely mature enough to take on the issue, and it thus remains to be seen what science can teach us about the potentialities and extraordinary capacities of the human brain/mind.

Again, I hasten to add that science is not the only valid approach to studying altered states of consciousness. As I have repeatedly implied, direct self-experimentation according to one's own terms and at one's own risk is also an option. At the end of the day, data is needed. From data we can derive theories. Because all entheogenic experiences carry data, we should not be in a rush to dismiss any self-report, whether garnered from a native shaman, an official study subject, or an independent researcher.

Does the Brain Recognize DMT?

There was another finding by Strassman that proved provocative. Strassman found that the human brain does not develop tolerance to DMT. Whereas the brain normally develops tolerance to psychoactive chemicals (repeated use means you need to use more to get the same experience), Strassman found that tolerance does not develop to the repeated administration of DMT. This suggests that, in the "normal" brain, DMT has some kind of *function*—that is, the brain recognizes DMT and repeatedly utilizes it instead of developing a tolerance to it. So far this putative function of endogenous DMT remains unknown, but it might well be involved in the process of dreaming. This is a tenable hypothesis because we must dream every night. If we are selectively denied that part of the sleep cycle in which we dream—known as REM sleep—we will subsequently have more dreams at some later time (known as the REM-rebound effect). And so if there are indeed dream-inducing chemicals such as DMT, then the brain would by necessity have to make sure that it does not develop tolerance to them because tolerance would stop dreams from taking hold. It is also the case that both dreams and DMT-induced visions are of a somewhat similar nature. Both represent dramatic psychological scenarios that experiencers may find themselves unwittingly involved in.

Strassman also recognized a new clinical use for DMT. He was able to administer DMT every half hour to his subjects, and after each session he was able to discuss their experiences. He found that the subjects' "psychological resistances" gradually wore down through these sessions, suggesting that DMT has therapeutic potential. Indeed, as DMT is only active for thirty minutes, it has an advantage over therapeutic drugs whose effects last much longer and that require more in the way of supervision from the therapist.

So What Does It All Mean?

Although the therapeutic application of entheogens seems apparent, it's less clear how these substances work and how we might address the various implications of their uncanny effects. At the very least, psychedelics alter consciousness in a dramatic fashion, and at the most extreme, as we have repeatedly seen, such substances can elicit a transcendental experience in which one apparently communes with an intelligence of some kind. Unsurprisingly, there is a popular belief among many of today's psychedelic researchers that the very origin of humankind's religious impulse is bound with our ancestors' discovery of entheogenic fungi, a notion that, as you may recall, was first introduced by R. Gordon Wasson. Professor David Nichols, president of the Heffter Research Institute, puts it this way:

> One can imagine an early hominid accidentally ingesting a psychedelic mushroom while foraging for edible foodstuffs. Knowledge of these drugs was handed down through the generations and led to the creation of rituals around their use. We have the hymns written to *Soma* in the *Rig Veda,* or the ancient Eleusinian Mysteries of Greece, as only two examples of the extreme importance attached to these substances. . . . Whatever you believe in this regard, it is a simple fact that the use of psychedelic drugs can profoundly alter one's understanding and belief about life and its meaning. Man has been on an age-old quest to find his place in the Universe, and these drugs can be important tools both in understanding this quest, and in gaining meaning about ourselves as conscious creatures.[5]

Whether or not these speculations about mushrooms are correct is not the main issue. The main issue is the conceptual paradigm that sees a naturally occurring psychedelic agent of some kind lying at the heart of humanity's sacred traditions. As it is, there is certainly some intriguing evidence that human civilization has been using psychedelic mushrooms since the earliest times. Dating from before 6000 B.C. (a long, long time before the Mexican use of psilocybin mushrooms described in chapter 2), rock paintings found at Tassili in Northern Algeria show mythical shamanlike beings covered in mushrooms. These Neolithic mushroom motifs are very distinct. Some have therefore argued that the Goddess-worshipping peoples who inhabited Tassili consumed locally gathered psilocybin mushrooms (such as the large species *Stropharia cubensis*) and that this practice influenced their spiritual beliefs. Whether the inferred mushroom use at Tassili was novel or derived from an even more ancient tradition is an open question yet to be resolved.

While the debate on the prehistoric relevance of psilocybin and its effects continues, we can end this chapter with a comment by Dr. Strassman. The comment concerns the value of researching the entheogenic experience to aid our understanding of human consciousness. With regard to the mystical claims made by native peoples who employ entheogens, Strassman says:

> Scientists ought to take all claims about the mind seriously. The DMT and psilocybin states . . . are basically non-material. They are not dependent upon the body moving through space, or interaction with other material objects. Thus, they are windows into consciousness, which, while it may have structural underpinnings, is essentially a movement of energy, rather than of matter. . . . So, at the very least, any claims by non-Western people about consciousness might prove very valuable . . . for speculation about how the mind works. In addition, these "non-literate" cultures are how we found out about DMT and psilocybin in the first place.[6]

FIVE

The Mushroom
and the Synapse

Now that I have acquainted the reader with the distinctly mystical nature of the psilocybin experience, it is time for us to focus our attention on psilocybin's physical modus operandi. If we can come to grips with how alkaloids like psilocybin work their spectacular effects within the brain and mind, then we will be one step closer to a preliminary understanding of the nature of consciousness and the underlying factors governing the switch from normal awareness to the mystical perception of an intelligent Other.

At this point, consciousness lies smack-dab at the center of our inquiry. All our paths of investigation lead directly to it. The psilocybin cultural history covered in the first few chapters of this book arose solely because of the radical change in consciousness induced by the mushroom in the Mayan and Aztec psyche. The pre-LSD investigations at Harvard were likewise galvanized into action by psilocybin-induced states of consciousness. Indeed, the whole 1960s thing happened, in part, precisely because of the new ranges of conscious experience originally kick-started into existence by the mushroom. The growing second wave of psychedelic research has likewise appeared on account of the compelling nature of entheogenic states of consciousness. One cannot escape the mystery of consciousness. Psilocybin simply highlights the boundless nature and mystical potential of the human mind lest we allow this fortunate state of affairs to pass us by.

As I pointed out at the very outset of this book, if we are interested in apprehending the ultimate nature of the reality process, it makes sense to focus on consciousness because consciousness represents the interface that links us to the "world out there." If we can understand what consciousness is, we might also understand how consciousness is able to be transformed and whether such a transformation can yield bona fide insights into the subtle nature of Nature. Nothing less than reality is up for grabs.

In the chapters that follow, I hope to develop a new, nontechnical, and user-friendly theoretical framework that can explain both normal consciousness and entheogenic consciousness. Essentially this conceptual framework derives from Aldous Huxley's reasonable assertion that the psychedelic experience results from an influx of information not normally available to us—hence the "doors of perception" being opened after ingestion of substances like, in Huxley's case, mescaline. What I eventually hope to show is that consciousness is actually a *form of information;* that physical matter can be described in terms of information also; and that reality ultimately consists of a flow of self-organizing information, with human consciousness occupying a significant functional role in the entire process. However, before we can explore the exciting ramifications that an informational model of reality yields, we must start from the beginning, that is, we must look more closely at the obviously important physical relationship between psilocybin and the human brain.

Neuromancing with Neuroscience

In any serious attempt to elucidate the brain processes underlying the psychological effects of entheogenic agents, one must utilize whatever relevant scientific data is at hand. In our case this means neuropsychological data, of which much has become available since the 1950s era, when Huxley wrote *The Doors of Perception.*

Neuropsychology is a modern scientific discipline based on the study of the nervous system, which consists of the body's entire network of nerve cells. These nerve cells, or neurons as they are more formally known, allow us to sense, transmit, and process information. Whereas other cells in the body are designed to form tissues and organs, neurons exist solely to transmit information in the form of discrete signals, or impulses. We are able to see, touch, smell, hear, taste, feel, and think because we possess a vast network of these neurons, which manage to continually process and communicate information about both the external state of the world and the internal state of the body.

Of particular interest to neuropsychologists is the detailed study of the brain (one component of the nervous system) and the way the brain's particular neurons function to produce thinking and behavior. Because psychoactive substances are known to influence the way brain neurons process information, neuropsychology has made some headway into understanding the chemistry of the brain and the actual way in which psychoactive substances work. Thus, we now know something about how common psychoactive substances like coffee, nicotine, and alcohol interact with the brain's neuronal architecture to cause their desired psychological effects of stimulation or stupor.

However, the study of psychoactive substances is far from being neuropsychology's key research area. Of perhaps most prominence is the study of the effects of brain trauma, a condition in which parts of the brain are damaged. A brief look at the rationale governing this kind of research reveals that we can approach the phenomenon of the entheogenic experience in much the same theoretical way.

For instance, medical patients with brain tumors and a corresponding psychological deficiency are, despite their misfortune, of great interest to neuropsychologists because a causal relationship can be ascertained between the area of the tumor and the particular psychological disturbance. This is equally true of brain-damaged victims of accidents, for where there is localized brain damage one invariably finds psychological disturbances of a definite kind that are associated with that area of the brain.

As an example, damage to the part of the brain known as Broca's area often leads to language problems associated with speech production. Patients of this type have no difficulty in understanding speech but have noticeable difficulty in producing speech, even to the point of being mute. The point of interest is that a specific area of the physical brain is damaged with an associated specific psychological disruption. Once the neuropsychologist has gathered a wealth of such examples, then psychological functions like language (which is often disrupted after brain injury) can be divided into various subsystems or "modules" operating in different areas of the brain, each of which can be differentially affected.

The upshot of this methodological enterprise is that scientists are now able to speculate about normal brain function and to link localized physical brain mechanisms with aspects of the mind. This is quite an achievement, resulting directly from the prevailing localization paradigm governing a major part of neuropsychology. It is therefore not unusual to come across references to the mapping of the human brain whereby different areas are associated with different psychological functions.

Bearing this in mind, it is clear that we could examine the entheogenic experience in a similar way. That is, by looking at the specific changes to consciousness arising from the presence of specific substances in the brain, we should be able to theorize about how normal consciousness arises. In other words, just as we can analyze abnormal language production and then speculate about how the language system works in normal people, so too can we analyze altered states of consciousness and speculate about the nature of normal consciousness. At any rate, by examining chemical changes associated with changes in consciousness, we ought definitely to come to some understanding about the nature of mind stuff and the ways it is possible to modify mind stuff through chemistry. On the face of it at least, this area of study promises a wealth of relevant psychological data with which to understand the elusive nature of mind.

Despite this reasoning, scientists, as should be clear by now, have unfortunately been hindered from investigating the psychedelic experience, and it is only in the last few decades that they have been permitted to resume studies in this fascinating domain. And yet enough information on the psychedelic experience has been generated with which to construct a user-friendly theory of consciousness. Most of this information I have outlined in previous chapters, in particular, information on the fundamental type of global change in consciousness caused by psilocybin. If we add relevant information regarding the physical details of psilocybin, we shall be able to reach some sort of sound theoretical conclusion about the nature of consciousness. Regardless of any legal issues, this mode of inquiry promises to be most fruitful. In fact it is rather apt that a mysterious phenomenon like consciousness should require such radical means with which to pry open its nature.

Introducing the Neuronal Brain

As mentioned, the brain consists of individual information-processing nerve cells, or neurons. It is estimated that the human brain contains up to one hundred billion of them. This is an astronomical number pretty much impossible to conceive. Regardless, these billions of neurons are the essential "wetware" of the brain, and massed together with other cells that provide support and energy, they form the spongy gray matter residing within our skulls. We should also consider that each of these billions of neurons forms interconnections with thousands or even tens of thousands of other neurons. We will learn more about this a bit later on.

Although the evidence is overwhelming, it still seems extraordinary that this convoluted blob of porridge-like neuronal stuff within our skulls is bound up with the elaborate properties of the human mind. Although one might have reservations in associating a spongy, wet blob with consciousness, the association is indisputable. Scramble someone's brain either through a severe blow to the head or through some other trauma, and that person's consciousness similarly becomes scrambled. Or, electrically excite the brain of a patient undergoing brain surgery who is under the effects of only a local anesthetic, and the electrical stimulation evokes definite and often vivid lifelike experiences. And, of course, certain chemical substances introduced into the brain serve to alter consciousness.

Hence, it is overwhelmingly apparent that the human mind with all its attendant beliefs, ideas, neuroses, fears, hopes, dreams, goals, and aspirations is intimately bound with the unsightly wet-blob brain inside our crania. Indeed, what distinguishes *Homo sapiens* from, say, our primate cousins, is the sheer size of our brains and the mental abilities that a relatively big brain grants us, abilities like self-awareness, language, complex social behavior, foresight, problem solving, metaphysical musing, and so on. We are what we are by virtue of our evolved brains, the phenomenon of human consciousness being determined by this fortunate evolutionary turn of events.

So what is the neuron exactly and how does it come to be involved not only in your reading of these words, but in the psilocybin experience? What is it exactly that these billions of units do?

Naturally Neat Neurons

Structurally, the neuron has four main components: dendrites; the soma (no relation to Wasson's Soma!), or cell body; the axon; and terminal fibers. This may sound somewhat complicated, but the basic principles involved are easily understandable and are essential knowledge to anyone interested in how the brain does its thing.

Imagine a big tree suspended in midair. The bottom of this tree has a dense network of roots, which are attached to a bulbous lower trunk. Above this fat lower trunk is a long, thin upper trunk that ends with a wispy network of branches. In this picturesque analogy of the neuron (which will be worth bearing in mind for the discussions to come when we try to imagine psilocybin's journey within the brain), the roots of the tree are the dendrites, the bulbous lower trunk is the soma, the long upper trunk is the axon, and the topmost branches are the terminal fibers. This is the essential structure of an archetypal neuron with its four distinct components, and all of the brain's neurons are basically made in this way. Neurons are akin to microscopic protoplasmic trees.

The dendrites are the root structures of the neuron, which serve to receive information in the form of signals, or impulses, from other neurons. In our analogy, the root network of the suspended tree receives signals from the branches of other trees suspended below it. These neuronal signals travel to the soma (lower trunk), where they are integrated. The singular result of this integration is then passed on to the axon (upper trunk), which in turn passes on the information to the terminal fibers (branches).

Already we can see that neurons transmit informational impulses in an orderly and well-defined manner; that is, informational signals progress or flow through the neuronal architecture in one direction only. But what exactly are these signals? Because neurons are living tissue, they operate by making use of their inherent electrochemical property, which is to say that their particular chemical molecular structure allows electrical potentials to be generated. The neuron has been constructed by Nature in such a way that it can either fire or not fire, depending on its input from other neurons. Firing here means that the neuron sends forth an electrochemical impulse (a rapidly traveling wave of electrical excitation) down its axon to its terminal fibers, at which point the impulse can be transmitted to other neurons.

This then is the way that neurons process information. The information they carry is *embodied in the electrochemical activity of the neuron*—its state of either firing or not firing, transmitting electrochemical impulses on to other neurons or not transmitting impulses. This all or nothing behavior is rather like the "bit" components inside computers, which store information by being either on or off, active or inactive. Neurons thus appear to operate in a kind of all or nothing digital fashion. Neurons can either fire or not fire; they cannot half fire. There is no room for doubt or indecision, only a logically determined discrete firing or nonfiring signal according to what other neurons in their vicinity are doing.

The purpose of the soma is to integrate all the incoming signals from its dendrites (signals that come from other neurons) and then yield a subsequent impulse down its axon—or not, as the case may be. The concept of threshold is therefore crucial here. For simplicity's sake, if there are a certain number of impulses received by the soma from other neurons, then the firing threshold will be met and an impulse will be passed on down the axon. Conversely, if the particular threshold is not met, there will be no impulse sent down the axon.

Don't relax yet, for there is one more important fact to consider. Neurons can be excitatory or inhibitory. If the neuron is excitatory, then if it fires, as its name suggests, its impulse will be one that tends to cause excitation in other neurons with which it connects. In other words its impulse will add to the chances of the next neuron in line firing as well. On the other hand, inhibitory neurons, should they fire, will decrease the chances of the next neuron in line firing.

To use the suspended tree analogy again, imagine that the roots receive one hundred impulses from the nearby branches of other trees below. The majority of these impulses, let's say, are inhibitory—that is, their inherent message being conveyed to the tree is "do not fire an impulse." After these signals are processed by the lower trunk of the tree, a resultant impulse is therefore not passed along to the upper trunk and branches, and therefore no signal is conveyed to subsequent trees above.

And there you have it—the essential features of the brain's highly sophisticated neuronal machinery in a nutshell. Information is transmitted and processed by the brain through the collective firing patterns of billions of neurons. Like the myriad on-off bit components of a computer, unbelievably large systems of neurons are able to carry out various computational processes and procedures, although the brain's capacity to compute and literally think far outstrips the ability of any currently existing computer. The emergence of a sentient HAL-like or Skynet-like computer system that worries about being turned off or wants to wage war on us is unlikely. For whereas computers might be good at numerical calculation and other well-defined logical operations, they fail miserably when it comes to carrying out the types of thinking that we do all the time, like how to cross a really busy street while simultaneously contemplating a Shakespearean metaphor. Perhaps if computers were born into a society of computers, were able to form intricately detailed models of reality, and were able to continually rewrite themselves, then maybe they might eventually come to possess mindful characteristics. As it stands, what partly determines human consciousness and the human self are the vast webs of social and societal relations that impinge on us, the complex internal models of reality that we build and store, and the continual learning processes we undertake.

When considering the organized neuronal activity of the human brain, what we must actively strive to appreciate is the enormity of the system and the different patterns of impulse firing that the whole system can potentially embody. Not only are there billions of discrete neuronal firing devices, the amount of connectivity between them almost defies calculation. It has been estimated that each individual neuron can potentially pass on impulses to as many as ten thousand other neurons and may be in receipt of as many as fifty thousand potential impulses from other neurons. In our tree analogy, each tree would therefore be able to receive impulses and pass them on to vast forests of other trees.

Based on the above figures it has been calculated that the informational-storage capacity of the human brain is comparable to the content of all the books ever written. It is this bewildering capacity to process and store information that makes the human mind as rich and as complex as it appears to be. Without the brain's ability to continually channel and organize billions of bits of information, the conscious human psyche as we know it could not exist.

This wealth of neuronal complexity that we all carry around in our big heads is staggering to say the least. At any one moment the entire network can be in an essentially infinite number of states of firing, and somewhere within this informational complexity lies our consciousness—who and what we are. Before dwelling on this obviously compelling mystery, there is yet more relevant data to consider. According to the outline of neurons given thus far, it might be assumed that they contact one another directly. We might suppose that the terminal fibers of neurons pass on their firing impulses directly to the dendrites of other neurons. In the tree analogy this infers that the branch tips of one tree touch the roots of other trees. However, this is not the case. What is more, the actual mechanism by which neurons relay their electrochemically mediated information to one another is the very place where psychoactive substances like psilocybin and your morning cup of caffeine-enriched coffee are believed to operate. To be more precise, the synapse is where it's all at.

A Fantastic Journey into the Synapse

The synapse is the junction between two neurons, the place where they communicate, and it is arguably the most interesting feature of neuronal activity, for it operates with chemical substances that psychoactive drugs resemble. In fact, as we shall shortly see, most psychoactive drugs work by mimicking the endogenous chemical substances employed at the brain's synaptic sites.

The chemicals employed at the neuronal synapse are called neurotransmitters since they are the chemical agents that allow neurons to transmit their electrochemical impulses to one another. Instead of one neuron directly fusing onto another, there is an intervening gap between them—the synaptic cleft—through which impulses must perforce be conveyed if they are to pass on their signal. This synaptic gap is so small that it can be discerned only with the aid of an electron microscope. Yet despite its microscopic size, a tremendous amount of chemical activity can and does occur in the synaptic cleft so that, in reality, the microscopic gap is more of a busy molecular chasm.

Basically, when an electrochemical impulse reaches the synapses at the end regions of the neuron's terminal fibers (the tips of the branches in our tree analogy), it causes a neurotransmitter substance to be released into the synaptic cleft. After this substance has flooded the intervening synaptic space, some of its molecules bind themselves to special proteins called receptors located on the surface of the dendrites of the receiving neuron. After the binding has occurred, these receptors cause changes in the biochemistry of the receiving neuron. These changes then alter the electrical properties of the neuron and, if a certain threshold of activation is met, the original impulse will be regenerated in this neuron and subsequently be passed on to other neurons.

To fully explain the scope, scale, and intricacy of synaptic information transmission, permit me to employ another picturesque analogy. Instead of a terminal fiber/dendrite synapse, think of two train tunnels that do not meet but have an intervening space of, say, ten meters between them. Furthermore, imagine that a train speeds along one of the tunnels at hundreds of miles per hour. This is akin to a high-velocity electrochemical impulse traveling along a neuron. Not dogged by track problems, this Intercity Electrochemical Impulse Express reaches the end of the tunnel and duly crashes onto specially constructed buffers. The dramatic impact upon the buffers causes a group of strategically placed gas canisters to explode, thus dispersing their gaseous contents into the gap between the two tunnels. The gases instantaneously diffuse across the gap and cause a reaction to occur in a stationary train situated at the start of the next tunnel. As soon as molecules of the gas reach the next train, a neat reaction occurs in which the engine roars and the train is off, at the same speed as the first train. Meanwhile the gas molecules in the gap are immediately mopped up (and then conveniently recycled) so that they do not cause the replacement train (that magically appears almost instantly to replace the one that just sped off) to start up also. And in the first tunnel the original train has also been removed in order to allow another to follow if need be.

This analogy captures in essence the manner in which information flows at a single synapse. Although one might argue that a speeding train is a physical thing and an electrochemical impulse is not strictly a physical thing, the most important feature is the *activity of the system and its informational state at any given moment.* We could equally imagine a speeding band of fluorescent light or even a speeding vortex of turbulent air traveling down the tunnels; it does not matter. What really matters is the informational state of the components of the system—their relations with one another. In the actual neuronal synapse these crucial relations are defined by the chemical constituency of the whole system, that is, where and what effects various neurotransmitters are having on the different parts of the synapse.

If the synapse is starting to sound ridiculously complex, we should also keep in mind that the synaptic transmission of an impulse outlined above takes place in no more than *100 microseconds*. In this outrageously short space of time, hundreds of thousands of neurotransmitter molecules are released from the terminal fibers of one neuron, are diffused across the synaptic cleft, come to attach themselves to special receptors on the dendrite of the next neuron, cause an electrochemical impulse to be generated (or not), and are finally reabsorbed and recycled for further use by the first neuron. All this in one hundred millionths of a second! Truly the mind boggles at the very processes underlying its boggling!

Despite the awesome intricacies of the neuronal system and any disbelief we might have that Nature could fashion such exquisite nanotechnological architectures, I have deliberately ignored many of the other important features involved in the neuronal transmission of information. For instance, the electrochemical impulse that shoots through the neuron is itself chock-a-block with chemical complexity. We find outrageously sophisticated potassium and sodium chemical pumps in the axon; we find vast oceans of charged particles, or ions, being continuously pumped in and out of the axon through special membrane channels so that an electrical current is created; and we witness, finally, the aforementioned emergent wave of electrical activity whizzing along the axon to the terminal fibers and on to the synapses. That is the least that can be said about Nature's wondrous evolutionary endeavors in crafting the mammalian brain.

In general, a major conceptual flaw in our understanding of the workings of neurons is the distinct lack of appreciation for their relative size and speed of activity, an unfortunate fact that I am at pains to rectify here. Our modes of inquiry tend to gloss over complexity. True, we don't have to marvel, gasp, and sit down in amazement at neuronal phenomena, yet to not do so (marvel at least) is to overlook the subtlest fruits of the evolutionary process.

So, although we can examine individual neurons and ascertain the mechanism whereby they transmit information, and although we can recognize the role of neurotransmitter substances in propagating information from neuron to neuron through the synapse, traditional scientific approaches tend to fail dismally in fully conveying, in a qualitative sense, the immense organizational complexity involved in the neuronal system as a whole.

Textbooks, for clarity, describe single neurons and single synapses in a fairly cold and reductive manner. What seems never to be stressed is the magnitude of electrochemical changes that zip throughout the conscious brain. Literally billions of coordinated and meaningful molecular events occurring in literally billions of discrete locations at every moment are somehow integrated so that organized sense results. This is information processing with a vengeance!

If, then, we are attempting to marry such neuronal activity with psychological activity (consciousness), that is, if we are attempting to bridge the conceptual gap between mental reality and physical reality, then we must appreciate the organizational complexities involved. If we were merely to skate over the immensity of these processes, we would miss an intuitive feel for the entire system.

Neuronal Patterns and Context

Returning to the concept of organized patterns of neuronal firing, this becomes useful when we consider the way the brain must work in everyday situations. If we take some important psychological function like, say, face recognition, we can see that the particular pattern of neuronal firing caused by nerve impulses issuing from the visual system when it is looking at a face will be, for any particular face, unique. In other words, each face we see will generate a unique pattern of neuronal firing—the face's neuronal signature—in our brain. Furthermore, the neuronal processing of faces appears to reside in a specific area of the brain that can be selectively damaged, resulting in prosopagnosia, a disorder in which the sufferer fails to recognize faces, even those of close family members.

Similarly, we recognize different people's voices by virtue of the fact that each voice causes a distinct pattern of neuronal firing that is conducted from the auditory senses to deep within the brain. Eventually this pattern of information reaches that part of the brain where acoustical information is analyzed and recognized. The same is true for different tastes. Each type of food or drink we consume causes a different pattern of nerve impulses to be generated, which finally reaches that part of the brain that deals in the perception of taste.

In each of these cases, the neuronal pattern produced through the sensing of a particular face, voice, or taste will, at some stage, need to be compared with other possible neuronal patterns in order to yield its particular meaning and significance. Therefore, the different processing systems of the brain must act, in part, to provide a *context* for ongoing neuronal patterns. Without a contextual effect, neuronal patterns would not be able to yield their inherent meaning. The brain's capacity to provide a precise context for ongoing neuronal patterns is thus crucial in understanding how neuronal activity and neuronal firing patterns become meaningful.

The Berkeley psychology professor Bernard J. Baars has noted the importance of contextual effects in giving meaning to ongoing neuronal patterns. In *A Cognitive Theory of Consciousness* he writes: "We generally gain information about a world that is locally ambiguous, yet we usually experience a stable, coherent world. This suggests that *before input becomes conscious, it interacts with numerous unconscious contextual influences to produce a single, coherent, conscious experience.* Consciousness and context are twin issues, inseparable in the nature of things."[1]

Although a detailed look at all the intricacies of neuronal firing patterns is beyond the scope of this book, for the time being it is enough that we grasp the essential principles that are likely to be involved in the brain's processing of information. Organized neuronal patterns arising from, say, visible external stimuli contain a wealth of latent information about the stimuli, which is to say that the neuronal patterns are representations of those stimuli. The latent information in these neuronal representations then gets "read" once the neuronal patterns are contextually processed. The brain, by supplying a context for neuronal representations, is able to access the meaning inherent in them.

One neurophilosophical approach to understanding mental states is that of functionalism, which, despite its dreary name, captures the important role of context in conscious brain processes. Essentially, functionalism views firing states of the brain as playing functional roles in an economy or *language* of possible firing states, which is another way of describing the type of contextual effects outlined above. Any neuronal firing state of the brain derives its significance and meaning from the functional role that it plays within a language of possible states. All possible states are related to one another (just as all words in the English language are related to one another), and it is the network of relations (stored within the brain's memory systems) that acts as context.

We now have at least a preliminary handle on the fundamental way that the neuronal brain operates. Patterns of neuronal firing embody information and meaning that is read or accessed by the brain through language-like contextual/relational effects. Conscious experience appears to be intimately bound somewhere within this information-processing system, since it is consciousness that comes to experience meaning. We see faces and we know who they are. We see pictures and we see what they mean. We hear sounds and we know what they signify. Consciousness is therefore substantiated within neuronal information processing, and it begins to look as if *consciousness itself is a form of information that emerges at the highest and most integrated level of the neuronal system.*

With these speculations in mind, let us look at the way that psychoactive substances influence neurons, synapses, and, of course, consciousness. This is where physical processes can be seen to be connected directly to changes in consciousness, an area of analysis teeming with profound implications, especially when we consider the effects of psilocybin. More important, we might ascertain still more clearly how consciousness can be understood as a form of information.

Chemistry and the Mind

There are drugs and there are drugs. To be precise, there are five principal classes of drugs that alter mood and behavior, some of which we
have already met and discussed. There are depressants like alcohol, bar-
biturates, Valium, and anesthetics; stimulants like amphetamines (speed),
cocaine, caffeine, and nicotine; opiates like opium, heroin, and morphine;
antipsychotics like chlorpromazine and risperidone; and last but by absolutely no means least, there are psychedelics or entheogens like psilocybin,
mescaline, LSD, and DMT. Cannabis and the synthetic club drug Ecstasy
(MDMA) are sometimes classified as psychedelics as well.

The substances listed here as psychedelic could be further divided
according to the precise effect they have, but this basic classification
will suffice for the following discussion, which focuses on the way these
substances are believed to work. Although we will briefly look at each
class of substance, the most attention will be paid to the known neuro-
physiological effects of psilocybin.

The predominant effect of depressants is to depress, or deaden, neuronal activity. Consider anesthetics. They are so strong in their depressant action that beyond the state of general anesthesia that they induce,
there lies only coma and death. It is believed that once anesthetics have
been administered, they reach the brain and inhibit neuronal firing
so much that consciousness is "lost." Therefore it is clear that without
adequate neuronal firing there can be no information processing or
information conductance and hence no mindfulness. Here we have yet
more proof that consciousness is bound up with the billionfold action
of activated neurons in the brain.

If we take another depressant drug, like alcohol, we find that it too
acts to inhibit neuronal firing throughout the brain, and hence consciousness becomes depressed or reduced. However, at low doses the
opposite effect takes place, whereby there is a certain degree of psychological stimulation because of the initial depression of the inhibitory
synapses, which, as you will recall, serve to diminish neuronal firing.
However, soon after these inhibitory neurons are depressed, excitatory

neurons begin to be depressed as well, and this effect comes to dominate the ensuing state of consciousness.

Not only do depressants inhibit neuronal firing in the brain, they also appear to depress the activity of the body's other nerves, heart tissue, and muscle tissue. More specifically, depressants upset the functioning of the arousal centers in the brain such that psychological arousal and stimulation are diminished. In short, the quantity of consciousness is reduced due to a concurrent reduction in neuronal firing, and there is less informational patterning and less informational organization happening within the neuronal systems of the brain once a depressant drug has been introduced.

Stimulants have the opposite effect of depressants. Cocaine and amphetamines each work in virtually the same way, causing almost identical stimulatory effects like euphoria, an increase in alertness, an elevation of mood, and a reduction in fatigue. Indeed, cocaine is derived from the coca plant, the leaves of which are still chewed daily by millions of native South Americans precisely for the resultant psychological stimulation and reduction in perceived tiredness and hunger. This latter "productive" effect of the coca leaf explains the fact that while the sixteenth-century Spanish conquistadors outlawed the religious use of sacred mushrooms, peoples like the Incas were allowed to continue their practice of chewing coca leaves as long as they slaved away in Spanish gold mines.

Amphetamines are believed to mimic and increase the activity of the neurotransmitters noradrenaline and dopamine (the brain uses many different types of neurotransmitter), thus interfering with the normal synaptic functioning of neurons using these neurotransmitters. This happens partly because amphetamines are similar in molecular structure to both noradrenaline and dopamine. Because of this resemblance, amphetamines literally invade those neuronal areas where synaptic transmission with these transmitters occurs and increase the rate of impulse generation. Once this occurs, the typical "speeding" psychological responses take hold.

With cocaine a similar tale unfolds. In this case, however, it appears that cocaine inhibits the recycling (the "mopping up") of noradrenaline and dopamine within synapses after they have done their work. Because of this selective interference, there are more neurotransmitters "hanging around" in synapses and therefore more of them to stimulate receiving neurons into excitatory action.

In both cases, the chief neurological effect is that of an increase in synaptic activity that causes stimulation of the nervous system. Again we see that the stimulating alteration in consciousness caused by these drugs is due to an increase in the information-processing activity of certain types of neuron, in this case, neurons utilizing noradrenaline and dopamine. Increased neuronal activity of this kind then generates the desired psychological stimulation, or "high." It is important to bear in mind, however, that the increased neuronal activity in this case does not lead to any kind of profound visionary experience. Such radical phenomenology is restricted to psychedelics.

With tea and coffee, the active ingredient, caffeine, is believed to increase rates of cellular metabolism, thus making more energy available to cells. The net result of this action is once again an elevated rate of neuronal firing, which explains the subtle stimulatory properties of tea and coffee and their widespread use.

The third class of psychoactive substance on our list is opiates, which are derived from the opium poppy. The opiates are interesting for their variety of powerful effects. The worldwide painkiller morphine is an invaluable opiate, and its chemical isolation from the opium poppy radically revolutionized medicine and pain control. Morphine seems to selectively bind to opiate receptors in the brain, which suggests that the brain has its own pain-control mechanisms. Indeed, it has been proposed that acupuncture and hypnosis might be able to reduce pain because they encourage the brain to generate its own endorphins, which are natural opiate substances that bind to opiate receptors (endorphins are also believed to be the cause of the high often experienced after rigorous exercise). Once these opiate receptors are activated, the emotional perception of pain diminishes—as opposed to a diminishing of the actual pain impulses arriving from the site of injury. Along with opium and heroin (a semisynthetic compound), morphine also generates euphoria, and this is associated with the emotional changes wrought through the activation of the nervous system's opiate receptors.

With the fourth class of drugs, the antipsychotics, we find synthetic compounds such as risperidone being used the world over to treat mental diseases, including schizophrenia. Perhaps the most common neuropsychological theory holds that schizophrenia results from an excess of the substance dopamine within the brain. Dopamine, of course, is a major neurotransmitter that we met when we looked at the neurological effect of stimulants.

The excess-dopamine explanation for schizophrenia is supported by the effects of risperidone, which can diminish the symptoms of this disease. Because risperidone operates partly by blocking dopamine receptors in the brain, it is logical to assume that an excess of dopaminergic neuronal activity lies at the heart of schizophrenia. This speculation leads to the intriguing conclusion that somehow an elevation in the activity of dopamine-using neurons is intimately bound with the strange delusions and belief systems of the unfortunate mind suffering from schizophrenia. By blocking the excess dopamine at the receptor sites, risperidone helps to block disorders of thought.

Here we have another strong clue about how to unravel the mysteries of the formation and emergence of complex consciousness—for schizophrenia is noted precisely for its disruptions of those higher levels of awareness that pertain to reality conception. Furthermore, these large-scale disruptions in thought appear to be nonrandom in that certain definite types of delusion are observed, often related to feelings of paranoia and the belief that one is being controlled by horribly malevolent external forces. If dopaminergic synaptic overactivity really is to blame for these global disorders of thought, we can begin to conceive how large patterns of abnormal neuronal firing yield large disorders of cognition, such as paranoid delusions and the like. If neuronal activity becomes too overactive and too "wild," then the resultant firing patterns might well be "flawed," which is to say that these patterns are essentially mistakes serving to mislead the experiencer. Or, if there is some negative disruption in the overall way in which the schizophrenic conceives reality, then the schizophrenic's model of reality will provide a faulty contextual effect on ongoing neuronal activity.

Obviously the human brain is a finely tuned information-processing instrument. If the neuronal events substantiating some kinds of information processing are pushed too far from some criteria, or if neuronal events are "read" by an erroneous contextual system, faulty processing occurs, with its resultant negative disruption of consciousness.

Neuro-alchemical Magic

Finally we come to the class of compounds known as psychedelics or entheogens. Admittedly it has been a little tough getting here, yet the journey is worth it. We are now ready to home in even closer to the link between neuronal chemistry and consciousness. Entheogens are by far the most interesting of all known psychoactive substances, although precious little is known about exactly how they are able to generate such a remarkable array of psychological effects. Entheogens are often referred to by unwary clinicians as *hallucinogens,* yet this term suggests that hallucinations are produced. The general definition of a hallucination is that of a perceived object in three-dimensional space that is in actuality not there—a bit like seeing a ghost or mirage. But this is not a typical effect, as I hope I have shown in previous chapters. In fact, one of the most prominent effects of substances like psilocybin is the production of complex visionary scenes that unfold behind closed eyes, along with a perceived increase in the realness of the external world as viewed with eyes open. More specifically, one does not hallucinate nonexistent objects; rather, one comes to see external reality in a new and more enhanced way. It is for these reasons that the term *entheogen* or *psychedelic* (literally mind-manifesting) is preferred to classify these particular substances.

It is believed that psilocybin works by mimicking the neurotransmitter serotonin (known as 5-HT), one of the most important and widespread of the brain's synaptic messengers. The mimicking occurs because psilocin (the active metabolite of psilocybin that is formed in the body) possesses a molecular structure almost identical to serotonin. Psilocin's shape is so similar to serotonin that it is able to infiltrate parts of the brain that process information using serotonergic synapses.

Serotonin is employed in a number of brain structures that control functions like sleep, mood, and general arousal. One of these structures is the raphe system at the base of the brain, whose serotonergic neuronal axons project to all other major areas of the brain, notably the limbic system (which controls emotional responses) and areas of the visual system.

Research indicates that the serotonin-using raphe system has a homeostatic, or balancing, function in which two primary effects emerge. First, in the waking state the system acts to enhance the activity of motor neurons, which govern the control of muscular movement. Second, and more significant, during the waking state this same serotonergic system acts to suppress sensory systems, which relay information about the external world. This second effect appears to screen out, or filter out, distracting sensory information. Furthermore, it has been speculated that this filtering mechanism allows us to perceive reality in a steady way, almost as if the serotonergic raphe system were a balancing stick enabling us to walk the "tightrope" of normal perceptual awareness. If this serotonergic homeostatic balancing system is interfered with, then the perception of reality will be correspondingly altered, so much so that we may plunge off the tightrope into new dimensions of perceived reality. Chemically dismantling the raphe system's screening effect would therefore admit the entry of latent information into consciousness. Is this how visionary agents like psilocybin work?

Most of the detailed physiological experimentation that was carried out with psychedelics in the 1960s concentrated on LSD and psilocybin and used rat brains, cat brains, and isolated rat neurons. Perhaps the most important finding was indeed that LSD and psilocybin depress the action of serotonin neurons in the raphe system (a neuronal system shared by rats, cats, and humans).

The usual activity of the particular serotonergic neurons that psilocin and LSD depress is inhibitory, which means that their normal firing serves to dampen or suppress activity in those parts of the brain with which they synapse. Thus it was believed that psilocybin and LSD's dampening effect on serotonergic neurons facilitated an increase in neuronal firing in those areas of the brain in contact with the raphe system (like the aforementioned visual and limbic/emotion systems). It was this effect, this enhancement of neuronal activation, that was believed to correlate with the psychedelic experience itself.

It seemed like a nice, neat theory. However, the above scenario does not take into account the recently discovered neuropharmacological action of mescaline, another classic entheogen. With not a little irritation we find that, like psilocybin, mescaline induces the full spectrum of visionary phenomenology, but it is not known to significantly influence the raphe system. Therefore our raphe theory cannot be the whole story.

Research over the past decade has revealed that there are distinct kinds of serotonin receptors, or serotonin binding sites, within the brain. In other words, neurons that are modulated by the release of serotonin from other neurons with which they synapse are not tied down to just one kind of serotonin receptor. In typical fashion, Nature has made things more complex and intriguing than that. In fact, there are different kinds of serotonin receptor (classified by grouping them into subtype receptors), and it is believed that different psychedelic drugs have differential effects upon these receptors. One particular serotonin receptor, however—the so-called 5-HT2A type—appears to represent a common site of action for both psilocybin and mescaline.

The 5-HT2A receptors are found throughout the cortex and also in abundance in the brain system known as the locus coeruleus, which, like the raphe, is situated at the base of the brain. The locus coeruleus processes so many sensory inputs (a flow of incoming data, if you like) that it is considered to function as a "novelty detector" and is able to influence one's state of arousal. By monitoring the constant surge of "electrochemical traffic" passing through it, the locus coeruleus is able to detect changes in the flow of data and alert other parts of the brain. When something changes in the environment around us, the locus coeruleus alerts the rest of the brain to the change. Both psilocin and mescaline bind to these 5-HT2A sites in the locus coeruleus and thereby alter the functioning of this system, ultimately raising levels of arousal. In other words, it once again seems that psychedelics function by making more information available to the experiencer.

This explanation is still not the full story, however, as pharmacology expert professor David Nichols attests.

> 5-HT2A receptor sites are located in a number of other key areas of the brain. Importantly, they are located on neurons in the frontal cortex called pyramidal cells. The frontal cortex is often referred to as the area where executive decisions are made. It is there that we make sense of all the information that is arriving. It is a sort of conscious integrating center where the brain makes decisions about what to do about all the information that it is receiving. Laugh? Cry? Get up and go to the bathroom? Experiments . . . suggest that stimulation of 5-HT2A receptors makes these pyramidal cells fire more easily, thus enabling them to process more information.[2]

Professor Nichols also points out yet another area of the brain that might be involved in entheogenesis.

> There is an area in the middle of the brain called the thalamus. The thalamus is a relay station through which all of the sensory information we receive (except for smell) is sent to the cortex. This part of the brain is sometimes called the "searchlight" of attention. It is wrapped in yet another layer of neurons called the reticular nucleus of the thalamus, and it is this layer that helps to control which sensory information actually gets through the thalamus and is sent on to the cortex. The 5-HT2A receptor is located on neurons in both of these two areas, so its activation has a direct effect on the control and flow of information that ultimately reaches the cortex. It is thought that psilocybin and LSD decrease the efficiency of this thalamic filter or gating mechanism, and allow much more information to be sent to the cortex.[3]

Despite introducing yet more areas of the brain, Professor Nichols appears to concur that the chief effect of psilocybin is *an increase in informational activity in those areas of the brain involved with consciousness*. As far as I can see, given all the scientific data at hand, a basic conclusion along these lines seems inevitable.

The Novel Orchestration of Information

We are now in a position to summarize the above findings in fairly straightforward terms: the net result of psilocybin's combined effects upon the locus coeruleus, the raphe system, the thalamus, and cortical cells is an increase in neuronal firing in the cortex, a concurrent increase in consciousness (an expansion of perceived reality), and the emergence of often spectacular visions behind closed eyes.

Only the second of those claims is in any way contentious, for I suggest an increase in consciousness. Others might argue that the increase in neuronal firing in the brain is more of an unwelcome dysfunction than a constructive effect. However, a negative judgment like this misses the implications of the entheogenic state of mind. After all, Huxley claimed that psychedelics could, through an act of "gratuitous grace," permit one access to perceptual information that was "out there," but not normally needed because from an evolutionary standpoint we need only information regarding things like food and safety. Or at least those are the sorts of thing it has been essential to know in our evolutionary past. Of course for Huxley and other champions of the psychedelic experience, the knowledge made available through visionary plant and fungal alkaloids was suddenly very important in the light of contemporary Western culture. A transcendental reality appeared to be awaiting us, ready to erupt amid the mundane and oft-profane trudge of human history.

Armed with modern data on serotonin receptors, we can see that Huxley was correct in his pioneering conjectures. Once entheogenic compounds have entered the brain, an increase in neuronal activity (that is, an increase in neuronal excitation and electrochemical information processing) takes place—hence more information does indeed become accessible to the mind. In particular, the parts of the brain that become more activated are involved with novelty detection, arousal, emotions, the relaying of sensory information, and making sense of it all.

But what exactly does it mean that there is an increase in neuronal informational activity? Just how valid and "real" are the novel patterns of neuronal firing galvanized by psilocybin? Indeed, how can novel patterns of neuronal firing *actually be conscious thoughts*? From here on, the ground gets more uncertain, mainly because the brain is such an astonishingly complicated organ. However, before we go on to speculate and deal further with what has been said thus far, there is one more piece of information we should consider, namely the role of serotonergic neurons in the process of dreaming.

Sleeping Dreams and Waking Dreams

REM sleep, or rapid eye movement sleep, is that part of the sleep cycle in which we dream the most vividly. Sleep, let alone dreaming, is a peculiar thing, especially since we spend about a third of our lives succumbing to it. Despite such a dramatic nightly encumbrance, science has yet to reach a universal consensus regarding why we sleep, for one can come up with plenty of arguments that counter explanations that view sleep as a purely restorative process. Proneness to attack comes to mind, for when else are we so passively oblivious to our surroundings? As for our need to dream, there are again numerous theories, from odd theories that we dream to forget, to theories that we dream to consolidate information.

Although we might not remember our dreams, it is vital that we engage in REM sleep each night. Sleep researchers have found that if periods of REM sleep are selectively disrupted, it results in a rebound effect whereby the next night, barring any more selective interference from researchers, there will be an extra amount of REM, or dreaming. We absolutely must dream, and therefore dreaming has to be related to some very important informational process of the brain.

Neuroscientist B. L. Jacobs has carried out experiments that show that a suppression of serotonergic neuronal activity elicits dreaming. If cats (unfortunately these most loveable creatures are often used for questionable brain-meddling sleep experiments) are injected with a chemical called PCPA, which is known to deplete serotonin supplies in all parts of the brain, the cats exhibit brain-wave patterns consistent with the onset of dreaming, despite the fact that they are fully awake. In other words, argues Jacobs, the cats are experiencing waking dreams. Therefore, waking dreams are somehow associated with low levels of serotonin. Indeed, during dream sleep, serotonergic cells in the raphe system turn off completely so that they cease having a depressant effect on other parts of the brain, a process that echoes the effects of psilocybin upon the raphe system.

The conclusion reached is that dreaming is associated with a form of neuronal firing normally kept at bay by inhibitory serotonergic neurons until the onset of sleep. More important, the visions produced by psychedelic agents like psilocybin might be the result of waking dreams, or at least they might emerge from self-organizing neuronal processes that are similar to those processes occurring while we dream. The essential principle appears to be the coalescing of information into meaningful patterns. This idea is not only compelling, it also seems intuitively correct; the psilocybin mushroom allows one to experience dreamlike consciousness while awake, which takes the form of intensely moving visions behind closed eyes.

According to the various documented cases of the shamanic visionary state, psychedelic visions are indeed dreamlike, the only difference being that one is immeasurably more conscious during visions than in dreams (even lucid ones) and one is able to remember them vividly, unlike dreams, which often fade quickly. Whereas most people cannot, offhand, recall most of the thousands of dreams that they all must have had, psilocybin visions remain fairly emblazoned upon the memory like favorite movie clips.

To be sure, the suggestion that psilocybin visions are dreamlike is theoretically useful, yet it seriously downplays their dramatic impact and

"Otherness." But because there is clearly some similarity in the chemical basis and phenomenological quality of dreams and psychedelic visionary episodes, their relationship—in terms of neuronal processes—demands further exploration, and so this is where we head, in part, in the next chapter. We must bear in mind though that the vision-generating side of the mushroom experience is only the half of it, since the altered perception of reality with eyes open is of equal interest. However, as stated, both these phenomena are intimately related to the processing of information within the neuronal systems of the brain, and we therefore need to begin thinking more deeply about the relationship between billionfold patterns of neuronal firing and consciousness. I have already introduced the idea that vast patterns of orchestrated neuronal firing *are* conscious experience, yet this concept is so profound that I shall repeatedly return to it in order to fully explore its worth as an explanatory model for understanding the nature of the brain and mind.

Whether it be a vivid dream or an entheogenic vision, the normal perception of an object or a psychedelic perception, the underlying structure of such experiences can now be discerned. The common mediating factor is *information,* and the way that information is transmitted, organized, and substantiated by the neuronal firing activity of the brain. Information, the "currency" of the brain, emerges as the key concept in explaining the normal conscious mind, the entheogenic mind, and the dreaming mind. We continue our avid investigations in the next chapter, as we spiral in toward the secret of the sacred mushroom.

SIX

The Stuff of
Consciousness

The purpose of this and the following chapters is to build on the ideas
previously introduced to further get a handle on the mind, or consciousness, and how it is possible for one to experience a transcendental communion with a seeming Other. At this juncture I repeat that I believe
mind stuff to be information, or at any rate that consciousness is an
informational pattern embodied within the neuronal firing system of
the brain. Moreover, it seems likely that psilocybin works by enabling
novel patterns of information to emerge that are not normally "permitted" due to the default constraints that usually operate in the brain.
This much seems clear from what has already been said about the way
in which neuronal firing substantiates informational states and how
such informational states are dramatically altered through the chemical
action of entheogenic compounds.

In other words, mind stuff resolves itself as being informational
stuff. This is perhaps not too controversial a claim, but what I eventually hope to show is that matter, or physical stuff, is also informational
in nature. *This would mean that everything, whether atoms, molecules,
organisms, or thoughts, could be described in informational terms.* The
mind and body could then be seen as consisting of essentially the same
kind of substance, that is, as particular forms of information.

Of course the concept of what information itself is, or what information actually means, is a decidedly muddy issue, despite the fact that

we now live in the Age of Information. Books carry information, as do DVDs, apple seeds, bank statements, fossils, fiber-optic cables, hormones, food wrappers, and the human genome. So too do vast networks of firing neurons carry information, whether infused with psilocybin or not. As to the notion of atoms (of which the above-mentioned information-carriers are all composed) being units of information also, the case is less clear. However, should I succeed in the coming chapters in defining both consciousness and matter in informational terms, then I should also be able to explain more clearly why psilocybin is able to generate both Other-derived visions and an altered perception of reality—all in terms of the flow and flux of information. In fact, armed with a sweepingly new informational view of reality, one might come to perceive oneself and the world with a new outlook. Indeed, the information paradigm of which I speak yields a whole array of truly stunning conceptual consequences.

Mind and Body

The issue confronting us—that of understanding consciousness—is, as you probably realize, a decidedly hoary beast, covered in thorns and about as amenable to close analysis as is the wind on a very blustery day. Formally speaking, it is known in the philosophical trade as the mind/body problem. At its heart lies the seemingly inseparable gulf between the world of physical matter and the world of consciousness. We know much about the structure and behavior of the former, yet relatively little about the latter. Before we go on with our quest to understand the nature of consciousness in the light of the psilocybin experience, let's take a very brief look at the history of this most murky philosophical quagmire.

The seventeenth-century French philosopher Descartes is generally credited with fully appreciating and documenting the mind/body dilemma. Descartes concluded that there were two sorts of universal stuff—mind and matter—and that they interacted in some mysterious ghostlike way. This dualistic "ghost in the machine" view of consciousness has annoyed many a philosopher and scientist alike. Especially scientists, for they do not like talk of incorporeal entities (elusive minds) not located in three-dimensional space being somehow able to interact with matter. Perhaps this explains why most psychologists have until quite recently been content to ignore the issue of consciousness. It is such an enigmatic phenomenon, and yet it is consciousness that is the very core of our being.

Consciousness defines you right now, for instance. This book might be physical and clearly tangible, yet what are your thoughts to know this? And even more problematic is the mind's ability to act directly upon matter through the body. How can a thought that is non-weighable and not made of physical particles nonetheless be able to move the collective atoms in, say, one's fingers? How can some sort of informational pattern embodied within the brain act upon so-called matter?

To reach some understanding we must either side with the old Cartesian dualistic belief or launch ourselves wholeheartedly into an alternative "informational monism," in which the reality process consists of only one stuff—information. As I hope to show, the nature of the psilocybin experience suggests that we embrace the latter scenario.

An Attempt to Exorcise the Ghost of Descartes

Since the musings of Descartes, philosophers have engaged in a veritable free-for-all in their attempts to either defend Descartes' ideas or do away with them and somehow unite mind with matter. Indeed, some academic philosophers make it their professional business to immerse themselves night and day in the mind/body problem. So annoyingly problematic is the existence of consciousness in an apparently physical Universe that entire academic careers have been built on this subtle paradox. Row upon row of shelves in the philosophy section of university libraries are given over to books dealing in some way with the mind/body problem.

Still, as far as I am aware, not one professional mind/body philosopher has become seriously involved with psychedelic experimentation in order to further our knowledge and insight into the dynamic interplay between chemistry and altered states of awareness. In fact, most books purportedly dealing with the issue of consciousness patently ignore psychoactive substances altogether, as if they had nothing whatsoever to teach us. I suppose that most traditional mind/body "specialists" balk and quiver at the very idea of psychedelic shamanism and its alchemical explorations of the mind. Maybe visionary plants are simply too scary for armchair-bound philosophers to confront. Whatever the case, entheogenic flora and fungi have remained a peripheral phenomenon, studied solely by anthropologists, ethnobotanists, and a handful of adventurous mavericks. It is hoped this state of indifference may soon be shattered and that science comes to properly address the delicate interface between chemistry and consciousness.

Chemistry and consciousness . . . what do such terms imply? The important answer is that, taken together, they directly address the boundary between the physical and the psychological. Chemistry implies chemicals and substances—material things, in other words—whereas altered states of awareness lie in the realm of the intangible mind. We established in the last chapter that various types of substance, particularly those with a close molecular resemblance to the brain's neurotransmitters, appear to elicit fairly predictable and characteristic changes in consciousness. If we consider psilocybin, we see that it bridges perfectly the conceptual gap between the two seemingly incompatible worlds of mind and matter, psychological and physical. The more we come to understand the modus operandi of psilocybin, the closer we get to divining the actual design of the bridge linking mind to matter.

A tall order then, this attempt to resolve the age-old mind/body problem. Still, no harm will have been done should I fail miserably in my theoretical endeavors. After all, untenable solutions inevitably aid the formulation of sound solutions, so the "psilocybin solution" should not have to be completely discarded. Bear with me then and judge for yourself as we embark on the next stage of the sacred mushroom mystery tour. This will take us further into informational territory as we focus more closely on the structural dynamics of psychedelic visions. Because such visions seemingly depend in some vital way on the integration and cohesion of large amounts of neuronal information, then above all else, an understanding of information is assuredly key to unlocking the mystery of consciousness, whether of the psilocybinetic kind or of the normal kind.

Symbols in Formation

We have seen that one major aspect of the psilocybin experience—the perception of vivid visions with eyes closed—appears to be the result of dreaming while awake, or at least something akin to this (this has nothing to do with daydreaming, which is something else entirely). According to our previous analysis, we can view such visions as being dynamic information patterns conveyed in the neuronal systems of the brain, information patterns that have been specifically "freed" to form themselves through the "liberating" action of psychedelic substances on serotonergic systems. Similarly, REM dreams would appear to be generated by the same "freed" neuronal systems.

The fact that psychedelic visions are loaded with powerful and often universal symbology might indicate that there are predetermined ways in which large amounts of neuronal information can be organized and integrated. This introduces an important idea. Just as elements like carbon, hydrogen, nitrogen, and oxygen naturally organize themselves into specific stable structures like water, carbon dioxide, and amino acids, so too may information in the brain, in the form of neuronal firing activity, organize itself in the same kind of way.

The fundamental quality that makes, say, water the same everywhere is its molecular structure—the exact way in which molecules of hydrogen and oxygen cohere. They form a specific pattern, a specific molecular expression. If my speculations are correct, information embodied in systems of neuronal firing likewise forms itself into specific structured patterns. And just as water molecules can organize themselves still further into stable macroscopic patterned structures like snowflakes, so too can more and more coherent forms of information coalesce by way of the patterning processes occurring in the psilocybin-influenced brain. Freezing temperatures (at least partly) help foster the structured patterns exhibited by snowflakes, whereas psilocybin helps foster the structured patterns of neuronal activity that come to be experienced as shamanic visions. Water molecules organize themselves according to the rules of a molecular language; neuronal firing patterns organize themselves according to the rules of a psychological language.

If specific patterns and structures emerge from expansive information-integration processes occurring within the brain, this would explain the existence of universal symbology, universal dream images, and mythical archetypes. Throughout the world, in all of the countless religions, cosmologies, and mythologies created by our species, we come across highly similar mythical images and symbols full of meaning and associative power.

The serpent is a good example of this universal symbology. It is found in the religious mythology of the Maya and the Aztecs (who worshipped Quetzalcoatl—the Feathered Serpent); the ancient Egyptians (the headdresses of the pharaohs incorporated the viper as a symbol of wisdom and intellect); the Australian aborigines (who worshipped the Rainbow Serpent); and the ancient peoples of India (who worshipped Nagas, literally wise serpents). Serpent mythology is also found in the ancient epic of Gilgamesh (a serpent tells of a mythical plant that can confer immortality) and in the Eden of the Old Testament (the wise but feared serpent who offers forbidden fruit from the tree of knowledge). More often than not, the serpent symbolizes a wise, divine, or spiritual life force or deity.

As we are on the subject of serpentine motifs, here is a relevant description of mine in which I describe some typical visions instigated by the mushroom.

Once, I remember seeing huge serpentine coils piled up upon one another and somehow turning as if the cogs of some organic machine. Then I found myself gliding toward a flexuous off-white mass which for the life of me I could not comprehend. This rippled white stuff was everywhere, and I was being drawn into it, suffocating almost as it surrounded me.

Suddenly, seeing this mass close up, I realised what it was. It was convoluted brain tissue. Spongy white cortical tissue, fold after fold of it. This was the immense brain of some mythical Serpent related, I thought, to Gaia. I felt that I was seeing a visual representation of the powerful intelligence of the Earth itself, the "Earth Brain" as it were.

The scene then changed and I found myself touring a building that was made of both artery-laced flesh and conventional material. Each room seemed to have a particular biological function. It was most bizarre. I appeared to be inside a kind of visceral architecture that was breathing gases, pumping oceans of blood, and digesting vast vats of food.

In fact, such visionary motifs indicating the fusion of man-made architecture with biological structure were repeated a number of times. I often perceived stately homes and palaces—or rather I would be gliding gracefully through such palatial places—and always, the woodwork, like the banisters, wall panels, or staircases, would reveal themselves to be made of the body of a living creature. To be precise, I perceived that these buildings were woven from the jewelled body of the Serpent. Everything was alive, all was part of one animate, constructing entity. And if I saw human figures in any of these scenes, they too were formed out of the transmutating body of the Serpent. Everything in these scenes had the stamp of the Serpent's hide upon them, in that a kind of pulsating grid of luminescent lines and scaly jewels pervaded every object.[1]

Serpent motifs might be universal because, as with other mythical symbols, they represent stable, organized concentrations of information. A symbol, such as the mythical Serpent, embodies a large set of relations or, to be more specific, it is the point where a huge web of psychological relations converge. To fully understand the symbol is to sense at once all of its relations to other objects of perceptual experience. In other words, visual symbols play a role in a psychological language. (Here, I again invoke the concept of language since language is essentially an informational system not restricted to words alone. Language, in the abstract way in which I refer to it, is a system of informational elements bearing definite relations with one another; hence a language of words, of molecules, of symbols, and so forth.)

Universally powerful visionary symbols can be thought of as *expressions* in the dictionary of a "higher" language connected with the human psyche. What I mean by "higher" is that the visual elements in this language are far more rich in meaning and informational content than the words of our spoken language. Moreover, seeing visionary symbols choreographed together in a movielike fashion—as occurs in the psilocybinetic state—is to experience meaning in perhaps its purest, most informationally rich way. To partake of a visionary dialogue is to be overwhelmed by the direct apprehension of pure, unadulterated meaning, which arises as a consequence of the highly integrative informational processes liberated by entheogenic compounds.

In the metaphorical and visual language emanating from the most integrated information processing of the human psyche, the serpent therefore appears to be a significant "word" or icon, itself derived from the natural environment. There are many such universally potent icons derived from the natural environment. Try now, if you would, to imagine in glorious Technicolor a volcano erupting, a butterfly emerging from its pupa, or a hand reaching into a flame. Further imagine all of the ways that potent symbolic images like these could be meaningfully put together by some agency dissociated from the self or ego to convey some message or idea to us. And finally, imagine an informationally rich creation like this being experienced directly by one's consciousness with no interference whatsoever. Here we begin to understand what the shamanic visionary experience is like, that it consists essentially of a communication transmitted in the higher language expressed by the Other, a language of symbols embodied in animated imagery.

See What I Mean?

Seeing, it seems, is the most direct form of perception. This is why one comes to "see the truth." It also explains why art is powerful. A great painting is unworded yet it may well speak volumes to us. Visual symbols and images can be truly effective in their capacity to inform. It is in this sense that I refer to a higher language of the psyche, a language not of words but of concentrations of information visibly beheld.

To really see something is to see what something really means, and to see what something really means is to instantly access all of its inherent relations to other things. To see a powerful symbol, whether in a shamanic vision, a dream, or a spiritual piece of art, is to behold a concentration of information, a supercondensed concrescence of meaning.

The idea then is that very large amounts of information can cohere and coalesce into symbols, and, since all brains work in the same way, universal symbols might emerge in a language of symbols, just as universal expressions and meanings emerge in all worded languages. But it should be stressed that universal symbols are related to real objects in the shared world. Even if they are not deified, snakes, for example, are generally at least feared the world over, and for good reason, since their venom can prove fatal. This automatically means that the real-world snake is going to be a good candidate for playing a role as a universal symbol wherever symbol-generating processes arise.

Designer Symbols, Designer Visions

In the case of entheogenic visions (or dreams), it might well be that they contain not only universal symbols, but culturally determined symbols that can be fully understood and appreciated only on a personal level. In the case of much of South American shamanism, like that practiced by the ayahuasca-using Tukanoan Indians of Colombia, we do indeed find culturally determined symbology in the visions experienced by the shamans, often related to powerful and revered jungle creatures like the jaguar, as well as the ubiquitous serpent. These Tukanoan shamans also experience imagery related to their particular brand of cosmology, which is known and fostered by all members of the tribe. An analysis of the varied pieces of artwork inspired by their psychedelic visionary experiences reveals a striking commonality, for the Indians invariably portray the spiritual entities encountered in the same way and in the same style. This clearly testifies to the culture-bound nature of their visions; that is, they experience one particular kind of visionary dialogue with the Other.

From the perspective of the informational approach being taken here, such culturally determined visionary dialogues still result from information integration within the psychedelically altered brain, with the attendant fact that the information used in the visionary communication derives, in part, from the shamans' personal store of knowledge. Because these native South Americans share the same culture and experience the same environmental forces, certain symbols and images will be highly significant to them in a way that an outsider would not be able to fully understand. It appears then that, in common with spoken language, there exist regional "visionary dialects" expressed in the psychedelic state, the dialect being determined by the tribe's unique physical and cultural environment.

Claudio Naranjo, a researcher who spent many years investigating the shamanic use of ayahuasca in the Amazon, reached a similar conclusion about the commonality of the shamans' visions. Naranjo wrote of visionary symbols as follows:

> The superimposition of the reptile, the feline's fangs and claws and the bird's wings (as well as the fish's watery environment and scales) results in the image of the dragon [synonymous with the mythical serpent]. Furthermore, through an examination of dragon myths and the content of subjects' reports, I concluded that the consciousness stimulated by *ayahuasca* involved an intuition of the inseparability of life and death, an apprehension of life as a self-consuming and self-devouring living-into-death or dying-into-life—and observed that just as mythical dragons may be symbols of good and evil, *ayahuasca* animals may be terrifying or friendly according to the readiness of the psyche to accept life-death or to reject, not only the "internal animal" but a greater Life, along with its deadliness and mortality.[2]

Whether Naranjo is wholly correct in his particular interpretation is not important. The point is that this kind of interpretation, in which the visionary elements are considered to be symbols replete with meaning, matches the theoretical approach being taken here. Visionary symbols can be understood as deriving from *the forced confluence of vast amounts of information*. In my own experience, psilocybin visions are accompanied by the unmistakeable sensation that huge amounts of psychological information are indeed being forced to fold, merge, and cohere and, moreover, that this process of forced coalescence mimics over a brief period of time what Nature at large is doing over a long period of time. In each case, self-organization is involved—whether of information or matter and/or energy.

It really is as if individual films of the utmost sophistication are forged by the Other and are forcibly screened before the mind's eye while one is in the psilocybinetic state. The visions well up magically from the depths of the psyche as though woven out of some undulating multicolored dream fabric, as if one's visual cortex were directly interfaced with some megapowerful intentional computer. Obscure items from memory are often strung together in some new creative fashion, or perhaps one witnesses scenes never before encountered but that are nevertheless immediately understood. In either case, the visions fairly burst with an overwhelming amount of information.

The material basis from which such designer visions are fashioned is one's store of memories and personal knowledge of the world. According to my interpretation, the Other is able to re-form idiosyncratic information in order to communicate in a highly personal way that one would likely be responsive to. Such creative artistry represents the meta-language spoken by the Other, the visions representing a higher, more informationally rich symbolic language being conducted deep within the innermost sanctums of the psyche. That which needs to be shown is shown. That which is poised to fall into place does fall into place. Information in the brain is like some living thing.

Stretching Credulity

If this is starting to sound too far-fetched, it is only because the terminology is new. What I am calling the Other is a dynamic information-integration process brought to life within the psilocybin-infused brain. To put it another way, the Other can be understood as an information-patterning phenomenon that spontaneously emerges when certain dynamic neurochemical conditions prevail, in the same way that a vortex pattern may spontaneously emerge in water if certain dynamic conditions prevail. The Other appears to be a higher, more integrated manifestation of the human psyche, so full of profundity and purposeful import that it can be considered to be fully autonomous and dissociated from the individual self or ego.

It is hard not to believe this when one has come to directly experience psilocybin visions. Think of the minister from Harvard's Good Friday Experiment who had profoundly religious visions of Christ. This is the way in which the Other "spoke" or "introduced itself" to him. Its language is that of symbols and images, creatively juxtaposed to convey some vibrant meaning. In the depths of the minister's psyche neuronal informational patterns of incredible complexity arose, informing him in a soulful way. Those particular arrangements of psychological information were generated out of the informational stores of his own personal psyche in a style that would be highly meaningful to him in particular.

The Other thus represents a name, or label, for the kind of information processing underlying the visionary state. An apparent communion with the Other demonstrates the inherent property of neuronal information to purposefully organize itself into streams of ideas laden with profound meaning. If one can conceive of the mind as being a kind of informational process, one can equally envisage the Other as being an informational process. Whatever the actual neuronal firing mechanisms involved, it seems likely that the self-organization, or forced coherence, of immense amounts of information underlies the felt presence of the Other.

The greater the facilitation of informational organization and informational coherence, the richer in meaning the resulting patterns will be. In a way, it is somewhat analogous to running a defragmentation program on a computer, whereby disconnected but related data are collated and organized in a more integrated way. In a brain/mind system under the influence of psilocybin, such a defragmentation process leads to the formation of mythical symbols and icons because this is the only way in which massive amounts of related information can be visually expressed. Because there must be limited ways in which huge amounts of information can be integrated—in other words, there are logical constraints—then this again explains the existence of universal symbology and universal mythology.

But why exactly should the focused embracing of large amounts of psychological information be under logical constraints? Could not any old image or icon do? Not really. Think of some short story and imagine trying to sum up the theme in one sentence or in a single visual image, the moral of the story so to speak. Although there may be a thousand and one ways of telling that story, to concentrate the moral (the point or overall pattern that connects the elements of the story) into one meaningful sentence or one meaningful image automatically constrains us to use certain key words or certain pictorial icons.

Consider also what it is like when one searches for a word that one knows will express what one wants to convey; that frustrating . . . what is it called? Ah yes, that tip-of-the-tongue moment. The word or term we look for is a logical consequence of what we need to express, and we might well be constrained into using that one word to capture the exact meaning we wish to communicate.

Likewise, in the language of the Other, there are certain types of meaning (large patterns of information) that can be expressed only with specific symbols and icons. The symbols and visual representations are highly organized fields of information. Such symbols and their drawing together into coherent progressing visions therefore reflect the ongoing language being "uttered" by the higher information-organizing processes of the Other.

We can also refer back to R. Gordon Wasson's vision of a mythical beast drawing a chariot or of the colossal doors opening. These are obviously powerful symbols teeming with inherent meaning, especially when perceived as close as is possible—that is, directly behind closed eyes while under the superconscious spell of the mushroom. These visions are not like simple pretty pictures; they are more like a confrontation with ideas and symbols issuing from some highly organized source of intentionality—like, say, the Platonic realm of pure Ideas, an inference you will recall that Wasson himself made in his attempts to come to terms with his experiences. The thing is, this Platonic realm, if that is what one chooses to call the transcendental Other, is not static, like an archival system. Instead, it is able to inform one through a dynamic stream of intentional information in which visual symbology dominates.

Various types of symbol can therefore be considered elements of a *higher language,* a language not of the individual ego-driven mind but of the communicating Other. The symbols are amalgamated concentrations of information coming to life in a mind illuminated by visionary alkaloids. Or, to use Huxley's terminology, the informational forms are *transmitted* via the psilocybinetic brain. As voluminous torrents of information "struggle" to integrate and coalesce, evermore elaborate forms and patterns emerge, and these are experienced as the felt presence of the Other actively communicating in a language of potent symbolic visual imagery. *Information appears as if alive and intent on self-organization.*

The Many Guises of the Other

As Terence McKenna repeatedly pointed out, it is quite common, for Westerners at any rate, to perceive UFO or extraterrestrial motifs in psychedelic visions. McKenna has suggested that the UFO is the Other in the guise of a contemporary symbol. According to McKenna, the Other is normally so remote from us that it dons the mask of the UFO in order to express itself, its Otherness.

Since the 1950s, a plethora of sci-fi films have focused on alien visitations to Earth. The predominant theme in these sorts of entertaining fantasy is the incredible impact that an alien presence would have on humanity. It is a modern reworking of the ancient religious idea of divine intervention. Some great alienesque force suddenly erupts in the midst of our culture in a way that upsets, or radically alters, human destiny. Everyone would have to take notice. People would, willy-nilly, be forced to cease their everyday business for a spontaneous alien-inspired holiday or two. Everything would have to change. Alien visitations are dramatic. They negate everything else.

Obviously, then, the UFO can be understood as a modern icon, an immensely powerful Western symbol packed with meaning. It also highlights the way to think about information, for, in terms of information, the archetypal UFO is the center of a whole web of psychological relations and associations. It embodies a concentration of information. It expresses a powerful set of psychological associations. As a simple word, *UFO* embodies information in the context of the English language, whereas as something visibly beheld in an entheogenic vision, the UFO, or indeed any kind of image of advanced alien technology, represents an utterance in the symbolic language of the communicating Other.

In *The Archaic Revival,* McKenna spoke of the UFO as:

> An autonomous psychic entity that has slipped from the control of the ego and approaches laden with the "Otherness" of the unconscious. As one looks into it one beholds oneself, one's world information field, all deployed in a strange, distant, almost transhumanly cool way, which links it to the myth of the extraterrestrial. The extraterrestrial is the human Oversoul in its general and particular expression on the planet.[3]

Here may lie the explanation for the rampant and often far-fetched stories of actual UFO sightings and alien encounters not reserved to closed-eyes visions. Perhaps for some people the Other emerges into the perceived world of external reality, although this would more than likely represent a genuine hallucination.

McKenna's use of the term *Oversoul* is yet another way of referring to the Other. Whereas McKenna readily assumed the Other to be the creative source of sacred visions, I am being more specific by asserting that an experience of the Other results from an inherent property of information just as the individual mind results from an inherent property of information. Through the redemptive action of sacramental alkaloids like psilocybin, the Other is able to become manifest and flow through the neuronal architecture of the brain. The Other, or Oversoul, is information, or at least it is the creative organizing principle underlying brain-based information integration and brain-based information patterning. Its language is that of symbols and cultural images, futuristically alien or otherwise.

To sum up the far-reaching speculations presented thus far: whether personal or universal, information becomes incorporated into entheogenic visions in a novel and creative way such that a definite message or meaning is conveyed, or at least appears to be conveyed. The resulting overwhelming confrontation with a spiritual intelligence is the result of information integration to the point where the integrative process appears to be alive, purposeful, and distinct from the self or ego. This is the transcendental Other, a sentient informative entity that is not us but something very closely related to us.

Can, or Should, We Banish the Other?

Alternatively, a cool, restrained, and skeptical approach might be to suggest that the self-organizing patterning of neuronal information does not reflect an information-composed Other at all, but is just the result of some incidental property of information. Just as gravity is a property of the Universe acting everywhere (on a macroscopic scale) to draw physical material together, so too might there be some inherent but incidental property of psychological material (or neuronal information) that acts to organize it. Although this organizational process can, if boosted by psilocybin or endogenous brain chemicals like DMT, result in the perception of a communicating Other, this Other will in fact be just a kind of illusory side effect promoted by the experience.

Having said that, however, in terms of the visionary shamanic experience, it is clearly so powerful and so emotionally charged that the inference of a transcendental Other is historically well established and seems indicative that something important and hitherto unknown to psychological science is occurring. As many Westerners who have sampled entheogenic flora will readily attest (this includes those brave anthropologists who have taken Amazonian psychedelic brews and experienced numinous visions), it is not simply "primitive" inference or hearsay that has led native shamans to speak of a perceived contact with gods or spirits. It is rather the case that the sacred nature of the entheogenic experience appears so dramatic, so persuasive, that the inference of an Other becomes unavoidable.

Even if we did still opt for the restrained armchair-bound explanation, it is not incompatible with the notion of the Other, but merely a kind of clever avoidance and reluctance to invoke a "big idea" that we are not accustomed to. For to reduce the Other to merely an incidental organizing principle inherent in information, with no real purpose, is like saying that normal consciousness is merely an incidental neuronal effect without any real purpose. But since we know that normal consciousness is purposeful (we have will, more or less), then it is tenable that the Other represents a kind of purposeful will above and beyond that of the individual ego. Indeed, if we also consider the many other self-organizing properties of the Universe—which are deemed fundamental—then the Other might well represent a similarly fundamental aspect of Nature, one that "comes alive" when conditions in the human cortex are appropriate.

Yet, if pushed, is it really necessary to speak of a dissociated communicating presence when a less fanciful explanation will at least partially suffice? Aren't we in danger of becoming overtly religious by invoking a kind of superintelligence dissociated from the individual self? Maybe so. But if the notion of an intentional Other still seems too bizarre to the critical reader, the idea can be further defended by examining a common analogous situation in which we infer a non-self-based other.

After all, do we not all assume without any doubt whatsoever that other conscious minds really exist? And yet this is also a big inference based solely on subjective experience. Let us pursue this, because it is, strangely enough, relevant to the validity of inferring purposeful entities.

Big O, Little o

To posit a transcendental communicating Other is really no different to the tacit inference that other human minds exist. Both these sorts of other, the big *O* and the little *o,* are equally conceived of as the focus points of intentional information processing. Yet there might not be other conscious minds apart from our own. Or there might be just a few. We cannot absolutely prove that others possess conscious minds like our own since we have access only to their external manifestations. Other people may in fact be, god forbid, soulless automata, no more than mechanical zombies masquerading as conscious beings. For all you know, you might be the only conscious entity existing, for what conscious experience are you familiar with but your own? Indeed, when Descartes began his philosophical career, he wanted to know what he could be absolutely certain about, with no room for doubt whatsoever. Gazing out of an ornate seventeenth-century window, he wondered if perhaps all of reality was a cunningly designed trick played on him by some artful demon with infinite powers of trickery. Entertaining such a sinister scenario, Descartes came to the conclusion that the only thing that he knew to be real for sure was the existence of his own self—he thought, therefore he was. There could be no doubting that at least. This deceptively simple realization became the bedrock on which much of his subsequent philosophy and science were based.

The philosophical belief that only one's own self really exists is known as solipsism. As weird as it might sound, it is a theoretical stance that many might be tempted to adopt, even for the sake of just playing with the idea in order to annoy and confuse friends. The point of raising this issue is that all of us make a big leap of faith in accepting that other minds like our own really do exist, and this way of thinking "works," so much so that most people have not the faintest idea what solipsism is and never even come to entertain the idea despite it being an essentially reasonable piece of personal philosophy.

Directly analogous with our tacit assumption that other conscious minds like our own exist is the inference that an intelligent, communicating Other lies at the heart of shamanic visions. This seems unavoidable if one is experiencing powerful visionary effects from entheogenic agents, and this makes it a valid and workable way of explaining the experience despite its distinct tone of grandeur. I would therefore claim that the notion of a transcendental Other is reasonable in light of the remarkably integrative information processing occurring in the entheogen-imbued brain. Such chemically inspired modification of neuronal activity is experienced as being so rich in symbology and meaning that for all intents and purposes it can be considered the result of a living, intelligent, and communicating agency made of information, an agency whose intent can become activated and focused should the chemical conditions of the human cortex be so conducive. Information must indeed be in some sense alive.

"Dreamformation"

A similar process to that outlined above would appear to govern dreaming, since complex and often fantastically stylized dream scenarios are something our dreaming selves confront. We literally find ourselves witness to the integrative information processes of our dreaming minds, often experiencing strange and elaborately scripted dream scenarios. But, and this is a major caveat, with dreams our dream self is not generally in a very consciously attentive state, so dreams remain ethereal and forgettable, unlike psilocybin visions, which one is highly conscious of and which are faithfully retained within memory.

It has been speculated that the reason we are unable to retain dream experience is because the normal neuronal mechanisms that underlie long-term memory are shut off during the dream state. This, however, is not the case with psilocybinetic visions, since the neuronal systems that facilitate long-term memory are still operative. Psilocybin is therefore able, perhaps, to bypass those brain mechanisms that normally serve to stop us consciously attending to information arising from the creative depths of the psyche.

The neuropsychologist and expert on sleep processes J. Allan Hobson has developed a model of dreaming that is compatible with the information-integration model outlined in this chapter. Hobson has offered an "activation synthesis" model of dreaming. He reached his theoretical conclusions after having studied in depth the neurochemical processes underlying REM sleep (also known as dream sleep), processes that include, of course, the cessation of the serotonergic raphe system.

On his activation-synthesis model, Hobson writes:

Activation is an energy concept: in REM sleep [dreaming], brain circuits underlying consciousness are switched on. Synthesis is an information concept: dream cognition is distinctive because the brain synthesizes a dream plot by combining information from sources entirely internal to itself and because chemical changes radically alter the way information is processed. So the term "synthesis" implies both fabricated (made up) and integrated (fitted together).[4]

Basically, then, dreams are associated with periodical bursts of firing in perhaps billions of neurons, with, of course, the attendant potential for an incomprehensibly large amount of networked communication (we should bear in mind that dreaming might be due in part to endogenous DMT). This wealth of activity is integrated in such a way that dreams emerge or are synthesized. Dreams are thus constructed of information, the information concerned being embodied in the unusual global firing state of the brain.

As we have already established, a related process appears to take hold when psilocybin is present within the brain. This "waking dream" situation takes place during the eyes-shut waking state, whereas dreaming takes place during sleep. So although the psychedelic visionary state and the dream state take place while the brain is in a different overall state (an awake state versus a sleep state), the general principle of vision generation and dream generation is the same in each case. To reiterate, this principle consists of the patterning and cohesion of vast bursts of neuronal information being generated from internal sources and not from external sources. The advantage of "waking dreams" induced by entheogenic alkaloids over normal dreams is that in the former one remains highly alert and highly conscious of the visionary dialogue, and it is generally not forgotten. Entheogenic visions also tend to be more sacred in character than dreams.

The Varieties of Dream Experience

Often dreams appear to be quite mundane, containing perhaps integrated scraps of information subconsciously perceived during the waking state. By joining these disparate pieces of information, a kind of learning might be facilitated. Indeed, it has been demonstrated that if rats (please excuse the ratomorphism) are selectively denied periods of REM sleep, then they are more likely to forget information previously learned.

Lazy newborn infants spend about sixteen hours a day asleep, of which half that time is spent in REM sleep. This means that they dream about three times as much as adults. As newborns have a strong need to learn about the world, dreaming presumably facilitates certain types of information integration—and hence learning. Through dreams, information acquired through waking perceptions can be sifted, consolidated, organized, and generally "worked out," so to speak. In short, one theoretical approach to understanding dreaming has it that dreaming allows information to become integrated within the developing psyche, a view fully compatible with my own speculations.

What of dreams not obviously connected with, say, diverse pieces of information, but that concern big themes? Especially those really vivid dreams that leave a lingering emotional impact on us? These might seem definitely to contain some meaning important to our inner well-being. Although we in the West do not have a cultural tradition that takes dreams, whether the mundane variety or the moving variety, too seriously, this has not always been the case with our species. It is presumably the phenomenon of significant-seeming dreams that led cultures like native Amerindians and Australian aborigines to take dreams seriously—so much so that dreams would often be discussed and acted on by the whole tribe. Such types of informative dream also led Western thinkers like Jung to conceive of a collective unconscious from which archetypal dream symbols could emerge. Although Jung's vision of a collective unconscious might be considered fanciful, it does highlight the fact that certain dreams can act as a source of useful information should we choose to contemplate them. Indeed, if this were not the case, then presumably native cultures would never have bothered with dream analysis in the first place.

Considering these properties of dreams, we can see more clearly how the brain is literally an information-organizing device able to continually forge illustrative patterns of meaning both consciously and unconsciously. The only real difference between dreams and psychedelic visions would appear to be the extent and scale of this important process. If information integration is allowed to reach a certain threshold of activation through the catalytic agency of entheogenic compounds, then the ultimate source of the information-patterning process can be divined and we come to directly experience a symbolic and unmuddied dialogue with the Other, where the Other is precisely the self-organizing property of the information embodied in the neuronal firing activity. In this sense the Other is a latent form of information that can potentially be brought to life through the processing mechanisms hard-wired within the brain. Neuronal information, by shaping itself in constrained ways, allows definite motifs to emerge, representative of the symbolic language of the transcendental Other. This language is activated and perceived during both the lucid dream state and the psilocybin-induced psychedelic state. Both states are natural and both derive from the capacity of the brain to coalesce and organize large amounts of information.

Reality Expansion

From what has been discussed thus far concerning the psilocybin experience, it might seem as if the eyes-shut visionary state is the prime effect, yet with eyes open one encounters equal perceptual wonders. The world appears as if new, bursting with a significance and beauty that literally brushes one's soul. One sees more clearly than one could imagine, as if an occluding cloud had been graciously dispelled to reveal the sheer unadulterated "isness" of reality. Visual perception is experienced as though it were the finest grain cinematography able to pick up upon a luxury of detail previously hidden. Objects in the environment may appear to be interconnected and part of a fluid coherent pattern. Great thoughts occur to one, unbidden yet full of profound import, as if the very secrets of existence were suddenly in one's grasp. This is the very least that can be stated. How can such phenomenology be accounted for in our information-integration model?

Regarding psilocybin's radical enhancement of visual perception, it seems logical to surmise that a change in the functioning of serotonergic systems facilitates a greater "absorption" of the external information impinging upon the eyes. More information inherent in light flows through the visual system and into the brain, and this is experienced as breathtaking visual clarity. Since we humans are effectively embedded in an ocean of photic information, by subtly altering brain chemistry we can allow a tidal influx of this informational sea of light to sweep over the visual system, leaving us awash in perceptual data.

All objects, whether organic or inorganic, possess an intrinsic meaning or set of relations to other objects. They possess informational content, linked as they are to a network of relations with other objects. As discussed earlier, to see an object is not merely to apprehend its shape or color, but to access its meaning. After all, the retina of the eye only records an inverted two-dimensional pattern of light intensities, much as computer vision records arrays of light intensity values. This is not seeing. Real seeing, as we know it, involves the perception of what the object signifies. To see an object is to perceive, all at once, its role, function, and relations—that is, its meaning—within a vast network of objects.

Under the spell of psilocybin, I suggest that one is able to penetrate deeper into the informational content of objects, akin perhaps to accessing a higher dimension that is otherwise occluded. This is a bit like looking up a word in a dictionary and noting *all* its meanings, thus coming to understand the word in its fullest sense. Normally we might not perceive the entire meaning of a word, accessing maybe only a fraction of its true semantic content, yet, in theory at least, we might come to ascertain more. This is what psilocybin perception involves: the accessing of latent information normally hidden to us by the hardwired constraints of the brain (my comparison to the comprehension of words is useful as, in the next chapter, I hope to show further how "material" objects in various domains—like the domains of physics, chemistry, and biology—are themselves elements within a hierarchy of language-like systems, playing functional roles just like words).

Informative Dialogues

As to the wealth of revelatory thoughts and ideas that erupt into consciousness during psychedelic ecstasy, these would appear to be, as with visions, a manifestation of the Other, in that they represent the holistic patterning of neuron-mediated information. This may often be experienced as a kind of internal dialogue with a wise being. Profound thoughts take on a rapidly flowing life of their own, generating further thoughts and insights. It is impossible not to once more invoke language here as a conceptual explanatory tool, though this type of inner psychedelic language involving complex thoughts and ideation works far more efficiently than the language system of the spoken word. Everyday language appears sluggish and cumbersome in contrast to the language of psychedelic contemplation, which moves at a profoundly different pace.

Indeed, the sheer fluency and dramatic insightfulness of psychedelic contemplation explains its emotional impact and ineffability.

If we conceive of language in whatever mode as a communicatory information system, we can see that its modes are many and varied, all operating at different speeds and with different properties. The principle however is the same. There is a flow of information and a natural progression that yields further information, just as with spoken dialogue. When we communicate with one another in conventional language, whether written or spoken, we initiate a dialogue in which information is exchanged. Regardless of whether this dialogue is one-sided or not, the process is dynamic in that information flows from one system to another, from one person to another, from one brain to another, from one mind to another.

With psychedelic contemplation, an internal dialogue ensues in which a flow of ideas takes place between the self and the Other, where the Other is a dissociated or higher-level informational source acting as one component in the dialogue process. Through psilocybin's activating influence, the psyche becomes a conduit to the Other, facilitating a dialogue of thought in which radical knowledge is received. It's an incredible idea to be sure, yet, as I hope I have made clear, the psilocybin experience demands these kinds of incredible explanation.

We are now equipped with a model that views consciousness as a particular pattern of information embodied in the rapidly flowing electrochemical state of the brain. And we also have an informational entity that we can call the Other that is activated and brought to life after the ingestion of psychedelic alkaloids like psilocybin. Both consciousness and the Other can be better understood as processes (or verbs) as opposed to things, moreover processes involving the patterning, or focusing, or coalescing, or orchestration, of vast amounts of information.

Now we must turn to the nature of information itself. In particular, we shall look at information outside of the brain and see if it too can be understood in the same way. Does an informational language underlie

Nature itself? Can molecules and atoms be interpreted as informational elements in a molecular or physical language? Is everything made of information? If so, does the reality process ultimately consist of a flow of self-organizing language-like information? Did our man Einstein emerge out of, grow up in, become famous in, and eventually die in an essentially informational reality process? Read on, then, for my psilocybin mushroom tale has hardly even begun. Information, it seems, cannot be stopped.

SEVEN

A Universe of Information

Nature's entheogenic agents have provided compelling evidence for the following two most interesting of propositions: first, that consciousness is a form of information substantiated within the brain's neuronal firing activity and, second, that this kind of cerebral information has a tendency to organize and integrate itself. Evidence in support of the first proposition was provided by looking at the ways that consciousness becomes altered according to subtle changes in brain chemistry, especially changes occurring at synapses. Chemically induced changes to global states of neuronal firing are synonymous with changes in consciousness, and since global states of neuronal firing must be global states of information (what else could they be?) we can conclude that consciousness is a form of information.

Evidence to support the second proposition—that cerebral information has a tendency to organize itself—came from an examination of psychedelic phenomenology and even dreaming, both processes highlighting the way that psychological information organizes itself without a deliberate effort on our part. Which is to say that we can *find ourselves* experiencing sacred visions after ingesting entheogenic agents or likewise *find ourselves* experiencing elaborate dream scenarios while we sleep (perhaps mediated by endogenous DMT).

The former experience, the psychedelic visionary state, seems to represent a very extreme manifestation of informational organization, so much so that a third proposition suggests itself, namely that an intelligent Other, distinct from the ego or self, lies behind the sacred thrust of psychedelic phenomenology. Such a dissociated Other can be considered to represent an organized source of intentional information that becomes activated when an individual's neuronal system is infused with psychedelic alkaloids. We can thus concur with Huxley in his assertion that psychedelics allow a greater amount of what he called Mind at Large to flow into conscious perception. The Mind at Large is the Other, which potentially interfaces with the human psyche, revealing itself in the visionary experience and possibly during symbolic dreams. Information is the stuff of both the Other and the human mind. Conscious experience is information in process, as is the entheogenic experience. The greater the field of information being processed or integrated, the more conscious we may become (the word *consciousness* means "knowing together").

In all three propositions, it is most definitely the term *information* that fits the picture. This chapter attempts to formally elucidate this information-based scenario and to explore further the nature of information and its role in the Universe at large.

Consciousness, Information, and Reality

At first blush, it might seem somewhat off the point to delve into the nature of information and its role in shaping the Universe. Are we not entering territory far removed from tangible entheogenic plants and fungi? Won't we be speculating beyond the call of duty? Can we really justify an attempt to understand of what the mystical experience and the Universe at large are made? Are they not two different things, two completely separate domains of inquiry?

In defense of such a bold move, I would remind the reader that the issue at stake in all refined psychedelic debates is that of the nature of perceived reality, in particular, whether the seemingly expanded field of reality unveiled by psilocybin, with its spiritual aura and its mysterious feel of interconnectedness, has any kind of firm foundation. My conviction, like that of Huxley and McKenna, is that entheogens like psilocybin really do allow us to glimpse the "bigger picture" (which falls into place when neuronal conditions are conducive) and that an attempt to understand this "bigger picture" should be pursued as far as possible. Since the psilocybin experience seems to depend on extreme levels of information integration, this strongly suggests, at least in my mind, that *a principle* of self-organization operates throughout the Universe on all levels, from star formation to DNA formation to the formation of minds, concepts, and perceived truth. In any case, the idea that the Universe consists of a purposeful flow of self-organizing information is precisely what visionary agents like the mushroom seem to confirm. For this reason, I think an attempt to understand reality in terms of information is justified. However, before we go on to examine these issues, a brief detour is in order. This will serve to drive home the point that entheogens have an important role to play in our conceptions of reality.

Shifting Paradigms

A genuinely mystical experience in which the presence of the Other is felt cannot fail but change one's conception of the world and, in particular, the significance one gives to life, particularly conscious human life, on this sensitive planet of ours. It therefore comes as no surprise that psilocybin phenomenology can be a tad religious in nature. Because the entire field of reality (the "bigger picture") is reconceived and reperceived in the psilocybinetic state, a kind of subjective paradigm shift occurs somewhat akin to paradigm shifts in science. These shifts in theoretical perspective involve thoroughly new conceptual frameworks with which to comprehend the fundamental nature of things. Similarly, traditional religious ideologies attempt to provide an overall scheme with which to understand reality. It is this holistic nature of religious thought that links it with psychedelic thought.

Entheogens, then, are powerful tools with which to forge a new set of conceptions about the reality process, and any competent person out to grasp the meaning of life should consider employing them. More to the point, newly acquired concepts can continue to be employed long after the consumed psychedelic catalysts have been metabolized into inactive by-products. In a sense, it is as if new conceptual insights into Nature, once divined, install themselves permanently within the mind. Entheogenic ecstasy, once tasted, is not forgotten. The difficulty, the overwhelming labor, is in trying to integrate the new view of reality with the old, to merge them so to speak, which is precisely what the rest of this book is about.

Huxley epitomized the paradigm-shifting effect of psychedelics through his interests and concerns during the last decade of his life. As we have seen, Huxley was convinced that psychedelics could grant one access to the sacred side of Nature as encountered by mystics and religious visionaries, an aspect of reality real but hidden to the secular mind. Indeed, he even asked his wife to inject him with LSD shortly before he died, so assured was he that a psychedelic state of mind could prepare him to face the final stage of human life. This is rather dramatic testimony to the fact that psychedelic consciousness connects one to the deepest mysteries that reality confronts us with.

Similarly, in the context of traditional psychedelic shamanism as practiced in South America, the mythological conception of reality held by the whole tribe stems from the effects of entheogenic plants on the psyche of the shamanic voyager. And, as the acid gurus of the 1960s testified, worldviews are very much at stake when it comes to the use of psychedelics. Chemically instigate a change in an individual's underlying concepts about reality, and culture transforms itself also.

In each of the above cases, reality is the issue at stake, along with the importance of the psychedelic experience in shaping it. Even without a psychedelic experience, Nature demands that we perceive it in some kind of organized way. Since we are woven into the very fabric of the Universe, we cannot ignore its true nature forever. Perhaps, for the most part, we conceive the nature of reality unconsciously, for we all carry around tacit assumptions and tacit beliefs about the world (this book, for example, carries a number of basic assumptions, such as the assumption that a "world out there" really does exist and that its nature really can be understood). Like our consciousness, we take many things for granted and may hardly ever reflect on them (like the stable existence of beneficent energy-emitting suns, for example, or the stable presence of oxygen in the atmosphere). What makes psilocybin so remarkable is its uncanny ability to take one's precious store of reality concepts and shake them about vigorously so as to reveal just how fragile and shallow-rooted these ingrained beliefs might be. If we imagine normal consciousness to be like a gramophone needle trundling along the groove of Nature's apparent "surface," entheogens like psilocybin can jog the needle of consciousness into a rarer, and indeed, more "groovy" surface groove. The true nature of reality then becomes a kind of "unfinished business" that simply must be dealt with. This is the clarion call of the psilocybin mushroom advocate. If we really wish to understand the reality process and the sense and significance of human life within it, entheogens offer us a direct path to the Other, a sentient and intentional agency made of information whose presence and teachings await us.

Assessing the Reality Situation

One cannot stop reality, and this makes its nature formidable regardless of what you believe. The sun warms us or burns us. The cold of winter bites at our flesh, and our homeostatic bodies automatically respond by shivering. The relentless rush of our billion-cell biology propels us toward sex, always it seems, making us grope, cling, moan, and shudder. This same biological march also puts us to sleep every night. We awaken, and again there it is—the reality process. We are inescapably bound up in it like grains of sand caught in an everlasting vortex of wind. More to the point, eventually this perennial condition kills us.

As I remarked in the introduction to this book, whatever you may have read, the ultimate nature of the reality process remains open to question. This may always be the case. Science seems always to reveal more mystery as it delves into the heart of "matter." What is more, science is conducted first and foremost to gather data. How this data is *interpreted* is another matter. What is a complex mechanical system to one scientist might be blatant proof of an organizing intelligence to another. And as for the long-sought-after supertheory that will be able to explain the totality of Nature in terms of, say, umpteen dimensional superstrings or in terms of some convoluted mathematical equation that only a few ivory-tower professors can really understand, these are likely to omit an explanation for consciousness and the mysteries of the mind. Indeed, such a final theory, such a final equation scrawled on a black-board with one fell swoop of chalk, will probably serve only to confuse the average mind rather than enlighten it.

It seems apparent that if we open ourselves to the vast cosmic mystery of existence, then we could do a lot worse than pursue the implications of the psilocybin experience. To consume the sacred mushroom is to launch oneself wholeheartedly into the mystery of being, the mystery of our short existence within this big system we call Nature. Our lives are defined by our conscious experience. We are led, prompted, and coaxed according to how we are informed. The remarkable feature of psilocybin mushrooms is that they can inform us in ways profound and sublime. To ignore their effects is to ignore new perspectives on reality.

As it is, the nature of the Universe is defined by the prevailing conceptual systems built into one's culture. In our case, the predominately reductive and materialistic paradigm favored by most of the science community shapes our views about reality. In the traditional scientific outlook that permeates Western educational institutions and the media, there is no real room for any kind of transcendental aspect to Nature. Nature is there, Nature is eminently intelligible, we can learn how it works, and that's really all there is to it. Suggesting that Nature has a spiritual dimension or an intentional quality is anathema to most scientists.

The entheogen advocate will doubtless have a stereotypical image of a hardnosed reductive scientist. It will be a he, and he will be old, scary, and grim faced, always waving a dry finger of admonishment at any talk of a so-called sentient and intentional Other. If psilocybin visions cannot be empirically measured in the lab, then forget it, he will say. And if one points to the few scientific experiments that have attempted to quantify the psychedelic experience in some way, our gloomy specter will doubtless pick holes in the methodology and ask for more proof. He would maintain that these experiences are simply too subjective and too personal to base any objective claims about reality on.

Still, as I hope I have demonstrated, psychedelic phenomenology flies in the face of claims that Nature lacks a spiritual side, or at least the psilocybin experience offers what I believe to be the most compelling reason to grant Nature an intent of some kind. This appears to be a neat and valid side step with which to bypass the bleak presence of the reductive materialist. Indeed, the real possibility that the reality process has a fantastically benign and purposefully smart aspect becomes readily apparent through psilocybin. Such a possibility will become ever more clear in this chapter and those that follow.

In short, psilocybin represents a catalytic agent of change in the domain of perceived reality, and this is why we shall now pursue the implications raised by the information-based propositions stated at the outset of this chapter. We are now armed and ready to re-view the "bigger picture" in the light of the psilocybin experience. This will prove to be astounding, so hold tight.

Elucidating the Nature of Information

What does it really mean to say that consciousness is a form of information? We seem to have merely replaced the intangibility of consciousness with another abstract entity. The question then arises as to what exactly information is. But even if we do succeed in adequately defining information, will we not then be in danger of trapping ourselves into one of those infinite regresses of terminology? Hopefully not. What we really want is a conceptual notion of information, not just another term. What I wish to develop is a broad understanding of what information is, and, in particular, whether it can be used to describe the world of so-called "matter" as well as that of mind. If so, then reality will have revealed itself to be made of different forms of information, almost as if . . . well, we shall see.

Information is notoriously difficult to get a handle on. The "slippery eel" that was consciousness has now become the "slipperiest eel" that is information. Apart from my hopefully reasonable assertion that consciousness is a form of information, it would also appear that much else besides consists of information. It seems to be everywhere, all over the place in fact, yet it defies a simple all-encompassing formulation. I am reminded here of the cult 1960s British TV series *The Prisoner* in which protagonist Patrick McGoohan, number 6, asks his mysterious captors what they want of him. "We want . . . information . . . IN . . . FOR . . . MATION!" he is repeatedly told. Perhaps he should have asked them to carefully define it. Anyhow, whatever it was, they never got it. Let's hope we fare better.

Someone once compared the modern status of information to that of iron in the Iron Age. The fashioning of iron lay at the heart of Iron Age material culture, yet no one knew of iron's atomic structure, that its useful nature lay in its atomic configuration relative to other matter. Similarly, we live in an Information Age, yet, if pressed, we find it difficult to get at the nature of information, at what exactly it is that links all forms of information, whether this information be in the form of consciousness, a bar code, a book, a weather front, or the current positions of the planets.

There are, in fact, specific ways to measure specific types of information. These were developed in the 1940s and 1950s by communication engineers who were concerned with the efficient transmission of signals along media like telephone lines. But before we look at the way they conceived information, let's first examine the commonsense view of what information means to us in its ordinary nontechnical sense. Since we use the term all the time, especially in our present culture, this must signify that we do know something intrinsic about its nature.

Take the following three deliberately evocative examples in which information is involved. They are not as trivial as they might at first appear; rather, they enable us to focus more clearly on the nature of information.

Example number one: At the end of the esteemed gangster movie *Miller's Crossing*, the main character shoots a fellow gangster but makes it look as though he was shot by someone else. He does this by putting the gun involved in the hands of yet another gangster, who lies shot and dead, so that it looks like the two gangsters shot each other dead at the same time. Now, when he plants his gun, our miscreant fails to wipe off his fingerprints. Why? Maybe he was unaware of the science of fingerprinting that was likely not as advanced and as pronounced in the 1920s (when the film is set) as it is today. In any case, the man simply places his gun in the other's hand. We know, of course, that had a modern forensic expert been around at the time, they would only have had to test the gun for prints for the real villain to become apparent. And what is the significance of said fingerprints? No one would doubt me if I said that the fingerprints contained information.

Example number two: A nervous student armed only with a fountain pen and a small bottle of ink enters an examination hall and takes an exam. After completing the exam the relieved student leaves, carrying his pen and his ink bottle, which is now empty. The ink he has left back in the examination hall is carefully distributed over the various sheets of the exam paper, and the distributional pattern of ink will, ultimately, decide whether he passes or fails the exam. Clearly, the pattern of ink set forth by the student contains a wealth of information.

Example number three: You crack open a boiled egg for breakfast. As you dip your toast into the yolk, you begin to reflect upon the nature of this tasty source of protein. In particular, you realize that if this egg were fertilized and had not been removed from beneath the warm body of the hen that laid it, then it would eventually have developed into a full-grown chicken with wings, a visual system, an innate repertoire of behavior, a digestive system, and so on. In other words, you become aware of the astonishing fact that somewhere within the soft yellow substance of an egg there must reside an inconceivably large amount of information.

Potential Information and Active Information

The first point to make about these three examples is that the information inferred is in a potential, or latent, state, which is to say that the unseen fingerprints remain as potential information until perceived; the distribution of ink across the exam paper remains potential information until the paper is read by an examiner; and an egg, before its untimely removal from beneath a hen, is also rich in potential information.

The second point is that this potential information can become active provided that it comes under the effects of an appropriate environment or appropriate *context*. As you will recall from chapter 5, I mentioned contextual environments in connection with their effect of providing meaning to individual neuronal patterns. We can now use this concept of context in a more general sense in order to understand how information can be made to actively flow or unfold from a potential state. As we shall see, context is an incredibly important word.

In the fingerprint case, a forensic expert armed with the tools of the trade can come to draw out the information embodied in the prints. The expert causes the information inherent in the fingerprint patterns to flow out into the larger environment, such that the information causes things to happen. The information has gone from a latent, passive state into an active state by virtue of the contextual effect of the forensic expert's psyche and equipment (that is, the expert's mind and equipment operate as a context). In other words, an appropriate contextual environment allows the meaning inherent in the prints to become manifest. To highlight the scope for causal effect that a transitional flow of information can have, we should note that information in fingerprint traces can penetrate a courtroom and induce a conviction. Information is a powerful thing, able to spread itself out into the greater environment.

With the distributed ink example, its analysis by an exam grader causes the potential information to flow out and be actively informative so that it comes to shape the grade awarded to the student. In the context of the psyche of an examiner, the information inherent in the precisely patterned distribution of ink is significant enough to indicate the intellectual capacity and communicational intent of the student.

As for the egg, its informational content similarly undergoes transition from a potential state to an active state when an appropriate environment draws the information out. In this case, a specific temperature acts as the initial befitting contextual environment, serving to elicit a flow of information from the sequential DNA patterns in the yolk (within the nucleus to be precise). Deny the egg the appropriate temperature context (take it away from warmth) and the information remains potential and inactive; hence a chicken fails to develop.

Subjective and Objective Patterns of Information

Besides the distinction between potential information and actively flowing information, there is also a distinction to be made between subjective information and objective information. In the case of the fingerprints and the ink distribution, the information is activated by us. The appropriate context is the subjective attention of human observers who come to channel the information. This means that the information is purely subjective in nature and depends on human observation to activate it. In fact, this subjective nature of information holds for the majority of the things we usually conceive of as information in our culture, things like TV and radio broadcasts, books, memos, newspapers, and so forth. To the fly crawling over the TV screen or the pages of a book, the visual or written information remains potential and dormant (unless of course the fly happens to be a cunningly designed electronic CIA bug), whereas in the context of the observing human psyche, the information actively flows out of these media and comes to be causally influential. It should be stressed however that this subjective nature of the information does not lessen it in any way; it is still very much a real part of the Universe. Relatively speaking, all and any kind of information is real.

The case is somewhat different with the egg, for human observers are not necessary to elicit the (genetic) information that they carry. The information in an egg is usually "read out" by the natural environment, and we can refer to an egg's information as being objective in the sense that the objective natural environment is involved as the appropriate context eliciting the process of information flow. The same goes for seeds and spores. They are informational entities that release their stored information when the natural environment is in a specific state. If the seeds or spores fall on "stony" ground (the wrong context), then their information remains unread, dormant perhaps for years. Indeed, a rather dramatic and apt example of this process occurred in the case of a freeze-dried Neolithic hunter found in the Alps a few decades ago. When his nondesigner straw footwear was thawed out, some fungal spores in the ancient straw came to life and grew. Scientists were astonished, as it was the first time that such a turn of events had been observed. Cryogenically suspended for five thousand years, the fungal spores went suddenly from a passive to an active state due to the warm environmental context of the science lab. The information in the spores began to actively flow, and this process manifested in the elaborate growth of the fungus.

But in both subjective and objective information, what is it that comes to flow? What is actually happening when the fingerprints are analyzed, when the ink is read, and when eggs and spores begin to grow? It is obvious that some kind of flowing process occurs wherein potential information becomes active information. But what exactly does this flowing process involve?

The Flow of Information

Above all, when information flows, there appears to be movement and change, in particular, a change in the state of at least one of the systems involved. In analyzing fingerprints, the information they contain initially affects the overall state of the forensic expert's psyche (the psyche being a system). Through analyzing the prints, the psyche of the forensic expert is provided with knowledge, a term often associated with information. Indeed, the concept of knowledge is bound with the theory of information developed by communication engineers, for information is conceived by them as representing a reduction in uncertainty. The richer the transfer of information, the less uncertain about something is the recipient of the information—hence more knowledge is gained. If I ask you to think of some famous person, and I try to guess who you thought of through the Twenty Questions game, then if my first question is whether the person is male and you answer "yes," then that single bit of information has halved my uncertainty. For the communication engineer, information is correlated with knowledge and a reduction in uncertainty regarding a choice of possibilities. Actively flowing information therefore comes to reduce the number in an ensemble of possibilities. It reduces uncertain possibilities and gives rise to the actual. The net result is a definite change, or resolution of many possibilities into one certainty, in the receiving system involved in the information flow. An uncertain "open pattern" becomes a certain "closed pattern" as it were. In the fingerprint case the receiving system is the psyche of the forensic analyst that changes its state, or at least part of its pattern, according to how it is informed.

Regarding the examiner case, before he or she comes to mark the paper, there is complete uncertainty about the ability of the student. As the exam paper is read, the information flow gradually causes a reduction in uncertainty, until an eventual mark is settled upon. So, akin to the previous example, we can see that the information contained in the patterned distribution of ink gradually changes the state of the examiner's mind or psyche. It is this sort of process that would appear to lie at the heart of subjective information transfer. A system of information on one level, or in one domain, connects to another system of information such that the state of the receiving system becomes altered. Or, to put it another way, one pattern of information is able to effect changes in another pattern of information. The human psyche is precisely a type of informational system, or informational pattern, able to change its state according to information coming from those other systems in which it is sensorially embedded.

It is apparent then that subjective information, when accessed through reading, hearing, smelling, tasting, seeing, or touching, comes to change the form of the receiving system substantiated in the receiver's brain. If we imagine the brain's neuronal system to be like clay, then as patterns of information impinge upon this clay, the shape of the clay is altered, and thus there has been a flow of information. The impact of the incoming flow of information leads to a gradual change in the form, or formal state, of the clay. The actual system that functions like clay is the neuronal system, or, to be more specific, the way in which billions of neurons are connected to one another. Indeed, learning, and by definition information access, is thought to be mediated through changes in neuronal connections. It is the overall network of connections that reflects the global form, or "shape," of the neuronal system.

The dictionary definition of *information* helps us here too, for it tells us that *information* comes from the Latin word *informare,* which means "to give form to." When information informs us, it alters the form, or pattern, of the informational system that is our mind. The mind is therefore an information-based system constantly re-forming itself (changing its pattern) through the accessing of information deriving from other kinds of information-based media, just as if it were clay being shaped by its environment.

For us, there is only information. Our minds are uniquely enduring patterns made of it. Information from other patterns, or systems, is continually being absorbed, integrated, and given out again. In this process, the form of the mind changes through alterations in the ways neurons are connected to one another. Consciousness emerges as a complex pattern of information whose form is constantly undergoing dynamic change due to the integration and accessing of other types of information through the senses. This is what I mean when I talk about the flow of information.

DNA Information

The case of the egg is somewhat different. When environmental conditions are conducive, the objective information in the DNA becomes active and is expressed through biochemical activity. DNA is seemingly "tuned" to operate when a specific environmental context surrounds it, just as our minds are tuned to our native language. The precise molecular details of DNA need not concern us here; rather, we need only grasp the general principle of how information actively flows out from DNA.

In our discussions of the egg, DNA represents "matter in a significant state" such that given a certain environment complex, organic activity will unfold. From a single fertilized egg cell an entire organism will develop because the information in the egg cell's DNA becomes activated. The DNA causes particular amino acids to form, which then cause various proteins to form, and hence various organs are assembled. Morphogenesis, the growth in form of an organism, is thus the reading out of DNA information, the expression of the meaning inherent in DNA (incidentally, if an egg is eaten, then another form of its information is accessed; in this case its "nutritional information" is absorbed by the consumer).

DNA information is read out through biochemical processes, and the resulting change in the formal state of the overall system itself acts as a contextual environment that allows the growth, or information readout, to progress. We can view the immediate chemical environment of the DNA as being both on the receiving end of the information transfer *and* able to feed back on, and influence, the information being accessed from the DNA. The form of the DNA, its specific information-rich pattern, comes to govern the form of the developing cells within which the DNA is embedded. In turn, the form of the cells (that is, their relative distribution as they multiply) will determine the formal development of the organs within which the cells are embedded as well as determine further DNA translation. In this way, DNA information comes to flow outward and be expressed on a macroscopic scale.

There is a strong suggestion here that informational systems (that is, meaningful patterns of form embodied within different media) are embedded within one another as in a nested hierarchical continuum and that they are continually influencing one another's form. This is rather dramatically illustrated in the fact that the reading out of DNA eventually leads to an organism moving about in the world at large. If some mutated DNA has fortunately produced some new advantageous behavior, then this eventually feeds back on the mutated DNA and favors its chances of being preserved. In a similar fashion, the form of the human genome is a direct consequence of the form of the environment in which our ancestors evolved. Thus, organisms and environment represent one continuous dynamic fluidic system. Informational systems, such as DNA, cells, organs, organisms, minds, and environments, are like the nested layers of an onion, intimately embedded within one another and able to inform (put form into) one another. All are interrelated states, systems, and patterns of information.

Information and Language

Since DNA is clearly a form of information, we can dispense with calling it "matter in a significant state." DNA is information in the same way that words are information or a string of Morse code is information. Both DNA and words contain meaning, potential or otherwise, which can be read and which can inform. DNA is thus a biological informational language that is expressed through biological growth and biological activity. I would go further and suggest that this language-like informational process is not merely a metaphor for spoken and written language, but that DNA really is linguistic in nature with its own grammar and semantics, albeit of an organic kind. If the DNA is disorganized in any way, then this corresponds to faulty grammar, and the development of the organism will proceed in a defective way. Consider the disease sickle-cell anemia, in which red blood cells are misshapen (they are shaped like a sickle). It is caused by just one faulty microscopic link in the DNA, yet this single error is enough to produce the disease. The faulty DNA link can be viewed as a grammatical error that interferes with the meaningful expression of the DNA.

The language-like processes so far suggested lead us to another concept, that of a dialogue. If we envision a dialogue as a communicatory process in which information is transmitted, then subjective information like the written or spoken word flows according to a dialogue between the source of information and the recipient. Imagine someone talking on a phone with no one on the receiving end. No dialogue and hence no communication of information takes place because there is no one to provide a receptive context—no one is there to be informed. However, if someone does take the call, then the information from the sender comes to be absorbed by the recipient, that is, there is a definite information flow between psyches. The form of the neuronal "clay" of the receiver is altered by the patterns of information being conveyed through the phone. The subsequent dialogue might be a one-sided affair in which the receiver merely listens, or it might be two-sided, in which case both parties are involved in the information flow. In either case, the dialogue facilitates a flow of information that leads to a qualitative change in the informational state, or formal state, of the receiver's mind.

If we now consider biological systems once more, a similar kind of informational dialogue takes place, this time between the organism (with its DNA) and the natural environment. Think of any plant as it grows. At the very tip of the plant, the leading edge of the growth process so to speak, there will be newly emerging cells. This unfolding growth will take place within the context of the natural conditions encountered, such as luminosity, temperature, humidity, gravitational force, and so on. A whole host of influential factors both inside and outside the plant will play an interactive role in shaping the form of the growing tissue. I suggest that this interactive process represents a kind of natural dialogue (as opposed to a dialogue in conventional spoken language) whereby information embodied in the plant comes to be provoked and stimulated into action by the immediate environment.

The resulting plant forms, in this view, are no less than natural, ongoing, organic "utterances," or expressions, shaped in response to the surrounding environmental context. The key point is that the interaction of the plant with the environment can be described in terms of a dialogue-like, language-like process of information flow. There are no rigid boundaries at all; rather, there exists a hierarchy of informational systems in which patterns and structures constantly flow and influence one another. Information is everywhere, residing in systems as diverse as biology and the human psyche. All systems can be viewed as patterns, or architectures, of information embedded within one another. Further, when one pattern influences the form of another, the process appears to be remarkably language-like.

Dissolving Matter into Forms of Information

But what of inorganic matter? Can we stretch the language-like informational paradigm to cover entities like physical elements? We should not forget that atoms underlie the various informational systems we have been discussing. If we take the most basic element, hydrogen, I see no reason why we should not consider it to be akin, in computer terminology, to a localized "byte" of information, divisible into even smaller "bits" (each byte in a computer's memory consists of a string of eight elementary digital on-or-off bits). What makes an element of hydrogen different from, say, an element of iron is its atomic configuration. The structural form of hydrogen (its pattern) is such that it bears specific systematic relations to other elements. Here again, we arrive at an informational and language-like conception of hydrogen. It is an atomic expression, a "word unit" in the language of physics. Put hydrogen in the context of another element, like oxygen, and their relational properties cause the formation of water molecules. Or, put an atom of hydrogen in the context of a star, and another aspect of its information becomes apparent, in this case its ability to undergo nuclear fusion. A star thus evokes one particular kind of information embodied within hydrogen, a fact of no small import for the existence of life on Earth.

An atom of hydrogen can therefore be understood as being a localization of basic information, *an element within the most primal language of the Universe*. With this view, the basic "matter" of the Universe starts to dissolve, and instead we see only information. All elements—from argon to gold to zinc—are here inferred to be units of information whose informational substance differs according to the relational role they play in a language of elements. This is the informational language of physics, as opposed to the informational language of, say, biochemistry, genetics, or psychology.

To gain a perspective on the sheer expressive capacity of the language system of elements, one has only to think of all the countless ways in which basic elements like hydrogen, carbon, oxygen, phosphorous, magnesium, and nitrogen can combine, yielding such varied forms as DNA, methane, ammonia, psilocybin, sugar, chlorophyll, amino acids, proteins, and so on. This implies that the language of physics underlies the language of chemistry, which further underlies the language of biology. Once more, one can divine that all these languages of Nature are part of an interconnected continuum wrought of information and within which the various kinds of information are everywhere flowing.

When we come to the various particles of which atoms themselves are made (protons, neutrons, and electrons), we are confronted by still more basic units of information, akin to on-off computer bits or the individual letters that make up words. The following relevant quotation on the nature of elementary particles comes from physicist and philosopher Fritjof Capra, who, through his examination of quantum physics, has also concluded that the classical Newtonian view of particles as being "material stuff" is no longer tenable. In *The Tao of Physics,* Capra writes:

> The high-energy scattering experiments of the past decades have shown us the dynamic and ever-changing nature of the particle world in the most striking way. Matter has appeared in these experiments as completely mutable. All particles can be transmuted into other particles; they can be created from energy and can vanish into energy. In this world, classical concepts like 'elementary particle', 'material substance' or 'isolated object', have lost their meaning; the whole universe appears as a dynamic web of inseparable energy patterns.[1]

Such a Universe of weblike energy patterns is entirely compatible with the language-like informational model being developed here. As stated, a language system like English consists of discrete informational elements (words) that derive their meaning from their relationship to things in the world and, more important perhaps, the specific functional role they play within a system of (words). If we take a French word like *bon,* we see that it plays the same functional role within the French language as does the word *good* in the English language. The word *good* is the point where a set of informational relations converge, and since all languages contain similar informational relations, they can be translated into one another.

Words can therefore be understood as being formal units of information that, when joined together, create further patterns of information. This also holds true for units of information like particles and atoms. They derive their meaning from their relations with other particles and atoms and, like words, they can form together to create an endless amount of new patterns or expressions.

The same principle applies to the languages of chemistry, biochemistry, and genetics. In each of these language-like systems, the elements involved bear definite relations to one another, and the relations determine the nature and meaning of each element. Although each particular language-like system operates on a different scale and uses a different kind of logic, all interpenetrate one another, and all foster the continual flow of information.

The Universe can now be understood as a kind of ongoing dialogue, or *story* even, in which language-like patterns of information are forever in the process of informing one another. As this universal tide of information flows, merges, folds, knits, weaves, and feeds back on itself, novel patterns of information are continually being stimulated and declared into existence. Particles, atoms, elements, molecules, cells, microorganisms, plants, animals, humans, minds, ideas, and so on—all are forms of information continually in process. Any "thing" or object is where a vast set of relations converge, and, ultimately, all these sets of relations form a coherent interconnected whole. Nothing is isolated; everything is relationally connected to, and defined by, everything else. Patterns within patterns within patterns. Whether potential or active, information is everywhere. Nature is made of it, fundamentally so.

Regarding this informational approach to understanding Nature, George Johnson introduces the same paradigm as championed by the Santa Fe Institute in his book *Fire in the Mind*. The scientists at the

Santa Fe Institute study complexity (in all of its incarnations), and some are convinced that information is a fundamental property of Nature. Johnson reports on one of their typical conferences:

> Most of us are used to thinking of information as secondary, not fundamental, something that is made from matter and energy. . . . But to many of those at the Santa Fe conference, the world just didn't make sense unless information was admitted into the pantheon, on an equal footing with mass and energy. A few went so far as to argue that information may be the most fundamental of all; that mass and energy could somehow be derived from information.[2]

A Contextual Web of Information

As the reader can appreciate, a number of key words help elucidate the new informational paradigm, words like *context, system, web,* and *pattern*. All these words infer interconnectivity, that all forms of information impinge upon one another such that no one thing can be fully understood in isolation.

Consider the following phenomenon that precisely highlights the contextual web of information uniting all and sundry within Nature, namely the formation of a snowflake in the atmosphere. An individual snowflake's particular development and form is dependent on a contextual web of informing relations (temperature, air pressure, and so forth) that ultimately extend out into the entire Universe. Because each snowflake bears a unique set of contextual relations to the rest of the world, each snowflake develops a unique form. This is amazing but true.

Similarly, every structure, object, or "thing" is an informational entity that achieves its meaning and significance according to its language-like role within the context of the rest of the Universe—language-like because, as with words, objects play a well-defined role within a language-like system.

Consciousness as a particular form of information can now be discerned with striking clarity. Any particular conscious state, as it flows, is determined by all the informing relations converging in the neuronal system at that moment. These relations will be the unconscious systems of the mind along with the environment that surrounds the individual. This contextual network of informing relations determines what the neuronal activity means. The brain/mind system exists in relation to the immediate surroundings, society, culture, the planet, and the rest of the Universe, and it is this network of relations converging in the brain that determines the state of consciousness. Furthermore, *to consume psilocybin mushrooms is to allow a new set of informational relations to converge within the neuronal brain.* Thus, one may suddenly "mean" more in relation to the rest of the reality process. Regarding consciousness, this is perhaps the most that can be gleaned from our informational model at this point.

So far, I have deliberately avoided putting the term *process* before the term *information*. Instead, I have repeatedly spoken of a flow of information in process. Everything—the entire substance of Nature—consists of information, and everywhere this information is in process—flowing, merging, coalescing, and informing in a language-like way. If we switch the terms *information* and *process* around, we unavoidably face yet another extraordinary idea, that in some sense the Universe must be a kind of computation, for computation involves the processing of information. That the Universe is akin to a vast computation (or even a simulation) is a notion currently voiced by a number of prominent scientists, and it is worth exploring in more detail as it might bolster the idea that reality is a system of self-organizing language-like information. Just when you thought it was safe to take a well-earned breather, we encounter yet more profundity.

Does the Universe Compute?

Before we try on the Universe-as-a-computation notion for size, let us briefly acquaint ourselves with the number-crunching background that provided us with computer systems in the first place. We are not so much interested in the details of computer hardware but rather the essential informational principles governing the operation of computers. This will reveal more about information and the way different forms of information can be processed. We will then be able to see if a computational description really is suitable for Nature (this is not as offensive as it might at first seem to some). If Nature can indeed be understood in computational terms—and I hasten to add that I am not the first to put forward this idea—we would have to view ourselves as living programs written in an organic, biochemical language. More to the point, we would represent programs whose destiny is to be *twice executed*—first by way of genetically determined growth and second by inexorable death.

In the meantime, of course, before the latter eventuality, we can, through the consumption of certain "access codes," come to experience information pertaining to the point or purpose of the overall master plan governing the reality process. Once more, it sounds assuredly fantastic, yet if the computational paradigm is in any way accurate in describing what Nature is about, then such radical ideas as these will have to be accepted or at least be debated. Anyhow, to get you in the mood to swallow the idea of an information-processing Universe, let us briefly look at the rise of computer culture, for, whatever your opinion of computers, these "infomous" machines are guaranteed to run and run. . . .

The Computer Revolution

It was the emergence of information-processing computers in the 1940s that heralded the arrival of the Information Age. Before 1950 there were just fifteen digital computers in the world, probably because there was no room for any more, given their huge bulk in those days. Now, of course, computers have shrunk in size and are pretty much a compulsory possession. Indeed, our culture thrives on computers, which explains the exponential growth in computer technology, that is, that computer science is evolving ever more rapidly. Trade and industry, the military, our education systems, financial institutions—all now depend on the constant processing and manipulation of information carried out by versatile computers. Information is the supreme currency of modern culture; it is everywhere being fed in and out of computer systems.

As with information and information integration in general, the emergence of computer systems and the proliferation of global computerized telecommunication systems like the Internet seem unstoppable. It is difficult to discern whether anyone has any real control over this development. So fast is computer technology racing that before we can assess the implications of one aspect of it, another dramatic breakthrough is made. Nostalgically recall the chunky portable digital calculators that suddenly appeared in the mid-1970s. At the time, these computing devices seemed excitingly futuristic. Whether or not they were understood, their various buttons and computational functions seemed to provide an instant gateway to esoteric mathematical knowledge. Input a few numbers and commands, and the little machine instantly responded as if by magic. Log books and slide rules could at last be ceremoniously trashed. And yet smaller mass-produced digital calculators are now given away in cereal packets. Similarly, those original home computers of the early 1980s, like the cute rubber-key Sinclair ZX Spectrum (with a whopping 48K memory!), are now all but worthless and primitive (in terms of capacity) in comparison with today's lightweight, high-resolution, portable touchscreen variety. And by tomorrow even these will have become passé. The digital computer revolution is happening so fast that it's a blur.

Formal Systems

Computers are popular because they are able to process information quickly and in so many different ways. Processing information, information in process—it's the same thing. At heart, information processing is all that computers do, whether the computer in question is used by the Pentagon, the Inland Revenue, or me to write this book. Computers might process musical forms of information, financial forms, meteorological forms, or even viral forms. Whatever the form, computers can be fed only with information, which they promptly process and return to the user.

As it is the form, or "shape," of the information that is processed by computers, a computer is an example of a formal system. When it comes down to the nitty-gritty, all a computer does is take one formal set of symbols (an informational pattern), which means nothing to it, and translates that set of symbols into another form according to specific rules. Likewise, the output of symbols (an informational pattern) means nothing to the computer either. The computers we employ only slavishly manipulate symbols; they do not think, they know not what they do.

In general, formal systems like a computer consist of a set of processable formulas such as strings of elements or symbols taken from some well-defined alphabet. In a computer the strings involved are sequences of binary numbers—ones and zeros—which are known as machine language. *Any information can in principle be coded into binary strings.* Think about it. Recall in the last chapter my contention that matter is informational. As we shall see, it is precisely because physical systems can be transcribed into digital bit strings (that is, physical systems are informational) that has allowed computers to model aspects of the world. Add to these bit strings (whatever they might represent) a set of transformation rules that govern the ways the binary strings can be transformed, and you end up with a formal system able to process information. The more powerful the computer, the more rapidly it can deal with its binary manipulations.

The transformation rules operating in a computer system are embodied in the computer's software, which is run by the computer's central processing unit (the CPU). The software instructs the CPU how to operate on its input information in a specified way. Built into the CPU are numerous logic gates (like AND, OR, and NOT gates) that transform sequential inputs of ones and zeros into further sequences of ones and zeros according to how input is fed into the CPU. Millions of such transformations occur each second, and the resulting output states (further strings of ones and zeros) can then be interpreted from outside the system. In other words, the context of human perception is needed to inject some meaning into the computer's output. For example, a computer system might take some input from a keyboard, process it according to its program, and then display the words *Are you sure you want to exit this program?* on the computer's monitor. Although the pixel array might well say this, for the computer it is merely a particular pattern of binary output absolutely determined by the logical processing of the input.

Other formal systems are things like dreaded algebra and heavy propositional logic (input *All sensible men hate propositional logic* and *Aristotle was a sensible man,* and according to the transformation rules of propositional logic, the output must read *Aristotle hated propositional logic*).

Chess is a more common kind of formal system. In chess, the pieces are the individual symbols and the strings are the possible positions of those pieces. The game proceeds according to transitions of the initial state, whereby the initial configuration, or initial start pattern, changes into another configuration through the movements of the chess pieces. This is the same principle involved with computers, as they too work by processing information via transitions of an initial input state. Thus, the rules of chess represent a kind of software that dictates how state transitions are to proceed.

The transition from one state of an ongoing chess game to another is discrete, as with the operation of any formal system. A bishop does not half move; instead, it "jumps" from one position to another. Also, since a formal system like chess depends solely on the form of the symbols and strings relative to one another, it is irrelevant what the pieces are made of. Indeed, they need not even be "physical" at all, for most professional chess players are able to play the game in their heads alone. Though that will not do much for avid spectators of chess, it does highlight the fact that a formal system can be realized in many different types of medium. Indeed, a computer system can be made of old tin cans and bits of string. The crucial aspect is the way the system's symbols relate to one another, regardless of the medium.

You could even take some people and use them to represent in binary code two numbers that you would like to multiply. Roughly symbolizing genital structure, the women could represent the number zero and the men the number one. After the two numbers have been transformed into a binary queue of men and women, one could multiply the two numbers by channeling the queue through a few logic gates operated by a couple of friends (instead of telling the binary people queue to go forth and multiply . . .). You could then take the output queue (the new pattern) and interpret the resulting encoded number, which, if you set up the system correctly, would correspond to the multiplication of the two original numbers. Agreed, a calculator app on a cell phone could have done the job more efficiently and with much less hassle, yet the point is that the calculator app itself works on the same principle, only it uses memory bits to embody the binary information. Formal systems like computers are therefore not tied to any particular substantiation.

Formal Systems and Language

Before we alighted on the notion of formal systems, I argued that not only was the Universe made of information, but that this information moved or flowed in a language-like way. I claimed that the elements in informational systems like DNA uttered their informative content in response to specific contexts, as if natural dialogues were unfolding. We have now reached the point where we can define language, in whatever mode, as a formal, and hence informational, system. Let me quote writer Paul Young, author of *The Nature of Information*:

> All languages are form dependent. In spoken language, arbitrarily selected symbols are manipulated as units that can be interconnected or arranged only in specific relationships according to specific rules. It is the form (relations), whether semantic, syntactic, experiential, or contextual, of the elements of language, and not the matter of which they are constructed, from which the mind generates meaning; the physical symbols themselves embody no linguistic meaning. ... It is neither the mass nor the energy content of the letters, words, sentences, and so on, whether expressed via mouth, pen and ink, stylus and wax, or computer printout, that contains the information in language, but their specific form or arrangement.[1]

I have gone one theoretical leap farther, however. Young refers to the so-called "matter of which they are constructed" with regard to the symbols of language. This "matter," in my view, is itself composed of language-like elements within some formal system or another. This implies that there is only information; the Universe is built on formal informational systems like those of physics, chemistry, and biology, and all are embedded within one another to form an integrated continuum. They are formal systems because it is the form (that is, the pattern) of the elements, whether they are particles, atoms, molecules, or words, and their formal relations to one another that determine the role, meaning, and subsequent behavior of those elements.

The language-like system of particles represents the Universe's most basic informational substrate. This system begets the language-like system of atomic elements. In turn, this system gives rise to the language-like system of chemistry, which itself leads to the language-like system of DNA. And so on right up to the substantiation of the language system of consciousness within our biological brains. Each language-like system of information utilizes its own kind of logic to express itself, namely the logic of physics, the logic of chemistry, molecular logic, the logic of genetics, bio-logic and, finally, the logic that underpins cognition. Each kind of logic gives rise to patterns that influence one another and that lead to more patterns, some of which produce, or come to embody, new systems of logic. Descartes was wrong; the dualistic mind/body problem is an illusion. Formal systems consisting of language-like information constitute reality. Information in process is everywhere and everything.

Some Inside Information: Are We Output?

If the above reasoning is correct, the Universe must in a real sense be an ongoing computation in which its information content is being continually churned and processed so as to yield new forms and/or patterns of information. At any one moment the Universe is in a specific state or form. This state is processed according to the "rules of the Universe," and another universal state is formed. And so on, from the moment of the alleged big bang to right now. The entire Universe can thus be considered a progressive state transitional computation, a kind of meta-formal system continually expressing its creative potential. And, more profoundly, we are inside the computation. Or so it seems.

Is such speculation tenable? Could we really be locked inside a vast Matrix-like computation as though we were all but hapless sub-routine prisoners, moving in time to some grand algorithmic dance? According to our foray into the nature of information and computational procedures, the suggestion that the Universe is a kind of computation would appear to be a spectacular probability, albeit a trifle claustrophobic, and an outrageous absurdity at the same time. We are so used to thinking of computers as neat boxes atop desks that we forget that they are formal systems that can, in principle, be embodied in anything. But, if we do take this fact into account, and if we also bear in mind that computers can manipulate all sorts of information, even going as far as simulating things like the solar system, then we might well be attracted to the idea of a computational Universe. Or am I merely resorting to the use of a convenient metaphor borrowed from our technological culture? If so, the metaphor might be useful but, ultimately, since it is temporal, its use will be limited until another, more useful metaphor becomes available.

Whereas it is true to say that metaphors have often been taken from the latest technological advances in order to support some novel theoretical conjecture, I would reverse the argument. I hold that the principle of informational computation reflects the actual way (or at least one way) in which Nature itself operates. What we have achieved in the digital computer revolution is a mimicking of Nature. We have come to realize that the name of the Universe game is information (everything is information) and its processing according to nonarbitrary rules and commands. Indeed, one has only to consider the fact that DNA, the very mainstay of life, is itself a form of digital information to begin suspecting that Nature is computational in some fundamental way. Four nucleotide bases make up all DNA—guanine, cytosine, adenine, and thymine—and because any given unit of DNA must be one of these four possibilities, then this system is clearly digital (quaternary as opposed to binary).

In his book *A Devil's Chaplain*, evolutionary biologist Richard Dawkins drives home this point about DNA being digital as follows:

> Watson/Crick genetics is digital through and through, digital to its very backbone, the double helix itself. A genome's size can be measured in gigabases with exactly the same precision as a hard drive is sized up in gigabytes. . . . Genetics today is pure information technology. This, precisely, is why an antifreeze gene can be copied from an Arctic fish and [be] pasted into a tomato.[2]

As if this digital quality of DNA was not striking enough, neuronal firing activity is also likely to be based on similar digital principles because neurons do, or do not, fire. Patterns of neuronal firing differ according to which neurons are firing and which are not firing (as well as the rate of firing). Thus, nervous systems (which include the brain) seem to employ an essentially digital form of information processing. As much as we like to think of ourselves as pioneering inventors and technological geniuses, Nature evidently beat us to it in terms of digital technology and digital computation. The Information Age is far older than we imagined.

State Transitions

If the reader is still not convinced that the essential fabric of the Universe is informational or if you still much prefer the safe and reassuring feel of "hard, tangible matter," let me introduce more support for the Universe-as-a-computation scenario. This comes from popular science writer Paul Davies. Davies is foremost a professor of theoretical physics, yet he is one of that rare breed of scientist who dares to ask the really intimidating questions about the fundamental nature of reality. He also attempts to answer such questions.

In his award-winning book *The Mind of God,* Davies labors hard to get to the heart of reality. While discussing the ability of computer simulations to mimic aspects of the real world, Davies inevitably asks us if the Universe is itself computational.

> Compare the activity of the computer with a natural physical system—for example, a planet going around the sun. The state of the system at any instant can be specified by giving the position and velocity of the planet. These are the input data. The relevant numbers can be given in binary arithmetic, as a bit string of ones and zeros. At some later time the planet will have a new position and velocity, which can be described by another bit string: these are the output data. The planet has succeeded in converting one bit string into another, and is therefore in a sense a computer.[3]

In the same vein, Davies goes on to discuss the various states within a system of gas molecules. An incredibly long binary sequence could be used to specify the velocity and position of all the gas molecules at one instant. After a set amount of time has passed, a new state will have been reached that can likewise be specified in terms of a bit string. Input information has thus been converted by Nature into output information, and this is clearly a computational process.

It is precisely because different aspects of the world can be coded into a binary form that computers are able to model different facets of reality. Of course, computers are not able to simulate the real world exactly, as that would require a calculation involving *all* the relevant information in the system to be modeled. Any inaccuracy in the initial configuration of input data tends to increase exponentially as the simulation progresses (if the simulated system is nonlinear). This is the so-called butterfly effect, in which the state transition of the system is highly sensitive to initial conditions. Alter the initial state of a computation in some minuscule way, and the alteration will inevitably have an increasing influence on the development of the computation, so much so that the end state might be radically different. This is why computer simulations of the weather are not accurate beyond a few days and why we should be merciful in our judgment of erroneous weathercasters. It is simply impossible to input all the information about the current state of the weather. Only the real weather system itself contains all the relevant information. Weather scientists simply simulate the weather as accurately as they can using as much input information as they can obtain. Computers merely model different aspects of the world; they cannot recreate them 100%, for that would necessitate inputting absolutely all the relevant information. For sure, computers and computations made by people are smart, only the real world is far grander and richer in information. And we conscious humans are part of its output.

The Original Software

If we go along with the notion of the Universe at large as being an ongoing computation, at least of sorts, we are unavoidably led to ask ourselves what precisely governs the state transition of the Universe from one moment to the next? In other words, what are the rules that control this vast information-processing system? After all, there must be some lawful control over the progress of the "Universal Computation," for we witness order and cohesive patterns on all scales of reality, from simple cells to spiral galaxies. What then is the basis of the meta-grammar or meta-software that runs the reality process?

It would appear that the fundamental laws of physics represent the Universal Computation. These laws constitute a kind of essential software governing the ongoing computation of the Universe. There can be no denial of this, for the four fundamental laws of physics (gravity, electromagnetism, and the strong and weak nuclear forces) reign supreme throughout the Universe and provide the bedrock upon which cosmological events unfold. However, these laws of physics—representing perhaps the ultimate contextual rubric—have generated new informational systems, like those of chemistry, genetics, biology, and the mind, which I outlined in the previous chapter and which I described as being informational systems in this chapter. These informational systems have themselves allowed new laws to emerge. This is also undeniable. Formal systems like genetics or the English language can in no way be totally reduced to physics. Nor can consciousness be reduced to physics. And yet physics and the fundamental laws that govern physics have somehow encouraged these subsequent systems to emerge.

Laws are essentially grammar-like because they govern the way information flows and integrates within different language-like informational systems. Thus, once new forms of information arise within the Universe, new laws emerge that control the relations between them; that is, new grammars come into existence. This is an important point to bear in mind when we talk of the laws of physics, for one might be suspicious that physical law alone is sufficient to cause, say, the evolution of life. It is rather that the laws of physics have allowed new laws to emerge once new forms of information have come into being. In this sense, the laws of physics are *primary;* they are the fundamental grammar, so to speak, or fundamental pattern that facilitates all else of interest. This is somewhat reminiscent of the fundamental role of the octave in music. The octave defines music since it holds all the major notes within it and specifies the vibrational relations between those notes. Once the fundamental octave system has been specified, then all music, all those compositions and melodies we love, can be generated out of that basic system. The same principle applies to chess, of course. Once the rules are created, then every chess game, whether a classic, an epic, or an embarrassment, can be generated from those basic rules.

We should also bear in mind that simple physical systems governed by simple laws can nonetheless generate novel behavior. Indeed, over the last few decades chaos theory has amply demonstrated the unpredictability and surprising behavior that certain seemingly simple physical systems can display. So even though the laws of physics may be understood, the long-term effects of those laws can be utterly novel. To suggest that the Universe is computational and controlled by software-like laws does not imply that the future is determined. Indeed, chaos theory teaches us that novelty and unpredictable surprise are an inherent feature of reality.

Is Reality a Bit Fishy?

The laws of physics, such as they are, require an initial input state in which to manifest themselves. This initial state would appear to be the initial conditions at the time of the alleged big bang, conditions that many cosmologists have argued had to have been highly specific in order that the Universe evolve in the way it has. Here we face a deep mystery. Why that particular set of initial conditions, and why those laws of physics?

In many of his books, Paul Davies (whom I quoted earlier) concludes that the Universe appears to be a bit fishy. Davies refuses to accept that the laws of physics and the initial conditions just happen to have been that way. It appears too good to be true, especially as we are around to speculate upon it. Either one accepts these fundamental properties of Nature as being unexplainable "brute facts," or one can try to account for them in some kind of metaphysical way.

As we are once more entering unusual territory, let's quickly recap. We have been trying to understand reality as an ongoing computation in which all of the Universe's information is being relentlessly processed via countless state transitions. This informational process has led to the (novel) formation of galaxies, stars, planets, life, *Homo sapiens,* consciousness, and subsequently conscious reflection on the nature of galaxies, stars, planets, life, and so on. The existence of such patterning is astonishing enough. But we have also concluded that these interesting and creative outputs are entirely dependent on the laws of Nature and the initial input conditions, and that these are special in some way, at least special in the sense that they have produced enduring forms of information like you and me.

If this line of reasoning already suggests the presence of a God of some kind, then it is because our vocabulary is severely limited when it comes to discussing these types of issue. This is a relatively new area of thought, for only in the last few decades have scientists begun to seriously contend with why things are the way they are, with why the Universe appears to be somewhat fishy. These are legitimate questions to ask, although they extend well beyond the limited scope of science.

I believe that since we are inextricably caught up in the unfolding Universe, wherever it might be leading, then it is surely in our interests to confront the situation head on. In fact, we should demand to be enlightened as to what is really going on here. As I have made clear, natural entheogens and their ability to foster transcendental forms of cognition are perhaps the greatest tools at hand for coming to terms with these questions about reality. Create the right sort of neurochemical alchemy, bring the right sort of natural ingredients into place, and information seems to conveniently orchestrate itself into revelatory patterns of understanding. This is the method, perhaps, whereby Nature resolves an understanding of itself through the vehicle of consciousness.

However, before we go on to form a conclusion from our informational view of things, it will be useful here to show in more detail how the computational processing of information according to a few very basic rules can nonetheless yield organized forms and structures. In particular I would like to welcome to this chapter the extraordinary world of the cellular automaton. This is not as dull as it sounds, and since such a system is very simple to grasp, it lends itself well to our computational/informational paradigm.

The Game of Life

A cellular automaton is a classic computational-cum-informational system able to yield lifelike phenomena, and it is therefore a model that captures, at least in part, Nature's life-making capacity. Oddly enough, the study of these systems has its roots in a novel Mexican mushroom, only this time the mushroom in question is the malignant mushroom cloud of the atomic bomb.

The atomic bomb was created in the army laboratories of Los Alamos in New Mexico as part of America's Manhattan Project. In fact, it was in response to the cautionary word of Einstein himself that the USA originally attempted to crack the atom for weaponry purposes. In 1939, Einstein, who was then seeking asylum in the USA, wrote to President Roosevelt concerning Germany's widespread and zealous search for uranium. It was painfully clear to Einstein that the implications of his $E=MC^2$ equation were being followed through to their ultimately explosive end and that the USA would do well to keep abreast of this disturbing development. On the strength of Einstein's warning, American authorities galvanized themselves into developing an atomic bomb before Germany managed it, and thus the Manhattan Project was born.

After the end of World War II, the Manhattan Project built a prototypical electronic computer system called ENIAC (Electronic Numerical Integrator and Computer). This was the first operational, general-purpose, electronic digital computer, and it was initially used to solve various ballistic calculations. The success of this "giant brain," as the press called it, stimulated the development of other computing machines and helped pave the way for the modern computer industry.

Computations on ENIAC were supervised at Los Alamos in part by eminent mathematician John von Neumann. Although von Neumann was a mathematical wizard, his ethical stance was a little questionable. Not only was he an extremely vocal advocate for the total nuclear destruction of Russia before that country developed a nuclear capability, and not only did he feel that it was safe to carry out and closely observe nuclear test explosions (he was later to die of bone cancer, probably caused by witnessing nuclear explosions at Bikini Atoll), he even devised plans to dye the polar ice caps in order to melt them. He also helped design the nuclear bombs that were detonated over Japan.

Despite these cheery idiosyncrasies, it was von Neumann who first began to study the computational properties of cellular automata on the bulky computers at Los Alamos. Von Neumann had always been fascinated by the idea of self-replicating machines, though he believed that ultimately this was not possible using only vacuum tubes, transistors, and the like. However, by utilizing the new computers that were at hand, von Neumann was able to implement a computer program in which simulated life-forms were able to replicate themselves. The program was the original cellular automaton. That these self-replicating, computer-generated entities were not made of flesh or machine parts did not matter, as it was their logical and organizational structure that defined them. This was one of the first real insights into the simulational power of computers. They could create convincing forms of life.

Von Neumann's work was given a whole new lease on life (literally) by Cambridge mathematician John Conway, who in 1970 invented a cellular automaton called the Game of Life. The game is deceptively simple, yet it is able to generate an endless amount of complexity and variation. It also mirrors the computational quality of biological life.

The Game of Life is referred to as a cellular automaton because it proceeds within a grid of cells (like graph paper) and because the game's progression is entirely automatic. The game progresses according to four rules. These four rules are applied again and again to the current state of the cells in the grid. Cells are either occupied or not—which means the system holds binary values. Cells are digital, on or off, alive or dead. These are the four simple rules:

1. Any live cell with fewer than two live neighbors dies, as if caused by underpopulation.
2. Any live cell with two or three live neighbors lives on to the next generation.
3. Any live cell with more than three live neighbors dies, as if by overcrowding.
4. Any dead cell with exactly three live neighbors becomes a live cell, as if by reproduction.

An initial configuration of on/off (that is, live or dead) cells is provided as input, and then the four seemingly vacuous rules are applied. The output from this process yields a new configuration of on/off cells. The rules are applied repeatedly, hundreds or even thousands of times. The results can be striking. Not only do slightly different start configurations yield wildly different outputs, various patterns can form that endure throughout the game. If successive states of the cellular automaton are presented rapidly on a computer screen as opposed to being drawn on numerous sheets of graph paper, a Life movie can be watched as it progresses. Patterns emerge, move around, collide, mutate, oscillate, and some even seem able to replicate themselves.

Conway's Game of Life grabbed media attention in the early 1970s through coverage in *Scientific American*. The various Life objects began to acquire names. Shuttles, beehives, and flotillas were born. Ships, boats, barges, and blocks were readily observed and documented as they meandered about the two-dimensional Life plain. (Animated examples of the Game of Life along with relevant freeware can still be found on the Internet—indeed nowadays certain interesting configurations can be iterated billions of times in just seconds.)

The genelike pattern with the capacity to replicate that sometimes emerged in the primordial Life soup was named the glider. Gliders were observed to collide with one another, resulting in the formation of a glider gun that shot out further gliders as though they were its offspring. It was even discovered that glider guns could be set up in such a way as to constitute a virtual computer. Conway proved that processions of gliders were able to code binary numbers, and that logic gates could be formed by making glider streams collide with one another in a specific way. The result is startling. The Life computer can itself embody yet another computer, and so on ad infinitum. A digital information process within a process within a process (this, of course, is reminiscent of patterns within patterns within patterns).

The fascinating feature of the lifelike patterns that evolved in the Game of Life was their origin. From initial simplicity, complexity was born. Furthermore, cellular automata were clearly computational, whether they were played out on a computer, a chessboard, or on graph paper. Through state transitions, information was being processed throughout the game. There was an unavoidable implication that life itself might represent a similar information-processing system. If so, then the Universe could most definitely be understood in computational terms.

We have now arrived back at the Universe-as-a-computation scenario. An ongoing computational system, the Game of Life vividly demonstrates how initial conditions and some basic state transition rules can give rise to organized complexity and the emergent phenomenon of self-replication. The real computational game of life in which we have been born similarly depends upon a well-defined initial state at some distant moment in the past and a set of rules. In this case the rules are the laws of physics and the constants of Nature (like the particular strengths of the various forces of Nature). This implies that we are inside the Universal Computation, much as gliders are inside of cellular automata.

A Discrete Look at Time

The case is still not watertight. Cellular automata, and indeed all computations proceeding within a computer, move in discrete steps. If the Universe is an ongoing computation, then, strictly speaking, it ought to proceed in discrete state transitions, frame by frame as it were. The late mathematician Martin Gardner, who originally introduced the Game of Life to readers of *Scientific American,* was one of the first to speculate about this. He wrote: "There is even the possibility that space-time itself is granular, composed of discrete units, and that the universe . . . is a cellular automaton run by an enormous computer."[4]

In other words, if the Universe is indeed a kind of computation, there is likely to be a smallest unit of time (time is granular) that cannot be broken down further. Such a hypothetical smallest unit of time is known as a chronon. A chronon is an absolute moment, or quantum of time, in which the Universe is in a particular state. This state will then proceed by a discrete "jump" to form the next chronon according to whatever laws are operating on that state, much like the movement of electrons, which are supposed to discretely jump from one orbit to another. There are believed to be no intermediary states between successive "jumps."

If time does indeed move in discrete jumps, one might well ask why we experience time as flowing. There is no surprise here, for to talk of discrete time is like talking of the successive frames of a movie. If the frames are presented quickly enough, the illusion of continuity becomes apparent. An illusion of continuity is also manifest in the Game of Life. The state transitions of Life automata can be processed by a computer so quickly as to give rise to patterns, which, on the computer monitor, appear to flow across the two-dimensional playing field. In fact, *all computer displays move in discrete stages,* even in the most advanced programs. Popular computer games and cell phone apps might look as if they are flowing smoothly, yet in actuality they are proceeding in rapid state transitional jumps (hence a still frame, or "RAM slice," can be observed if a computer game is paused).

The continuous flowing forms that seem to constitute the Universe must therefore be due to the presence of stable patterns that endure from one moment to the next. If one were to take one snapshot slice of reality, a single, all-encompassing chronon as it were, one would not be able to properly discern any patterns; rather, the patterns we observe, like planets and people, are patterned structures that emerge over a multiple succession of such slices. Likewise, I would assume that consciousness seems to flow precisely because it is an informational pattern that endures across successive frames of granular time.

There have been attempts to quantify the hypothetical chronon. For what it's worth, it is assumed to be the shortest conceivable length divided by the velocity of light. For obvious reasons, I'll take this definition on trust. Anyhow, this yields what is sometimes called the "Planck time," and this may represent the elusive chronon. Intuitively it seems there must be discrete time, for otherwise a second could be divided into an infinity of moments. If so, then it is hard to see how time appears to flow at all. An echo of this "timely dilemma" is found in particle physics. Are there any smallest bits, or does scale and size continue indefinitely? It makes more sense to think of a smallest unit of matter (or information) and a smallest unit of time. The case remains open, however, though it is doubtful that any measuring instrument could be built to observe any discrete moves in time. Alternatively, it may still be possible to hold the computational view of the Universe with non-discrete time. This is a task someone else can tackle.

What Gave Our Universe Its Lucky Break?

Once more assuming that reality is indeed a kind of ongoing computation in which language-like information is everywhere being processed, and in which the moment "now" is the leading edge of the computation, we can return to the question of its software, that is, the laws of physics that determine how the Universe develops and progresses. As previously noted, the nature of the Universe is completely tied up with the laws of physics and the initial conditions prevailing at the beginning of time.

Now, just how significant or arbitrary are these two sets of variables?

With the Game of Life, Conway's four rules were specifically designed to ensure that enduring and interesting forms of information could arise as the game proceeded. *The four rules were chosen from what is basically an infinite amount of possible rules.* Indeed, it took Conway a great deal of time to discover these four rules. If you took just any old rules and applied them to the game, then nothing much of interest would happen. And if anything of interest did crop up, it would only be likely to vanish soon after. It is because Conway's Life rules were so permanent, precise, and constraining that his game took off and was ultimately able to yield lifelike forms. Moreover, to obtain really interesting results (like getting a virtual computer to emerge), one must carefully engineer the initial state, set it all up in advance so to speak, to ensure that the system develops in the way you wish. Conway was clearly God of the Game of Life, or at least his intelligence was. For a glider speeding merrily about the Life plain, it could do a lot worse than worship the great and holy Conway of Cambridge as its creator.

So, what about the laws of physics and the initial conditions in the real game of life? Just how precise do they need to be to allow us to be here now to reflect upon them? This is somewhat hard to ascertain since we know of only this Universe. We can't examine other Universes with slightly different laws and initial states to see if they also bring forth life and consciousness. However, many scientists have concluded that for conscious life as we know it to have evolved, the laws of physics and the initial conditions had to have been *exactly* the way they are. Indeed, it seems that there are many "cosmic coincidences" that have "conspired" to elicit life. In *The Mind of God,* for instance, Paul Davies has commented upon the combined effects of hydrogen, subatomic neutrinos, and physical law in their impact upon the emergence of organic life.

It is particularly striking how processes that occur on a microscopic scale—say, in nuclear physics—seem to be fine-tuned to produce interesting and varied effects on a much larger scale—for example, in astrophysics. Thus we find that the force of gravity combined with the thermodynamical and mechanical properties of hydrogen gas are such as to create large numbers of balls of gas. These balls are large enough to trigger nuclear reactions, but not so large as to collapse rapidly into black holes. In this way, stable stars are born.[5]

Davies goes on to describe how some stars eventually explode and how the remains of supernovas (exploding stars) form the basis of planets like the Earth. Apparently, every heavy atom in our bodies had to go through many supernova cycles before ending up as an integral part of terrestrial life. The force of an exploding star derives, in part, from the presence of neutrinos, which Davies refers to as "ghostly entities."

In other words, the long and complex chain of state transitions of the Universe that eventually yielded life and consciousness was determined by the precise manner (both microscopic and macroscopic) in which the universal dialogue unfolded. An appropriate set of grammatical rules/ physical laws that would eventually generate life and consciousness was seemingly "set up" at the very beginning of time. Once the laws of physics and an initial input state had been specified, they eventually went on to facilitate the evolution of planets and people made of stardust. Even dour Mr. Skeptic must concur that this has been a somewhat fortuitous turn of events. One has to be near dead not to marvel at least a little at our conscious existence at this stage of the Universe's evolution.

Consider also the so-called constants of Nature, like the mass of the electron and Newton's gravitational constant. Their value is considered absolutely precise, and they determine how the language of physics is conducted. These constants also seem to be fine-tuned to allow organic life to emerge. If their value was but a fraction different, then life as we know it could not exist. Some scientists have introduced the *strong anthropic principle* to account for this phenomenon. This principle holds that the fundamental constants of Nature have the value they do precisely to allow life and consciousness to develop somewhere and somewhen in the Universe. It sounds like design. Needless to say, other scientists balk at such talk, preferring to seek a less astounding explanation.

The "life-friendly" nature of Nature is seen elsewhere. The element carbon, which is so crucial for life on Earth, is generated inside stars by an extraordinary series of "lucky flukes." It just so happens that normally rare high-speed collisions of three helium nuclei are favored to occur within stars due to fortuitous quantum effects. The resulting carbon that is formed eventually gets blasted out into space when stars go supernova. Because carbon is the basis of all organic chemistry, we really can thank our "lucky stars" for its biologically constructive presence here on Earth.

Even the expansion of the Universe is precision-based so as to allow time enough for galaxies, planets, and life to form. If the expansion of the Universe were too fast, then galaxies could not form, and if the expansion were too slow, it would recollapse before anything interesting happened. According to some estimates, if the velocity of expansion in the first second of the big bang was a mere trillionth slower, the Universe would have collapsed within fifty million years, during which time the temperature would have remained above ten thousand degrees, clearly a state unfit to yield life as we know it.

And let us not forget good old water. Water is indispensable for life. The various unique physical and chemical properties of water—as utilized by life in such processes as photosynthesis, nutrient transport, osmosis, heat reduction through sweat evaporation, and so on—make water a form of fluidic information fundamental to the art of living.

Then there is DNA. Not only is it remarkable that something like the genetic code was always waiting to fall into place once certain precursor events had unfolded here on Earth, but it is equally remarkable that DNA has the specific kind of variability and mutability that it does. If it were much more subject to mutability and change, then it would not be robust enough for life to take hold; and if it were too accurate in terms of replicational fidelity, then it could not become subject to natural selection. As with many other creative properties of Nature, it seems there are specific windows of opportunity present, and it "just so happens" that DNA has all the qualities necessary for it to work.

These are but a handful of the countless examples that show how finely tuned the Universe must be to bring forth organic life. This situation echoes the precise conditions needed in the Game of Life for cellular automata to bring forth elaborately organized forms. In both cases, the real world and the model world, it is clear that specific fundamental laws in association with specific fundamental constants and precise initial conditions are needed to ensure that interesting organized patterns evolve.

Now, Wait Just a Goddamn Chronon!

We might protest here and argue that life has merely exploited the conditions that happen to prevail. In that case, life has just seized on whatever "chances" are on offer, where *chances* is the appropriate word. Life might therefore reflect what can be achieved in an essentially uncontrived Universe. But how can we be positive that life and consciousness could have evolved in "any old kind" of Universe? Could one just throw some dice to determine, say, the mathematical nature of the laws of physics, and then still expect to get life and consciousness at some stage in the resulting reality? Could one think of any number between 1 and 1 million, add 5, randomly shuffle the decimal point, designate this number as the value of a constant, and then still expect to come up trumps with the subsequent Universe? Come to think of it, why should there be any laws, energy, and dimensions at all?

It appears impossible to conclusively prove that an evolutionary process in which consciousness is eventually formed depends on our particular type of Universe with its particular initial conditions, physical laws, constants, and so on. And yet it is easy to imagine stupid and very silly Universes in which nothing of interest happens. Letting our imagination go, we can picture Universes in which the laws of physics stop complex structures from forming or in which the constants of Nature force the Universe to form into a bland and stagnant conglomeration in which nothing creative happens. More chaotically, we can imagine Universes with little or no law and order at all, or with just a couple of unstable dimensions. Or, even more absurdly, we can imagine a Universe in which life starts, only to be inevitably destroyed soon after by some immutable principle of physical law. There are trillions and untold zillions of possible boring lifeless Universes, just as there are billions and untold zillions of possible uncreative cellular automata. So, why is our Universe so very, very interesting? And why us?

One "fast-food" solution is to suppose that the Universe expands from a big bang only to eventually contract into a "big crunch" at some later stage. Out of a big crunch a new Universe evolves and the cycle continues, only this time the successive Universe has slightly different laws and initial conditions. This "pulsation of Universes" is presumed to have been going on forever without any reason whatsoever—an infinite chain of Universes with no end and no beginning. One of these, ours, just happens to be one of the significant ones among a literal infinity of boring ones.

A similar scenario to this is the arch-cunning multiple-Universe theory touted by a disturbing number of quantum physicists. They view the Universe dividing whenever a quantum event takes place in which more than one outcome is possible. This happens more than a lot. Thus, the Universe is forever branching into an endless amount of Universes. Again, we merely happen to be in one of the more interesting ones.

Finally, there is the "birthing Universe" theory, also of appeal to some cosmologists. This imaginatively fertile scenario views black holes giving birth to new Universes with slightly different laws and constants, one of which . . . well, you know the score by now.

Are the above proposals tenable in explaining our very special Universe? On reflection, these "you want it your way, you got it" schemes are a tad ridiculous, for in them there must be, by definition, not only an infinity of Universes but an infinity of ones like our own, differing perhaps only in some minor detail like, say, your surname. In one of this infinity of Universes, or perhaps in 582 of them, each of my readers will be called Mr. or Mrs. Banana. But, since we can never observe or experience these other Universes (apart from in *Star Trek* or *The Twilight Zone*), then what on earth is the point of invoking them? In other words, is it really legitimate to speak about that which cannot in any way be verified by direct experience? I think not.

The popular principle of Occam's Razor (perhaps we should now call it Occam's Laser) holds that one should always stick to the simplest theory possible whenever one has to choose among competing theories. This tenet has attained a kind of hallowed status within science. If we introduce it here, we see that *there could be no more blatant departure from the use of Occam's Razor than in an inference that a literal infinity of unobservable Universes exist.* And, as Davies has pointed out, even if you do endorse one of the cunning multiple-Universe scenarios, *they all fail to explain why an infinite chain of Universes exists in the first place!* Basically, what all of these imaginative multiple-Universe scenarios reveal is that physicists and cosmologists are in expletively deep water when it comes to accounting for the "why" of our most creative Universe. In other words, it is becoming more and more apparent that Nature is extremely fine-tuned, yet no one really wants to invoke an intelligence to account for the fine-tuning.

Alternatively, some people just shrug their shoulders at the presence of life and consciousness in the Universe, happy to heed the Beatles and just let it be, let it be. As long as dinner is on the table and there's a good film on TV, who cares why the reality process is so organized, coherent, and conducive to consciousness? And as for agnostics who deny that people can acquire knowledge about the ultimate nature of the Universe, unless they have explored all possible approaches to the mystery, then they are merely being lethargic, happy to shrug and shrug again at unexplainable brute facts. Alas, we have no time for such shruggers here.

I happen to think that it is a bit of an intellectual cop-out to dismiss the fine-tuning of our Universe as being no more than a brute fact to be mindlessly swallowed and forgotten about. It is not just that a Universe with specific laws, dimensions, and free-flowing energy should exist in the first place (why not dimensionless nothingness—it seems a lot more simple), and it is not just that a Universe should endure for so long. Why should the something that does exist be so creative and reach a state where it can contemplate itself through the mind of *Homo sapiens*? How come we ourselves are so highly attuned to the mystery?

Ultimately, the choice about the significance one attaches to the Universe is a personal one. One can only mull over the facts about reality, the rules of the game as it were, and then interpret them in the light of contemplation. One's unique life experiences will also help shape one's conclusions about the nature of reality. If you tend to notice and be awed by beauty and purpose within Nature wherever you might care to look, you are perhaps more likely to be dissatisfied with brute-factual explanations. What I have tried to highlight is the sheer fantastic nature of reality, for Nature deserves this at the very least. For my part, I side with Davies. There is most definitely something fishy going on both in and around us. What is more, this fishiness is very subtle and mystifying. And an immense source of wonder.

At the end of *The Mind of God,* Davies sticks his neck out and suggests that one cannot get at the ultimate meaning of reality by logical and rational thought alone. These are brave words coming from a respectable scientist with an award-winning reputation to defend. And Davies knows that an appeal to other forms of thought for ascertaining answers to the "why" of the Universe is controversial, to say the least. He writes:

> Although many metaphysical and theistic theories seem contrived or childish, they are not obviously more absurd than the belief that the universe exists, and exists in the form it does, reasonlessly. It seems at least worth trying to construct a metaphysical theory that reduces some of the arbitrariness of the world. But in the end a rational explanation for the world in the sense of a closed and complete system of logical truths is almost certainly impossible. . . . If we wish to progress beyond, we have to embrace a different concept of "understanding" from that of rational explanation. Possibly the mystical path is a way to such an understanding.[6]

There ends Davies' exploration of God's mind. Whatever one concludes about the fine-tuning of the Universe, there will always be some factor involved that cannot be grasped by our normal conception since the factor in question is uncaused. If we side with the clumsy and arguably nutty multiple-Universe scenario, we must admit that the infinite multitude of Universes were not caused by anything, that they just are, were, and always will be. And if, like me, you opt for just this one remarkable Universe, there is still the matter of the initial setup, which also indicates some uncaused factor. In other words, there must always have been a timeless and eternal "something" that existed. A chain of causes and effects cannot be extended back in time indefinitely because time itself is believed to have had a beginning. Even if we smugly assume that the Universe sprang out of "nothing," *a potential of some kind, quantum or otherwise, must have always existed.* In fact, such a potential must be the richest and most powerful potential imaginable, as it gave rise to everything! Thus, however we look at things, we have no choice but to invoke an eternal something that cannot be explained in terms of something else. One cannot escape this disturbing yet mildly innervating conclusion.

A Return to Entheogenic Wisdom

If we want answers to these most difficult questions, we need to be armed with new forms of consciousness. Our normal frames of thought cannot cope with notions of eternity and the like. And here we must once more face up to the potential power of Nature's entheogenic allies in elucidating the living mystery of existence. The knowledge attained during the entheogenic experience as well as the revelatory insights gained through superconscious perception of the world arguably represent the most direct path to the kind of metaphysical understanding alluded to by Davies. As far as I am aware, Davies is not clued in to the epistemological virtues of visionary agents, for he explicitly states that he has never had a mystical experience. Open-minded scientists like himself would therefore do well to explore natural entheogens like the psilocybin mushroom, since their numinous effects are in the here and now and not limited to the pages of mystical religious literature.

Psilocybin can potentiate new and enhanced states of consciousness, and it is precisely in such a state that one may glimpse an answer or two to the riddle of reality. Of course, if you are happy with a simple god scenario in which an omnipotent being just sits around studying its creation and maybe dabbling with it now and again, then good for you. However, many of us will want to pursue the mystery in more depth, hoping to attain some deeper and less supernatural insight into the nature of reality. Without doubt, psilocybin can be utilized in this noble and justified pursuit. Entheogens work, just as mathematics works. And it is precisely because they *do* work and because they *do* allow one to confront big truths that they elicit fear and mistrust in the West. Indeed, as McKenna attested in his book *The Archaic Revival,* much of the New Age movement—ostensibly a movement devoted to forging spiritual awareness—is actually a move away from Nature's psychedelic dimension.

> People love seeking answers. If you were to suggest to people that the time of seeking is over and that the chore is now to *face* the answer, that's more of a challenge! Anyone can sweep up around the ashram for a dozen years while congratulating themselves that they are following Baba into enlightenment. It takes courage to take psychedelics—*real courage.* Your stomach clenches, your palms grow damp, because you realize this is real—this is going to work. Not in twelve years, not in twenty years, but in an hour! What I see in the whole spiritual enterprise is a great number of people supporting themselves in one way or another on the basis of their lack of success. Were they ever to succeed, these enterprises would all be put out of business. But no one's in a hurry for that.[7]

A somewhat harsh evaluation, perhaps, but the point is taken. We are so immersed in the hypnotic spell of our material culture that we are unaccustomed to forms of perception and conception in which our normal frames of reference fade into obscurity. In the innervating and inspirational glow of the psilocybin experience, we suddenly find ourselves transported to a spiritually charged realm where metaphysical musing and theological speculation all but dissolve, giving way instead to a direct perception of the Other, an Overmind, or biospherical mind, that somehow holds the keys to the purpose of life and consciousness.

With the continued emergence of information relating to the psilocybin experience, we now have a raised platform upon which to stand to further our understanding of the nature of reality and consciousness. Just as Newton claimed to have stood on the shoulders of giants to discern more clearly the nature of the Universe, we have reached the point in our culture where we can relaunch the shamanic spirit now vanishing from the rainforests of the Amazon and use it to blaze a trail into the depths of the mystery of our existence. Psychedelic agents, especially the fungal variety indigenous to most regions of the biosphere, can yield knowledge otherwise unobtainable through traditional modes of perception and conception. Herein lies their greatest virtue. Until we make full use of Nature's ambient psychedelic resources, our understanding of reality will remain incomplete.

We have seen how the Universe is a kind of ongoing utterance, or self-writing story, built upon the language-like integration of information; that information is everywhere being organized; and that consciousness is itself a "finer" form of information arising from the web of informing relationships converging in the neuronal architecture of the brain. Thus we are like playing pieces in a universal game of chess, pieces whose function, role, and meaning are determined according to our relationship to all else. And, in our attempt to apprehend this computational game, we have reached the point where we wonder at the ultimate software whose rules govern the field of play.

If, as seems highly probable, the major pattern-inducing properties of the Universe are not accidental, then we might discern some will or intention lying at the very heart of Nature. We might wish to shake hands with Nature and say "nice work" or "good game." I have to employ a modicum of humor here as the situation we are now in is somewhat bizarre. Because an accelerating flow of self-organizing information appears to be focused upon our planet, it must surely be directed toward some culmination point. What then will be the final output of this particular evolving part of the Universe? What on Earth is the point? Where are we being drawn? What pattern has yet to evolve or be resolved?

A Vision Shared

Before we take a final look at the implications of the psilocybin experience for an understanding of "the meaning of it all," let me summarize the heady ideas outlined in the past few chapters in the form of a vivid visual metaphor. This metaphor embraces everything of significance in the computational/informational paradigm, allowing us to view everything at once, in one great image. So, relax and get your mind's eye ready as I present to you the River of Life thought experiment. (I should point out that I came up with this metaphor independently of Richard Dawkins, who uses a somewhat similar metaphor in his book *River out of Eden.*)

Picture a big lake of still water. This is an informational void, endowed only with capacity and potential. All the myriad particles of the water can be likened to potential bits of information, though all are in the same uniform state. There is just still water, no forms or patterns whatsoever, nothing of interest, no dialogue-like flow of information or anything. Still, it is an initial state; the lake of formless water exists. You and I creatively imagine it and format it that way.

Now, take a monstrously big stick and begin to stir the lake. The stirring action corresponds to a law, or rule, or intent operating on the state of the lake water. Already, the stirring action begins to create currents, eddies, and vortices of turbulence. As you continue to stir the lake, ever more of these forms and patterns emerge in the water. Notice that the ripples, patterns, and waves that are forming and that flow across and beneath the surface of the lake are all facets of one whole entity—the entire lake. No one part of the water is isolated; rather, there is just one system of water swirling and slopping about. This is the fluidic, interconnected "informational stuff" of the lake that has been transformed from a featureless state to an informed state through the stirring action. The stirring action represents the rules or laws commanding the behavior of the water. If you cannot picture the water in the lake as an interconnected continuum, then scale the lake down to a bathtub of water. When you slosh the water around in a bath, it is clear that there is just one fluidic entity lapping about; no single region is isolated.

If we continue to stir the lake in a particular way, more and more complex patterns emerge. Let us also allow the water in the lake to gradually flow out and form a river, the leading edge of which contains the most organized patterns so far generated within the water. Swirling vortices are created that persist indefinitely. Now imagine these forms meeting with one another in the frothy forefront of the rushing river. Somehow they replicate themselves according to the precise manner in which we have done the stirring. So now we have a flowing river containing replicating patterns of information bearing definite language-like relations with one another. When these fluidic patterns meet, a kind of dialogue ensues in which the patterns inform one another, creating yet more diverse patterns.

We can add to the laws inherent in our stirring by incorporating new laws in the form of precisely shaped rocks over which the river flows (akin to constants). These rocks will further determine what kinds of forms arise in the water. As the river progresses over the contrived rocks, perhaps different types of swirls are generated, such that new patterns emerge even more complex than their predecessors. As the number of enduring patterns increase, so too will the amount of relations between them. And yet all forms remain part of the same integrated fluidic stuff. What one pattern of water does in one part of the river will eventually be felt everywhere else, for there is but one single interconnected substance in which all these events unfold.

Let a long span of time elapse. If we look to the leading edge of the river, we might find that the patterns that have now emerged are truly lifelike. Patterns that bear a specific and enduring role in relation to the rest of the water behave like organisms. It does not matter that these patterns consist only of water; what matters is their robust and self-sustaining structure and their formal relations to the other patterns around them and to the rest of the water.

Now we reach the climax of our metaphor. Picture the river cascading over a rocky cliff face, creating a waterfall. Take a close slow-motion look at the leading splashes, the leading edge of the creative flow of water. Elaborate humanoid life forms have now emerged, representative of the most evolved patterns of flowing information. Minds might eventually form within these creatures, minds being yet further patterns born out of the informational fluid, albeit of a highly evolved kind dependent on a huge amount of informational convergence. History foams into being across the face of rocks, cities flow in and out of existence, cultures come and go in the complex splashes emanating from the turbulent onrush of water. And at the very edge of the torrential flow we see informational entities like ourselves. And yes, such conscious beings might even come to wonder at the nature of the stuff around them. They might even conclude that it is all but one integrating confluential substance—that of fluidic information in process.

It is important to hold in mind that the eventually conscious property of the fluidic flow of information was determined by the precise way in which we stirred the water and the precise form of the rocks over which the river flowed. It was not accidental; rather, the flow was deliberately organized and configured so as to eventually produce consciousness, the most evolved kind informational pattern. In this way, the river of information has come to know itself and its origins. The river literally woke up to its true nature. A reflection of some sort arose.

Perhaps, then, the actual river of organic life that has spawned us has already attained its ultimate purpose, for we are the means by which Nature has become self-aware. Does this mean that we should now sit back comfortably because all is complete? Is the goal of Nature self-awareness of the kind we have already attained? Surely not. There must be more to it than that. I would surmise that the "climax" of reality has yet to become manifest, at least in our neck of the woods. After all, complex computer programs often yield a final output, this result depending upon what the user wanted from the program. In our river metaphor, this would mean that there would be a climactic state emerging at the bottom of the waterfall, a kind of final solution verily propelled and coerced into existence.

Because the information-integration processes displayed by our culture in the wake of evolving computer technology and computerized telecommunication systems shows no signs of abating and appears to be speeding up at an unprecedented rate, and because of the type of information accessed during the psilocybin experience, I believe that the destined output of the biosphere is something that human culture will eventually usher in. In other words, the "intent" of Nature is now being conveyed through the evolutionary development of human culture and human consciousness. If so, this implies that conscious human culture with its attendant technology represents the fulfillment of some kind of cosmic imperative. This is the sort of highly speculative idea taken up in the next chapter.

NINE

The Fantastic Hypothesis

Our aim now is to discover more about the nature and intent of the intelligence that would appear to underlie the reality process. This intelligence, whatever it is exactly, seems to be causally manifest through the specific law, order, and self-organizing properties of Nature. Hence we witness the inevitable progressive emergence of phenomena like stars, molecular compounds, organisms, and even consciousness. In other words, because the laws of Nature *force* the reality process to give rise to stars, molecular compounds, organisms, and consciousness (the means by which Nature can know itself), then this is strongly suggestive that there is some sort of purposeful intelligence connected with those laws. In any case, the patterns of information forced into existence by Nature appear to behave according to various systems of logic that we can loosely refer to as physics, chemistry, genetics, biology, psychology, and so on.

The forms of logic cited above are language-like, computation-like, and enfolded within one another in a kind of nested hierarchy. The language-like logic of physics acts as a substrate from which the language-like logic of chemistry emerges. In turn, the language-like logic of chemistry gives rise to the language-like logic of molecular biology. And so on. Eventually, highly advanced bio-logic leads to brains that embody patterns of information we call minds. Conscious minds are subsequently able to contemplate the intelligence that likely governs this astonishingly creative set of processes. All creativity, all order, and all life must derive from a fundamental creative property of Nature, a property that is best explained by invoking a willful, ubiquitous intelligence, the very same intelligence that entheogens like the psilocybin mushroom can bring into sharp focus.

We can boldly refer to this quixotic reasoning as being but one corollary of the *fantastic hypothesis*. The fantastic hypothesis views reality, or Nature, as a deliberate and intelligently behaving system. According to the fantastic hypothesis, we are woven into a tide of self-organizing information, interconnected throughout, whose spectacular final purpose awaits us. For if the natural tendency of the Universe is to foster the integration and cohesion of more and more information; then, as with gravity in the "physical" realm drawing together atoms and elements, the result of this integrative tendency in the realm of human consciousness might be to draw some kind of "truthful solution" into being, like an ultimate pattern falling into place.

Such a fantastic hypothesis is waged against the prevailing null hypothesis. The null hypothesis decrees a morose state of affairs in which our Universe is accidental, but one of an infinite number, devoid of reason and purpose, and in which the earthly psilocybin experience is no more than a trap, an aberration distracting us from more pressing concerns.

However, it really does seem evident (sometimes obviously so) that some mysteriously intelligent presence pervades Nature. We have seen that life and consciousness were poised to emerge out of the Universe right from the start, maybe in many locations throughout the cosmos. Now that we are here and now that we have realized the breathtaking situation in which we are so intimately involved, we can rightly demand that the mystery of the Other reveal itself to us in more detail. The momentum gathered by our inquiries is thus set to lead us into yet more rarefied territory. There is no point in backing down now. If I were to stop before making a last leap into idea-space, I would be no more than a psychedelic *homme fatale,* withdrawing supposition before a climax worthy of our subject matter had been attained.

That we have already posited an intelligent Other made of information that can manifest within an individual psyche through the medium of sacred plants and fungi is perhaps not so controversial at this point. Such an "intelligence of sorts" has been a kind of soft, conceptual pillow upon which to rest our stretched minds once the visionary effects of entheogenic compounds and the implications thereof have been acknowledged. But whereas the religiously minded might well be firmly acquainted with the notion of a creative intelligence at work in the Universe, those of us who eschew traditional religion might be willing to entertain the idea of some kind of intelligence over and above that of *Homo sapiens* only if the idea can be properly fleshed out. This is especially true if one has not personally experienced the tremendous spiritual power of psilocybin.

Anyone can suggest, or imagine, that some sort of distributed intelligence infuses reality. Many might intuit so. But to develop a coherent conceptual framework with which to understand the inferred intelligence and grasp its agenda is another matter entirely. Indeed, the risk of heresy and banishment from the scientific community can only escalate if one prosecutes such speculation to its furthest limits. However, since I have no scientific tenure to defend, no academic office to be summarily kicked out of, I am at liberty to set forth more radical ideas. These ideas will hopefully bind all that has gone before into an aesthetically pleasing whole, which is, after all, the way reality looks to be—an integrated whole. So, keeping our minds open, let us ponder the idea that Nature is blessed with a sophisticated intelligence above and beyond that of our species.

Facing the Options
Should We Go Whole Hog, Including the Postage?

If we accept, even just for the duration of this chapter, that consciousness is the preordained output of an immense computational system, then the future surprises in store for us might be great indeed. Since we are presumably the first species of earthly life to be able to fully confront the mystery of being (at least through science and art—although who knows what dolphins think about), then it seems likely that our conscious role within Nature's informational hierarchy must be of functional import. If some of the ideas that I will shortly be introducing have any bearing on this issue, then our collective future will be awesome, to say the least. If we consider for a moment the dramatic leap in complexity and information integration that separates the primeval emergence of a single-celled bacterium (in itself highly complex) three and a half billion years ago from, say, the emergence of Tokyo, with its inconceivably vast concatenation of informational activity, then what would a comparable leap in evolution produce? If reality is being driven by intelligence, then what surprises still lie in store?

Before we can assess these questions, it makes sense to step back a little and look in more general terms at the idea of a "higher intelligence" (let me add that from here on, when I discuss such an intelligence, I mean it to be synonymous with the Other, or at least that the Other is an expression of it). As far as I can see, if we invoke some kind of higher intelligence in operation within the reality process, then there are three basic options concerning its nature: the intelligence exists outside the dimensions of normal reality, just as a programmer lies outside a computer system; the intelligence is representative of an extremely advanced form of life existing elsewhere in the Universe; or the Universe is like an organism and the intelligence exists throughout Nature.

Already we appear to have gate-crashed the pulp storylines so beloved by sci-fi writers. In defense of this move, we should bear in mind that, whatever the case, reality is *already like fiction*. Why things should be the way they are in this neck of the cosmos is decidedly strange, with or without psilocybinetic speculation. To suggest that reality is anything but remarkable and mysterious is to be a victim of either tiredness or depression. In fact I am prepared to go so far as to say that there is nothing quite as strange as human history and human consciousness within the ongoing reality process. You don't need crop circles or ghosts or faces on Mars or convoluted notions of semi-reptilian illuminati controlling the world to be stimulated and awestruck. The Universe *as it is,* with conscious human observers, is more impressive and far more worthy of our awe and attention. Indeed, it is only because we are so used to being self-aware components of Nature that we do not continually marvel at the fact. Upon careful reflection, however, the ability of Nature to evoke the tree of life and nourish its evolution to the point of conscious brains is truly extraordinary and indicative that some sort of cosmic imperative is being fulfilled. Curiously, we seem willing to accept plenty of other far more radical notions about Nature without as much as a murmur of disbelief. Not surprisingly, Terence McKenna repeatedly made the point that a belief in the big bang, in which the entire space-time continuum is considered to have sprung out of a minuscule dimensionless point, requires an inordinate stretching of credulity. Indeed, if you can believe this, then you can surely believe anything.

If you still don't see the strangeness to reality, then locate some pictures of galaxies and supernovas, study them closely, and then step into a packed train during rush hour. Do you not detect a curious twist to reality here? Is it not a trifle telling that the Universe should have yielded such organismic arrangements of information, that it should have engineered us sentient, bipedal, hominid creatures, who patter busily around the surface of a rock circling a star? Above you lie billions of miles of space and billions of suns. So too below you and all around you. In fact, some estimates suggest that we are surrounded by *125 billion galaxies,* which means there are more stars in the heavens than grains of sand on the Earth. We are literally a suspended anomaly within a twinkling, starry mystery whose solution remains suspended. And yet it apparently all sprang out of nothing and for no good reason!

Given the astonishingly fictional quality of existence, I feel totally justified in outlining the possible nature of an inferred creative intelligence in more detail. In the last analysis, it makes just as much sense to do this than it does to enthuse upon the null hypothesis, which asserts that all this "astonishingness" is without reason. Indeed, it is arguably nuts to suggest that all and everything exists for no rhyme or reason. One even suspects that this kind of mindless interpretation of life and consciousness stems from an ego-obsessed psyche that is only prepared to describe our own abilities in terms of high intelligence. Hence, the tiresome popular sentiment that we are very smart and purposeful while the rest of Nature is very dumb and pointless.

Back to the chase. The aforementioned three options concerning the nature of a higher intelligence (or Other, as we can also call it) have been explored in one way or another by the well known sci-fi writer Philip K. Dick, who used fiction as an unbounded medium in which to put across some decidedly mystical ideas about what he believed to be the true nature of reality. By looking at some fictional scenarios that he created, we shall be able to more clearly divine the feasibility of at least one of the options open to us.

Do Psychedelic Shamans Dream of VALIS?

For most people, Philip K. Dick (hereafter known as PKD) is best known through films like *Blade Runner, Total Recall, Minority Report,* and *A Scanner Darkly,* which were all based on his writings. Classic movies like *The Matrix* and *Vanilla Sky* also owe a great debt to PKD's work. What is not so well known is that PKD was a bit of a latter-day mystic, a man who spent the last decade or so of his life struggling to come to terms with a series of visionary experiences (not related to psychedelics) that befell him in the early 1970s. In these experiences, PKD felt as if some vast cosmic intelligence was communicating with him, as if a deity was slipping him secret information. Such was the impact of these theophanies that he chose to incorporate their thematic content into a number of novels as well as an eight-thousand-page exegesis. To the consternation of his peers, PKD began to be not a little obsessed with ideas of "divine invasion" and the like, his last books testifying to his escalating interest in theology and theistic philosophy (interestingly, his last novel, *The Transmigration of Timothy Archer,* partly concerns the search for a sacred mushroom).

Since his death it has been speculated that PKD suffered from what is known as temporal lobe epilepsy—a brain disorder that can lead to hallucinatory experiences—and that this explains his mystical encounters. However, leaving aside the contentiousness of this claim, it does not deal with the burning issue of immediate mystical experience. To label an experience in order to explain it away is to avoid the very real nature of the mystical experience, however it should arise. In fact, as Huxley noted in *The Doors of Perception,* we should not be surprised if there is *always* unusual neuronal activity concurrent with a mystical experience, for, as we have seen, modified neuronal firing patterns are related to expanded forms of consciousness. Altered forms of awareness demand altered brain processes, and such a change in brain state can be achieved in many different ways, whether through psilocybin mushrooms, endogenous DMT, yoga, meditation, fasting, or spontaneous epileptic disturbances. Mystical experience is therefore not to be conveniently disposed of with a diagnostic label.

Even before his visionary experiences, PKD had long fought to discover the true nature of reality. It was his pet fascination. In a talk he delivered in the late 1970s, he admitted that for all the years he had thought about the question "what is reality?" he had gotten no further than concluding that reality was that which remained even if you stopped believing in it. Admittedly a thin definition, it is nonetheless indicative that the true nature of reality is not so easily pinned down.

PKD juggled with countless explanations for his mystical experiences. Some involved a Judeo-Christian God, others involved the Logos outlined in some of the Gnostic gospels (these are the "alternative" gospels dug up at Nag Hammadi, Egypt, in 1945), while others even opted for an advanced extraterrestrial intelligence. Whatever the case, PKD was certain that he had been "contacted" by some form of advanced transcendental intelligence-cum-Other.

One of his more enduring theories concerned VALIS, which is an acronym for "vast active living intelligence system," a notion that accords well with our intelligent Other. In the semiautobiographical novel of the same name, VALIS is a hidden entity of immense power and sentience that is in the process of infiltrating our reality by establishing communication with certain individuals. These disclosures are experienced as theophany. For our purposes, the key point is that VALIS is essentially outside of our dimension, but able to penetrate our world. The question arises as to the feasibility that a superior intelligence exists in another dimension with the capacity to move across into ours. This is one of our fanciful options concerning the Other.

To more fully understand what PKD was suggesting, consider the plot of his acclaimed novel *Ubik*. In this story, the main characters are seriously blown up in an explosion at the start of the story and then placed in a kind of collective suspended animation machine that keeps a portion of their brain processes functioning. In this way the characters enjoy what PKD calls a "half-life." What is more, the collective nature of their half-lives ensures that they experience a simulated reality, a reality so real that the half-lifers fail to realize that they are no longer in the real world. In other words, they don't realize that they are actually wired up in the half-life unit of the Beloved Brethren Moratorium. Indeed, they falsely believe that they survived the explosion with just a few scratches (you can now see why *The Matrix* is a decidedly Philipdickish movie).

Our interest grows when we see what happens when someone outside of their simulated reality system attempts to communicate with them (using the standard electrode headphones of course). At one stage in the tale, the protagonist, Joe Chip, who is unaware that he now exists inside a simulated reality, is contacted by someone from the "outside." This communication is experienced by Chip as an eerie sequence of synchronistic events in his simulated world. For instance, he begins finding significant messages everywhere—scrawled upon washroom mirrors and turning up on matchbook labels and in bits of consumer junk. Personal messages even begin interrupting TV shows (this idea was borrowed to good effect in the Emmy-award winning BBC sci-fi drama series *Life on Mars*). In short, the communicator has invaded Chip's world in such a way that the communication gets distributed across different media, turning up in the most unlikely of places rather than manifesting as a big booming voice coming out of the sky.

I think it is this cunning idea, which PKD used on many fictional occasions, that captures his views on the nature of VALIS. VALIS was an "outside" intelligence able to penetrate our world, revealing itself through mystical experience and through the unlikely juxtaposition of meaningfully related events. Can we possibly utilize this notion and map it onto our idea of the Other?

If we were to do this, then it would be tantamount to suggesting that the "programmer" of the Universal Computation is able to "jump into" the program, reaching in as it were to influence the state transition of the computation. Or perhaps this transcendental influence can only be felt in the psyche, in which case all theophanies would represent the manifestation of the Other as it penetrates our reality.

But what does it mean to be outside the system, outside the Universal Computation process? Can there really be an outside? It is possible to imagine that in the future we will be able to create a kind of simulated universe or an elaborate virtual-reality world that we can enter for years, if not a lifetime. And yet despite the fact that there will indeed be an outside to a simulated reality, we cannot say with certainty that there is also an outside to our present reality. If we do entertain the notion of a dimension outside of our world, we run up against the old infinite regress pit of despair, for surely the "outsides" could be continued indefinitely. In other words, if the intelligent Other exists outside our (simulated) reality, then what lies outside the Other's dimension?

It is these dilemmas, which would appear to be insurmountable, that lead me to think that the solution to the Other cannot be found by appealing to a supernatural "outside the system" option. Indeed, we have already seen that the Other appears to represent a creative process conveyed by the mind whereby information organizes itself and takes on lifelike properties. The Other, therefore, is surely more likely to be found firmly entwined within the Universe along with ourselves (even if only as a mysterious potential expressed under certain circumstances). If we once more restrict ourselves to this one Universe, then at least our theoretical model will be somewhat constrained and more amenable to a single holistic explanation. This does not deny the existence of PKD's VALIS; rather, it locates VALIS within our reality. Somewhere.

Sophisticated ET's

Could the Other somehow be connected to a highly advanced extraterrestrial intelligence? I don't know about you, but I have a strong dislike of talk of precocious ET civilizations. Perhaps this is due in part to the often-ridiculous depictions of aliens in sci-fi movies (the film *Contact*, based on a novel by the late Carl Sagan, is a rare exception). Be that as it may, the notion that highly advanced life forms exist elsewhere in the Universe is far from an unacceptable idea. Indeed, NASA has spent millions of dollars funding SETI, the search for ET intelligence.

This use of the term *intelligence* is interesting. It is not the search for ET life, ET art, or ET real estate, but the search for the communicatory signals of some other intelligence apart from our own. The assumption is that intelligence is a universal phenomenon, a mental capacity if you like, that will be similar wherever it should arise. Furthermore, such an intelligence is presumed, like ourselves, to have a strong urge to communicate its presence across the vast depths of space in order to search for another intelligence. This is why the SETI program has sent out radio signals bearing mathematical formulas (like chemical formulas and atomic numbers). These signals are assumed to embody the sort of universal significance that an advanced ET intelligence would appreciate. If the Earth were to detect signals from some other star system, it would indicate beings similar to us. Alas, no such signals have been detected thus far.

Our assumptions about ET intelligence determine how we go about trying to establish interstellar communication. We know only of human intelligence and human thinking; it is by no means certain that an alien intelligence would be exactly like our own. If intelligence is a capacity—moreover a capacity to exhibit purposeful behavior and intentionality—then as intelligence evolves, so too might the intent of intelligence evolve. The intelligence of an advanced ET civilization, should one or many exist elsewhere in the Universe, might have evolved way beyond our ken, so much so that we would not recognize its presence should it be upon us already. Alternatively, an ET intelligence might be so far away as to make it a practical impossibility to establish effective communication. Although there are estimated to be untold millions of planets potentially hospitable to life in the Universe, most are millions of light years away. Should intelligent life forms on one of these planets have sent out a radio message, by the time it is received elsewhere the senders might well have become extinct.

If we put aside notions of radio broadcasts, it may still be possible to conceive of other types of communication involving radically different means. Here, I can once more look to McKenna, who suggested various alien scenarios to account for the psilocybin experience. Before I lay his ET ideas on you, I should stress that McKenna liked to oscillate in his psychedelic speculation. On the one hand, he consistently pushed for an earthbound biospherical explanation for the Other (which I will deal with later), while on the other hand, he invoked the idea of an alien intelligence as lying at the heart of the visionary state. He was led to entertain extreme speculation because of the equally extreme nature of psychedelic phenomenology. This I understand and I completely support his claim that the Other often appears distinctly alien in nature, though I am less enthusiastic about attributing this alien quality of visions to an actual ET presence.

In *True Hallucinations,* McKenna speculates that alien probes might have once visited our planet in the distant past and injected "seeded genes" into the prevailing ecology. These "seeded genes" are the DNA portions of plants that code for tryptamine alkaloids like psilocybin and DMT. These alien genes are carried along in the terrestrial flow of evolutionary events until they are encountered by a species open to the information that is broadcasted from the probes. The precise communication issuing from the alien probes depends on the intelligence of the particular species that encounters and consumes the "loaded" plants.

The first point to make about this controversial suggestion is that interstellar automated probes with the ability to transmit information is not a new or crass idea. A number of SETI scientists, in thinking about ET communication and the major problem of galactic distance, have concluded that one solution would be to design self-replicating probes that are able to multiply at an exponential rate during their voyages through space. Through such replication over aeons of time, the network of probes would eventually cover entire galaxies. This is an intriguing idea that has its origin in the work of Von Neumann, who, you will recall, proved that it was possible in principle to design self-replicating machines. If machines like this could be built by an advanced ET intelligence, it would offer a way to eventually make contact with other life forms in distant star systems.

McKenna has taken this idea a step further and argued that once probes of this sort locate a life-bearing planet, they do not send out binary radio broadcasts or "How do you do?" signals, but carry out a much more subtle and long-term form of communication. In McKenna's view, the probes have engineered specific message-conducting genes whose signal becomes active after ingestion of those plants and fungi carrying the alien genes. In his final analysis, McKenna claims that once a species like our own has reached a certain point in its cultural development, then the probes will yield information on how to complete the contact.

Well, these are truly quixotic claims. I also detect the spirit of PKD in them as well, for in the book *VALIS* an ancient ET satellite (somehow connected with an "outside" intelligence) circles the Earth, selectively firing information into people's brains. There is nothing intrinsically wrong with alien probe scenarios. On the contrary, they serve to remind us that an advanced alien intelligence might well have radical technologies at its disposal—after all, we grant that they are alien and advanced—and that we should maybe think again about how we go about sending out signals and looking for signals.

The biggest problem I have with such an ET scenario is that it fails to account for the significance of the software-like laws of Nature that, as we now know, are bound with our very existence and all forms of informational patterning. Furthermore, we are left without an explanation for how the alien species itself came to be. It is also not clear why the alien intelligence would want to use seeded genes to conduct communication. Though they are potentially long-lasting, it still remains a rather haphazard and totally unpredictable method of information transfer, and it runs the very real risk of total failure through plant extinctions. If an ET intelligence were indeed able to build sophisticated probes with which to scour the Universe, then surely when the probes have encountered an intelligence worth contacting they would use some direct and unambiguous method of communication rather than having to construct "tailor-made" genes. And then there is the problem with the age of the probes and the distance of the probe senders. If such an intelligence were a million light years away, is it really feasible that a useful contact could be made? Unless faster-than-light technology has been developed (which immediately introduces paradoxes), then any hope of interstellar communication across really vast distances is all but futile. And if the ETs had telepathy or some kind of advanced capacity like that, then why bother with cumbersome probes in the first place?

On other occasions, McKenna concedes that the alien is merely the Other in one of its many symbolic guises, and I think that this is more likely to be the case. As I discussed earlier, the alien or the advanced ET is a major symbol peculiar to the modern era. Perhaps this is one of the Other's "favorite" metaphors with which to express its nature. If this is so, we can dispense with all notions of ET civilizations millions of light years away and concentrate upon our final option, namely that the Other is somehow built into reality like ourselves and that its intelligence is not far away but all around us. What follows is a prelude to the final option.

Is the Reality Process Intelligent?

One scientist who believed the Universe to be home to a vast and highly evolved intelligence was the late unconventional British astronomer Sir Fred Hoyle. However, the intelligence conceived by Hoyle and outlined in his little-known book *The Intelligent Universe* does not belong to some ET species existing elsewhere, nor does it refer to God, for Hoyle was at heart an atheist. Rather, Hoyle believed that a non-omnipotent intelligence preceded us in existence and helped to create life on Earth. Let me explain.

Hoyle suggested that life did not start in the turmoil of the soupy primeval oceans of the Earth as is commonly accepted. Hoyle argued instead that pre-life molecules and simple microorganisms might exist throughout the Universe amid interstellar dust clouds and within the interior of comets and meteors. Comets often contain the same proportion of carbon, hydrogen, oxygen, and nitrogen as the Earth's biosphere and are therefore potentially capable of giving birth to primitive replicating microorganisms. Through their "free lift," such microorganisms could be dispersed onto the planets that lie in the path of their cometary hosts. Because the Earth and indeed any planetary body is continuously bombarded by cosmic bodies, it would only be a matter of time before the microorganisms and molecules surviving their trip found themselves in a sustainable environment in which to further evolve. Hoyle reckoned this is how life started on Earth—that the Earth has been seeded by simple life forms and organic molecules.

To bolster his theory, Hoyle pointed out that what appear to be fossilized microorganisms have been found inside some of the various meteorite fragments that have been recovered here on Earth. In addition, many microorganisms have evolved such a hard protective layer that they are able to withstand massive doses of radiation (some bacteria have even been found living contentedly within nuclear reactors!). This form of protection is an essential requirement should microorganisms have formed in interstellar space but an inexplicable adaptation according to the conditions here on Earth. It has also been found that microorganisms exist up to forty-five miles above the Earth's surface, which is consistent with the theory that the Earth is being continually bombarded with life-bearing cosmic debris.

Hoyle went further. He claimed that not only did life originate from space, but that the evolutionary process on our planet has since been "directed" through the continuous arrival here of microorganisms. Hoyle suggested that some of these "invading" microorganisms are able to attach their own DNA to the host organisms that they encounter, much as viruses function by incorporating their own DNA into the host's genome. While some of these viruslike interstellar microorganisms might be harmful, some would be sure to confer an advantage should their DNA successfully incorporate itself into the DNA of a compatible host organism. (Think of mitochondria, the energy-producing organelles inside animal cells that have their own DNA and are thought to have once been free-living bacterial organisms that developed a symbiotic relationship with animal cells.) In this way more and more genetic information is integrated from the basically unending source of DNA reaching the Earth from space.

Hoyle did not give up there either. In accounting for the unbelievable series of cosmic coincidences that have facilitated the emergence of organic life, Hoyle speculated that the microorganisms in interstellar clouds also serve to influence the formation of stars and planets (by means of physical processes). In other words, the creative cosmic processes we observe are the result of an active intelligence that is forever striving to survive—with the added difficulty, according to Hoyle, that the physical laws of the Universe are always changing. In *The Intelligent Universe,* he writes:

> The apparent coincidences which allow carbon-based life to exist throughout our galaxy and in other galaxies might well be temporary possibilities in a Universe where the applications of the physical laws are changing all the time. This point of view . . . suggests that in the future the Universe may evolve so that carbon-based life becomes impossible, which in turn suggests that throughout the Universe intelligence is struggling to survive against changing physical laws, and that the history of life on Earth has only been a minor skirmish in this contest.[1]

Are we to believe then that the laws of Nature gradually change and that at some distant time in the past a powerful intelligence engineered things so that in the future, carbon-based life would utilize the newly prevailing cosmic conditions? This is indeed what Hoyle asked us to believe. He summed up his thinking in the following singularly profound sentence in which he states this about our species: "We are the intelligence that preceded us in its new material representation—or rather, we are the re-emergence of that intelligence, the latest embodiment of its struggle for survival."[2]

When I first encountered Hoyle's radical panspermia theory (the notion that life is being seeded throughout the cosmos), I was naturally curious. Shortly after this, new scientific evidence coincidentally emerged that seemed to support at least part of his theory. A news flash in *New Scientist* declared that "molecules of life" had been detected in space. Hawk-eyed American radio astronomers had spied glycine—an amino acid and a potential building block of organic life—in a dense interstellar dust cloud near the center of our galaxy. This kind of finding is totally in line with Hoyle's speculations. Indeed, a few years later, the comet Hale-Bopp was analyzed as it passed near the Earth, and it too was found to contain the molecules of which amino acids are made. Therefore, we cannot rule out all of Hoyle's theory, and we must consider his assertions more closely.

The compelling aspect of Hoyle's proposal is that it is assuredly grand, employing as it does a mix of science and near-mystical speculation. Hoyle attempted to account for the fortuitous nature of the Universe by arguing that the initial widespread presence of microorganisms somehow influences star and planet formation. Everything was engineered by some previous intelligence. However, we are still left without an explanation as to how this previous intelligence emerged. In fact, Hoyle appealed to the so-called steady state theory of the Universe that he himself helped to develop in the late 1940s as an alternative to the big bang scenario (it was, in fact, Hoyle who originally coined the term *big bang* in order to make light of such an explosion-from-nothing-theory). The steady state theory holds that there was no big bang at all (only "little bangs"), and that the Universe has existed indefinitely. Within this eternal Universe an intelligence has been forever modifying itself in order to survive the subtly changing laws of physics. Hoyle even concluded that the religious impulse of our species arises because we are born with an instinct that leads us to remember our origins, an instinct written into our DNA by the intelligence that preceded us.

It all seems very neat and tidy, and I am sure that there is some grain of truth in Hoyle's "eternal intelligence" theory. However, the element that is lacking is the role and effect of entheogenic agents, unless of course they were also engineered by the intelligence that preceded us. If they were, then Hoyle's theory might well offer us the ultimate truth about reality. Then again, we must accept that the Universe has been in existence forever with the caveat that the laws of physics continually change and force the intelligence to re-create itself. To my mind, this is not an aesthetically "clean" solution. As I said, how did the intelligence develop such sophistication and creative power in the first place? Moreover, how come the Universe has bits and parts conducive to creative manipulation? And how and why should the laws of Nature change? If the laws were to continually change, the Universe might surely run the risk of losing its existence completely at some stage due to destructive physical laws. And Hoyle did not convincingly show how microorganisms are able to mastermind the formation of stars and planets, nor was he able to deal a deathly blow to the big bang scenario currently accepted by most cosmologists.

As we have seen, it seems much more likely that all of the cosmic coincidences necessary for life and consciousness to arise are connected with the way the Universe was originally configured at the time of the big bang. If this is the case, we are again left with this one significant Universe fine-tuned from the start. Or, to put it another way, we are left with Nature, a system in which the capacity for ever-more-exquisite forms of self-organization reflects some kind of intelligence and intention.

Still, Hoyle's intelligent Universe is certainly one of the most cogent scenarios I have yet come across that attempts to explain the mystery of reality in essentially scientific terms, even despite its failure to specifically address altered states of consciousness. I think it is possible to utilize some of Hoyle's ideas and rework them. The prelude to the final option is over. Armed with the fantastic hypothesis outlined at the start of this chapter, we are now ready to focus on what I consider its most likely and most brilliant implications.

Recalling the Biospherical Mind

On a previous occasion I referred to the Other as a biospherical mind, a term that, although doubtless too far-fetched for some, nonetheless captures the planetary character of entheogenic flora and the rather spectacular organic visions they often induce. Sacred plants and fungi appear like carefully distributed "access codes" that create a different set of informational relations to converge within the brain/mind system, allowing one's meaning in the context of the rest of Nature to shift up a notch. In this way, as if tuning in to the otherwise occluded "higher frequencies" of Nature, one can come to behold the numinous and intentional presence of the Other. Can we therefore locate the Other here upon the Earth, somehow woven into the evolving fabric of the biosphere?

Contemplating Evolution

The fine-tuning of the Universe really comes into effect through the evolutionary process that has dominated the Earth's surface regardless of whether this process originally began on Earth or in space (we can concede that Hoyle may have been correct with his panspermia theory). Either way, organic evolution can be looked on as an *information-gaining process*, for life has gone from simplicity to astounding complexity, from relatively simple arrangements of organic information to highly organized arrangements, from simple proto-genes to hugely elaborate genomes, from primitive sensing to five fully fledged senses, and all because the fabric of the Universe encourages the evolution of carbon-based life. That evolution is essentially an information-gaining process is an important concept to bear in mind for what follows, for information-gaining is strongly associated with intelligently behaving systems, and I am from here on arguing that the biosphere is just such an intelligent system. Once again, information is a key factor in the ideas under discussion.

In its broadest sense, the evolutionary process is currently being channeled through human culture. The knowledge acquired by our predecessors can be stored in computer networks like the Internet, books, folklore, music, dance, spoken language, and so on, and this information accumulation—the growth in advantageous wisdom if you like—can be passed on directly to successive generations. In this way, accurate information about the world grows as uncertainty decreases, and this process of information accretion allows our species to dominate and understand the planet in next to no time compared with the otherwise slow rates of (biological) evolutionary development that preceded our species.

With computerized telecommunication swiftly evolving and connecting the Earth's store of information, the biosphere looks to be wiring itself up into a bioelectronic superorganism. Our physical bodies may no longer be evolving, but our culture and our technology are, especially our digital-communications technology. Just as the neurons in our brains are able to transmit information to one another at astounding speed, so too are we now able to electronically synapse with one other across the globe.

This leads me to think that the assertion that the human brain is the most complex "device" we know of is in fact a fallacy and that the biospherical system in its interconnected totality is far and away more complex than a single human brain. It must be. A brain cannot be understood properly unless the context in which it exists is taken into account. This context is the environment, with its vast network of language-like relations. Nothing remains isolated within the environment. All organisms derive their meaning and their function according to the role they play and the relations they have within the entire biospherical system. The biosphere is thus unimaginably more complex than the parts of which it is composed.

Since the human brain is complex enough to embody intentional intelligence and since much of its firing activity can only be understood in the light of its intentional intelligence, I believe it tenable that, in an analogous way, evolution itself represents the ongoing intent of an intelligence somehow distributed throughout Nature, and brought into focus through the biosphere (or any biosphere for that matter). In other words, somewhat like Hoyle suggested, the evolutionary process that has dominated the surface of the Earth is the articulation of an intelligence of some kind.

Returning to purely biological evolution, the idea that this process represents an intelligence in action is not to deny the reality of natural selection. Far from it. After all, to argue against natural selection (the process whereby certain genetic variations and mutations are favored due to their ability to better replicate themselves) is to commit perhaps the cardinal sin against the life sciences. I would not dare embarrass myself like that. No, I am simply suggesting that evolution through lengthy sequential instances of natural selection represents a natural intelligence in action as opposed to, say, human intelligence in action.

If we selectively breed dogs or cats, then we are carrying out a process of artificial selection whereby we select those animal features that we would like to see strengthened. In the case of selective breeding, therefore, human intelligence governs the process. In the biosphere at large, natural selection governs the process of evolution over longer stretches of time than artificial selection. Biological evolution is slow—exceedingly slow. So slow in fact that we can't really see evolution happening. Whereas this is taken to mean that Nature is essentially dumb and mindless, I believe that we can view Nature in its entirety as a form of active intelligence, though of an order of magnitude well above that displayed by our species. And by "Nature in its entirety," I mean that we can view the biosphere as a continuum within which individual organisms are in fluidic connection with each other and their surroundings. Influences pass in all directions. There is but one interconnected system in which evolution occurs. Remember our River of Life metaphor, in which all forms of the water were part of a coherent, interconnected whole? This is how we can think of the biosphere, as representing a single sensible system in which information is continuously being churned and integrated into greater and greater patterns of coherence and complexity. Moreover, natural selection can be interpreted as natural intelligence at work, quite literally a response of Nature to its own significant contextual configuration. In other words, the environment, as a context, always serves to highlight the sensibleness of certain genetic variations and thence sustain them—rather like the way our minds will spot and highlight a word amongst a scattering of random letters. This being so, genetic changes that lead to some kind of sensible life-enhancing behavior will tend to persist and have the opportunity to further evolve within any gene pool. Because Nature represents a meaningful and ordered contextual system (in other words, it is intelligently configured), evolutionary events can unfold in *response* to that meaningful context. Indeed, the very tree of life germinated in accordance with this significantly configured context.

The Importance of Context

To get a firm handle on this highly salient notion concerning intelligent contexts, consider that well-worn story of the monkey at the typewriter. We are asked to imagine this monkey typing feverishly away at random for ages and ages, most of the time producing gibberish. Eventually we can see how, by pure chance, the monkey manages to type some words or even a short meaningful sentence (in which case any grinning on the monkey's part becomes suddenly apt). Now, although this story is meant to show how meaning can be generated from a nonmeaningful system by pure chance (meaning coming out of nothing and for free), this is patently not true. Indeed, if one can grasp why such reasoning is false, one will simultaneously grasp the point I have been driving at—namely that Nature is an intelligently configured contextual system *guaranteed* to grow the tree of life by highlighting its sensibleness.

In the monkey yarn, we do not get meaning out of nonmeaning. Far from it. First, we have two meaningful systems from the outset:

the monkey and the typewriter. Second, and more important, it is the *context of the human psyche that gives meaning to the typed responses of the monkey.* This means that one is not getting meaning out of thin air, but that there was a priori meaning present in the system of monkey, typewriter, and us-as-observer. It is precisely this a priori meaning—in the form of an intelligent and patient observer—that serves to highlight that tiny fraction of the monkey's typed responses that make sense. If there is no meaningful context surrounding the monkey and its typed output (that is, no intelligent observer is present), then no meaning can be highlighted and thus nothing that the monkey types will ever make any sense.

The same holds true for evolution. *If Nature were not already a sensibly configured system, if Nature were not highly organized in terms of its laws and its lawful logical relations, then organisms and DNA-writ structures would not make any sense. That they do make such good sense and that more and more sense can be made through organic evolution reveals the* a priori *intelligently configured context provided by Nature.* As an all-surrounding context, Nature notices and minds, as it were, what happens within it, in the same way we would notice if a monkey typed something sensible. In this way, Nature selects sensible changes to genomes, those variations and modifications of DNA that yield life-affirming behavior. If the reader can grasp this, the notion of natural intelligence—the ultra-smart quality of Nature—becomes self-evident, and everything that we take for granted changes.

Environmental Awareness

It is apparent that Nature has an unfailing contextual capacity to continually select smarter and smarter biological forms. Look at the evolution of the hominid brain, for instance. The remarkable evolution from cortex version 1.0 to, say, cortex version 7.0 happened only because the environment continually and invariably selects genetic changes that enhance a brain's ability to make sense of the intelligible information that the environment provides. Thus, environment and evolving organ (or evolving organism) are part of one interconnected fluidic system. This role of environmental context in cultivating the evolution of complex living things is unfortunately taken for granted by most evolutionary thinkers. In other words, it is not usually remarked upon just how much a role Nature, as an environment, plays in the evolutionary process. It surely did not have to be that way, for we can imagine a state of affairs in which Nature would not continually foster the evolution of complexity—in the same way that we can imagine a monkey typing away at a typewriter for eternity and never ever making written sense because there is no context available with which to highlight any sense.

It seems though that Nature is arranged in a way that literally demands that a real kind of self-stimulation occurs in which information—in the form of genotypes in this instance—continues to organize itself due to continual contextual feedback from the environment, that is, the combined system of organisms and the environment feeds back upon itself and provokes ever-more evolutionary progress. In this way organisms can continually evolve and become smarter, because the environment surrounding them acts as the context that highlights and sustains newly sensible structures and newly sensible behaviors. By making biological and behavioral sense within the larger context in which they are embedded, organisms can be selectively evolved. The point to bear in mind is that sense and meaning of one kind are clearly required in order to elicit further forms of sense and meaning. Only meaning can beget meaning; only intelligence can beget intelligence; only something smart can construct something else that is smart. The fabric of Nature is therefore smart throughout (some of these smart qualities were discussed in previous chapters and were referred to as the Universal Computation).

As a good example that demonstrates the role of the environment in eliciting sensible and ingenious biological structures, think of the shape of dolphins and sharks. Each species has evolved a similarly sleek body shape along with musculature that affords swift movement underwater. Such creatures can move extremely efficiently in water. What their bodies, musculature, and behavioral patterns have done (through evolution) is to home in on, or gravitate toward, the lawful and sensible properties of water, these lawful and sensible properties acting as a sensible context. Because water is replete with various sensible properties, these can be made sense of, or be reflected. The sleek body shape of dolphins and sharks and their precise techniques of swimming therefore reflect the presence of a sensibly ordered environment. If we concede that dolphins and sharks embody impressive natural design, this is only because Nature itself, serving as a context that invokes the design, also embodies impressive natural design. Order and intelligence are everywhere, inherent in both the lawful behavior of the environment and in the organisms and biological behaviors that evolve therein.

Let's return to the rapid evolution of the hominid brain from version 1.0 to version 7.0. Each incremental increase in size and capacity (presumably derived through mutation and variation) must have met with specific environmental circumstances with which to immediately highlight those improvements such that a reproductive advantage was achieved. Each mutation in hominid brain size was therefore *nourished* by a contextual set of environmental conditions to ensure that its new capacity had an edge over nonmutated hominid brains. In other words, Nature was able to make sense, or highlight the sensibility, of these mutational, variational changes in the hominid brain. If this were not so then it is difficult to imagine why so many small changes in brain size were so rapidly selected for by the environment.

One assumes that the cerebral capacity we humans have is a highly neat adaptation to living in the world. Indeed, if more and more refined methods of sense-making are the stock and trade of natural selection, consciousness and language are capacities that almost certainly had to evolve somewhere and somewhen, as they are capacities that enable good sense to be made of the environment on a moment-by-moment basis (consciousness and language allow us to "swim" well through the world just as a fusiform shape allows dolphins to swim well through water). And the only reason consciousness and language were able to evolve, the only way they manage to make sense of the world, is because Nature is already sensible and can be made sense of. This is most apparent when thinking of language. Nouns, adjectives, and verbs exist in Nature—old leaves fall gracefully to the ground, for example. Even before we had language to speak about old leaves falling to the ground, they still did. The language we possess merely reflects the language-like property of Nature itself. This means, in effect, that Nature is, and always has been, eminently sensible, and this is reflected within organisms through the "mirror" of bio-logic.

What I am really driving at is that Nature can be viewed as a *single system of self-organizing intelligence*. That's the gist of it. Through the evolution of life, Nature feeds back on itself and generates an ever-more refined reflection of its inherent intelligence. In particular, this intelligence is reflected through the language of DNA, which Nature edits so as to express precisely those structures, organs, and behaviors that make good sense in the larger context in which they are embedded (think of eyes, ears, lungs, livers, fur, seasonal migration, bone structure, wing structure, light sensitivity, semipermeable membranes, metabolic pathways, hibernation, and so forth). Not only are genome variations and genetic mutations crucial for evolution, but the intelligent configuration of Nature must also play a key role—if not the main role—in highlighting and nourishing the advantageous potential of a tiny fraction of the mutants and variants whose altered genes are not deleterious. Eventually, nervous systems and brains endowed with consciousness were destined to emerge somewhere along the evolutionary line. This line happens to be the primate line and our species, *Homo sapiens*. Although this creative capacity of Nature is commonly considered to be a simple brute fact and not worth a second thought, it can also be interpreted as evidence for the presence of natural intelligence throughout the contextual fabric of the Universe.

An Exquisite Unfolding Potential

That some form of highly organized carbon-based life was always poised to emerge out of the Universe is a remarkable fact that seems to be peculiarly downplayed by mainstream science. I once remarked on this immanent aspect of life to a university philosopher. "Look," I said eagerly. "Here's this nucleic acid stuff, which, when put together in precise digital strings, codes for precise strings of amino acids. And these cause precise proteins to form. And the proteins integrate to form fully functional organs more complex than computers. Why is that? From whence cometh this astonishingly inventive capacity of Nature, this remarkable computational precision? Why should Nature be endowed with such an inordinate amount of latent creative power?"

Well, this academic chap thought little of it, declaring that the things humans invent are just as much latent within "matter" as is life and that we do not marvel at that. At the time I was unable to come up with a rejoinder to his careless dismissal. Now, however, it seems clear that his university salary was undeserved in that moment, for most of our inventions are based on principles already expressed by natural intelligence. Airplanes were preceded by natural bird and insect flight. Our electrical telecommunication systems were preceded by the natural electrochemical communication occurring in nervous systems. Our solar energy technology was preceded by natural photosynthesis. Our sonar technology was preceded by natural echolocation in bats. Our nanotechnology mimics the nanotechnology first invented billions of years ago when life began. Our prototypical nuclear-fusion generators were preceded by natural stars. Our information-processing computers were preceded by natural information-processing systems of which the Universe is made. The list goes on. In fact, had Nature not provided us with the above examples, we might never have been prompted to develop our own technological equivalents (surely no one would ever have conceived of flying were it not for the tangible presence of birds or winged insects). Not only has natural intelligence in one form or another taught us all we know, but the evolutionary process is itself a manifestation of this intelligence at work. What we are witness to here on Earth is the unfolding genius of Nature. The evolution of life is no less than a wondrous promise woven into Nature and, over time, coordinated and delivered by Nature.

Are We Smarter Than Nature?

Despite the above reasoning, the notion that Nature represents a self-organizing intelligence working over immense time scales is an idea that, I am sure, many of us will probably find hard to swallow (unless swallowed with a dose of psilocybin mushrooms!). And yet to assert that evolution is not an intelligent process is to rate the process that allowed this assertion to arise to be less smart than we are. In other words, over the course of three and a half billion years the evolutionary process has managed to forge conscious human intelligence (the capacity of the human cortex) that is then able, if it so chooses, to deny that the evolutionary process is itself intelligent. Think about it. Can a nonintelligent process really yield profound intelligence? Can we expect a computer simulation of evolution to produce a smart virtual organism without first ensuring that the computer software is itself smartly designed? Or could one of Conway's Life games have yielded a virtual computer able to exhibit artificial intelligence without having first been set up in an extremely intelligent way? Can we really explain all and everything without recourse to invoking intelligently configured contexts?

Clearly, the average neo-Darwinist alleges that the evolutionary process is not intelligent. Yet life is undeniably more complex, organized, integrated, and smart than we can possibly grasp. Indeed, science, especially biological and genetic science, is still coming to grips with the elaborate complexity of living systems. It seems that the more closely science examines life, the more ingenious life turns out to be, as if there is little that evolution cannot achieve. Evolution through natural selection undoubtedly happens, yet how we *interpret* the meaning of *natural* is not necessarily a foregone conclusion. To suggest that natural selection represents a manifestation of natural intelligence is merely a new way of evaluating the reality of evolution in the light of contextual considerations. No new supernatural mechanism is being invoked—rather we are reinterpreting and reappraising the facts at hand.

Have We Stolen Nature's Glory?

Scientific discoveries, whether in biology, chemistry, neuropsychology, or physics, invariably point to the ingenuity of Nature. Every university science department in the world owes its existence to the smartness of Nature—a smartness that science merely reflects. Almost every scientific researcher, almost every doctoral student is sailing on a sea of sensible knowledge provided by Nature. Whether a geneticist marveling over replicating mile-long, compact strands of DNA, a botanist spellbound by bee-mimicking orchids, or an entomologist fascinated by fungus-cultivating ant colonies—all are caught up in the engineering finesse wrought by Nature over billions of years.

Similarly, almost every science book available owes its existence to Nature's intelligent manipulations. Science is therefore to be understood as *an attempt to mirror or reflect the intelligence of Nature in a worded form.* And yet whatever facet of Nature we care to investigate, whether this be the intricate structure of a single cell, the elaborate grip of the Venus flytrap, or the delicate balancing mechanism of the inner ear, science is always committed to accounting for such phenomena as being no more than the end products of a natural but purposeless process, a process that *just happens* to be extremely constructive and that *just happens* to arise because the contextual laws of Nature *just happen* to allow interesting evolutionary events to unfold at some time and in some place. Things just tend to happen that way. And a lucky thing it is, too, for if Nature did not possess intelligible and sensible contextual qualities, then the scientists would be out of work and out of life.

However, it does not matter what science comes across in its pursuits, for no matter how smart some animal, plant, or biological process is, it can always be reduced to a "mere" aspect of natural selection, where *natural* means only "the way things tend to happen." If we were to discover, say, some new plant that yielded a massive fruit out of which popped an organic flying machine complete with a steering wheel and a comfy seat, then two things would probably happen. First, scientists would immediately account for the machine in terms of "mere" natural selection by inferring that the fruit was a potentially advantageous adaptation. Second, the machines would be seized upon by people and exploited to the hilt without a second thought as to the nature of the process that led to them. In no time at all, both scientists and the lay community would be completely used to this useful new production of Nature. It would have become yet another "mere" incident of the natural world.

The imagined state of affairs above parodies the often-blithe attitude of the science community toward the nifty creative processes exhibited by Nature. All organisms, no matter how intricate, no matter how refined and sophisticated, no matter how well adapted, are "merely" the products of a blind process that just happens to produce smart and enduring structures over vast spans of time. Brains certainly convey intelligently driven processes, but not so Nature, we are told. Yet natural selection is itself a process, and since it is the most stunning and successful information-gaining process we know of, then it can justifiably be deemed an intelligent process.

Perhaps Nature should be awarded Nobel Prizes and not the scientists who discover Nature's smart mechanisms and pathways. If a scientist begins a learned discussion about the double-helix structure of DNA and the genetic code, we might well be taken aback by his or her grasp of the subject matter. We would say that someone who understands the complexities of DNA is very intelligent and deserving perhaps of prestige, respect, and admiration. Yet he or she is in actuality merely reflecting the creative ingenuity of Nature. Thus, it is the discoveries of science that should be described with a liberal sprinkling of the popular adjective *mere* and not the actual processes that science documents. Nature is ultrasmart, and it is we who "merely" reflect that fact.

Similarly, terribly thick textbooks detail the physical and mathematical processes underlying cosmological phenomena like star formation and supernovae. Again, the neat equations and so on that govern precisely these phenomena are in a real sense written by Nature. Consider also the text in a leather-bound book about the highly organized microstructure of paper and leather—the integrated and mathematically precise atomic configurations of carbon and other organic elements of which leather and paper consist. You would certainly require a fair degree of intelligence to really understand such a book. But surely *the book itself* (the actual paper and leather) is more representative of intelligently constructed units of information than the text it carries? Science serves only to reflect the intelligent structures already "out there" in reality.

The living proof of natural intelligence is everywhere around us and inside us. Our bodies are spun from it. The text found in a biology book detailing the fantastic inner wisdom of, say, the immune system, is merely a reflection in the formal system of words of the formal system that we call biology. Both are intelligible, and a hallmark of intelligent systems is precisely their intelligibility. This means that biological systems and their evolution can be regarded as a manifestation of natural intelligence. Thus, NASA's hubristic SETI program in which communicatory cries are broadcast out into space reveals a distinct failure to look closer to home, for it is Nature in its totality that is the highly advanced intelligence we are so keenly interested in locating.

Ah, but Can Nature Pass an IQ Test?

If we find it difficult to accept that Nature is intelligent, then perhaps this represents a too-limited view of what constitutes intelligence. Or maybe we confuse intelligence with consciousness. In any case, don't be fooled into thinking that intelligence is something to be measured solely by IQ tests. These are mere inventions of the psychologist, designed to tap specific aspects of intelligence. In its strictest sense, *intelligence* means "the ability to learn and to understand." This definition implies the capacity to increase information such that sense is made and uncertainty is reduced. If you use intelligence, you can work things out, make sense of things, and thereby increase your internal state of knowledge. Intelligent processes foster the integration of more information. In my book *Darwin's Unfinished Business,* I discuss this at length.

> The absorption of information, the storing of information, and the ability to learn from that information are, I contend, the principal ingredients of intelligence. Indeed, they are precisely the sort of thing

that we do so well and that the robots of AI engineers attempt to do. Our senses continually take in information about the environment, our brains store this information, and then we use the information to learn more and more about the environment. These are all processes, not static things. Bearing this in mind, it should be apparent that the end result of these three processes working in combination is intelligence. Intelligence is all these processes combined into one, the term *intelligence* being a convenient way of explaining their combined action. So intelligence is definitely not a thing like a table is a thing. Nor is it merely an attribute. It's more of a process, moreover a process concerned with information and the constructive manipulation of information. The science of AI is all about substantiating this process in robotic form, or "in silico," as some AI scientists call it.[3]

Evolution is precisely an information-gaining process and can be considered a form of natural learning. As information is built up within the biosphere and its gene pools, uncertainty is reduced, the result being specific organisms with specific behaviors and specific relations to the environment. The natural intelligence that is life has learned to express itself through the language of DNA, has learned to utilize the sun's energy through photosynthesis, has learned to fly through wings, has learned to breathe, sleep, dream, think, communicate, reproduce, recycle, and so on. The evolution of the tree of life therefore represents a natural learning process that is inscribed in DNA and that emerges in response to an environmental context that serves to elicit the learning.

Natural Intelligence Is Everywhere

Although natural intelligence becomes apparent everywhere we care to look in the natural world, the modern version of *Homo sapiens* seems to miss it. If, say, we were to venture into a desert and stumble across some strange, whirring, solar-powered machine that transforms sand into circuit boards so that it can replicate itself, repair itself, and even reproduce, then we would certainly take notice and infer that the machine embodies some measure of artificial intelligence. Yet if we later stumble across a hardy cactus quietly converting sunlight into usable energy and constructing reproductive organs that cunningly lure insects into transferring its pollen, then we immediately infer it to be "merely" the result of natural selection and not of intelligence. No doubt we would pass over the cactus and return to the ostensibly more interesting manufactured machine. To date, most scientists stubbornly refuse to equate the process of evolution with intelligent information processing, despite the fact that the most complex things we know of are living organisms.

Recall Mr. von Neumann. He was considered a highly intelligent man because, among other things, he showed that in principle, self-replicating machines could be built. *Von Neumann was himself a replicating machine,* albeit of the organic kind. Why should he be considered intelligent while the process that generated him is not? Given the fact that, like us, von Neumann was built of a hundred trillion cells tightly woven into a triumph of organic engineering, the case for natural intelligence becomes even more conspicuous. Nothing von Neumann did came anywhere near matching the genius of evolution itself. Only the human ego can deny this. And yet the human ego is itself dependent in some way on the human cortex for its existence. And we already know how brilliantly Nature has designed the cortex.

Let us also consider photosynthesis a tad more closely, embodied as it is in the green film covering the Earth. Without this downplayed biomolecular wizardry (which has yet to be technologically mirrored in a globally viable cost-effective way) there would be little life at all, for almost all life is based on this ultrasmart process. Because photons (of which light consists) behave sensibly and have sensible energetic properties, biological photosynthesis can evolve in response to this (just as dolphin biology and shark biology have evolved in response to the sensible properties of water). Yet it is easy to play the imagination game and hypothesize a reality in which organic chemicals could not in any way form themselves into neat, energy-utilizing organisms. For life to flourish it had to reside as an immanent potential within organic chemistry, and the context of the Universe at large had to be conducive to eliciting such a potential right down to the formation of suns that eventually go supernova. In short, I would argue that it is valid for us to wonder why reality is so amenable to the process of biological evolution, just as it is valid to ask why the Universe is intelligible.

Traditional Darwinism cannot adequately answer these questions. It can only shrug and state with nonchalance that Nature just happens to be that way, that Nature has been, well, lucky—lucky in the sense that it eventually brought forth conscious brains able to grasp the processes that led to conscious brains. However, if we conceive of evolution as the ongoing expression of a natural intelligence, we can connect it to those other fortunate aspects of the reality process that have allowed interesting things to happen in the Universe. Eventually we can discern that Nature is, at heart, a creatively intelligent system. Don't forget, I am not implying some new phenomenon here or introducing something supernatural; rather, I am suggesting that overall, in its entirety, Nature is a smart system and that biological evolution is a direct consequence of this. Such a view, such a new angle through which to conceive reality, is not merely a case of words, but an attempt to redefine our place within Nature and to reappraise the significance and meaning of our conscious existence.

Unnatural Bias

I think there are three principal reasons why evolution is not generally viewed as an intelligent process. First, intelligence often has connotations of consciousness, and many of us would doubtless find it hard to attribute consciousness to Nature (at least akin to the kind of consciousness we have). Second, evolution happens over lengthy time spans, as opposed to the relatively short time spans over which human intelligence operates. Third, we are a terribly proud and arrogant species that likes to imagine that we ourselves are the smartest thing on two legs. Intelligence belongs primarily to us and not to the more abstract systems of which we are a part (I presume that this outlook is connected to the human ego, as alluded to earlier).

However, intelligence, when understood as a process, does not necessarily entail consciousness (intelligence can also be *unconscious*), nor does it have to be limited in its method or time span, nor should it necessarily be confined to brains alone. If intelligence is tied up with information-gaining processes and learning, then clearly evolution is natural intelligence at work. Life on Earth, in all its manifold organismic glory, has ably learned how to live, cope, and behave sensibly—that is, life has mastered the subtle art of sustainability. The only real difference between this kind of natural acumen and human acumen is in magnitude and success.

Reductive science does not recognize natural intelligence because reductive science looks to isolated entities and attempts to seek explanations for their existence on lower levels. To glimpse natural intelligence is to view the larger system of which the components are a part. This larger system is, ultimately, the entire Universe, a specifically configured backdrop that provides the essential conditions necessary to promote the digital computational procedure that is evolution. These essential conditions are things like the sensible flow of energy throughout the Universe; the convenient formation and enduring presence of suns; the facilitated formation of DNA, with its conveniently plastic and linguistic nature; the continual presence of factors that conveniently induce DNA to vary and mutate; and, most important of all perhaps, the instructive nature of the environment that ensures DNA can be expressed in ever-more sophisticated ways. If we contemplate in large-scale holistic terms, then natural intelligence emerges. Darwin's groundbreaking legacy therefore resides in his discovery of the *methodology* of natural intelligence.

Superfluous Icing on the Darwinian Cake?

Some might object here and claim that to infer that evolution represents an intelligent process is to introduce superfluous and scurrilous gossip-making baggage into what is already a sufficient theory. In other words, why infer natural intelligence when it is not absolutely necessary to use such terminology for our understanding of the mechanisms by which evolution proceeds? Well, this might be true, yet to refuse to elaborate on evolutionary theory is to impose limitations on our understanding, especially if we desire a holistic and metaphysically satisfying view of Nature. Perhaps this is why there have been so many attempts to do away with Darwin's theory, not because it is wrong but because there is some conceptual element missing, an element that can more properly capture and appreciate the amazing power of evolution.

As far as I can see, if we don't infer that Nature is smart, we can't explain why exactly Nature should allow, and indeed encourage, biological evolution. Why, for instance, should the emergence of self-replicating, self-repairing DNA be an inevitable consequence of the laws of Nature? Why does DNA have language-like properties that can be expressed through proteins? Why are millions of proteins able to effortlessly fold into exquisite organismic patterns? Why, through genetic variation, is life continually able to forge solutions to various problems? How come there is a biological way forward most of the time? Why are DNA and genes so plastic and flexible? Why, indeed, is Nature made of such elegantly versatile, Lego-like components? And why should something as amazing as consciousness eventually be facilitated by life? The questions go on. The fortuitously creative brute facts mount up. The smart self-organizational properties of Nature abound. Something important is clearly happening everywhere.

The Ultrasmart Complexity of Organisms

Allow me to reiterate a previous reiteration: your own self-repairing body, your visual system processing these words, your autonomic breathing system and autonomic digestive system—all are far more smart than any manufactured computer or fabricated device currently in existence (especially when one considers how the body's various functions are integrated into a coherent and enduring unity). Perhaps you are familiar with some latest piece of computer software, some brand-new nifty program embodied in computer code. You will certainly concede that this code is smart. Yet reflect on the huge store of digital DNA coding etched into almost every one of your many trillions of body cells and you will realize that human-derived programs pale in the face of those written by Nature.

This becomes more apparent if we bear in mind that the DNA is essentially the same in all our cells, whether liver cells, lung cells, skin cells, or brain cells. Yet somehow that self-same information can be expressed in many different ways. The final orchestrated result—a living organism—is so wonderfully complex as to defy a complete understanding.

Somewhat paradoxically, I would suggest that it is precisely because Nature is so very, very smart that we do not acknowledge it. Biological processes, in the main, are so perfected in their natural execution that we fail to comprehend just how much complexity is involved (recall my detailed discussion of neuronal events, for instance). It is only when biology goes wrong that we suddenly become aware of just how ingenious it usually is in its operation. And yet, more often than not, we do not awake in the morning with a broken eye, a crashed memory module, a faulty connection in our ear, or an intermittent lung. Unlike our machines, our nervous systems do not tend to blow a fuse or suffer incongruous shutdowns. Thus, for the most part we may take life for granted and fail to grasp the very real miracle of our conscious organic existence. Similarly, if computers were so perfectly designed that people were able to utilize them for a thousand years without one single breakdown, we would soon lose sight of just how smartly they were designed. We would become completely accustomed to computers and take them for granted without a thought as to their intelligently designed infrastructure. However, should malfunctions begin to occur, we would suddenly wake up to their underlying contrived functionality.

Returning to human biological processes, they are generally so impeccable that they take care of themselves, which is to say that Nature is a pretty smooth operator. For most of us, we grow from babies to adults faultlessly, yet the myriad steps in this morphological feat are absurdly sophisticated. Think of a couple of identical twins and the amount of steps involved in turning them from microscopic single-celled entities into macroscopic trillion-celled entities. Yet after all that incomprehensibly complicated development, they both look exactly the same!

Such fine biological precision is a creative manifestation of what I am calling natural intelligence—a naturally smart process that has yielded as part of its output we beings endowed with consciousness, a process moreover that has been operating over an immense stretch of time. Yet just because the information-gaining evolutionary process that led to you and I took billions of years does not mean that it is nonintelligent, as we have been led to believe. To surmise that high intelligence exists only in our species is to be blind to both the natural intelligence that facilitated evolution and the natural intelligence embodied in all biological systems.

We have arrived back at the idea of the Universal Computation (or cosmic seed even), for it would appear that all the information necessary to construct suns, planets, molecules, amino acids, cells, microorganisms, plants, animals, and conscious brains was somehow written into primeval Nature, lying dormant as it were until the right conditions had developed somewhere and somewhen in which this information could be "read out." This is a breathtaking idea, and if it should generate a small gasp of wonder, this is but nothing compared to the awe generated by entheogens like the psilocybin mushroom, an awe that is intimately connected to realizations of our potential significance, as conscious agents, in the reality process.

Nature thus emerges as being incredibly smart as well as deadly, and I can close this chapter with an apt quote by Einstein, this time pertaining to the reverence felt by at least some scientists toward the Universe with which we interface. Einstein openly notes that this emotion "takes the form of a rapturous amazement at the harmony of natural law, which reveals an intelligence of such superiority that, compared with it, all the systematic thinking and acting of human beings is an utterly insignificant reflection."[4]

I almost second that emotion. Human thinking might not be an "insignificant reflection" at all. Far from it. Indeed, I presume that if we divine natural intelligence, acknowledge it, and really feel it, then this represents a *highly refined reflection of that intelligence*. Which implies that such a cortex-embodied reflection is of functional import, facilitating a sort of self-realization factor of natural intelligence as it were. We explore these issues in the next chapter.

TEN

A Neo-Shamanic Climax

As we have seen, the impressive fine-tuning of Nature is most clearly indicated in the evolutionary process that Nature has facilitated here upon the Earth. Over some three and a half billion years, our planet has transformed itself from a lifeless mass of rock into a veritable metabolizing organic matrix in which countless elegantly patterned organisms swarm about the Earth's surface, each organism an informational expression of natural intelligence. Yet, like the hour hand of a clock, scientists have failed to discern the context-driven intelligence of evolution, claiming instead that evolution is essentially a dumb and mindless process. But this can only be a subjective inference likely drawn according to the perceived duration over which evolution manifests, a duration so great that the intelligence operating over such a span remains all but invisible. If we instead imagine viewing a time-lapse film of the biosphere wherein three and a half billion years of information-gaining evolution are compressed into but one intense second, then modern electronic human culture and human consciousness explode instantaneously into existence, bursting forth out of the Earth's ocean of elemental constituents. This awesome pattern of self-organization can be no mere accident. To those who would still scoff at this assertion, I can only ask them this: If the aforementioned capacity of the Universe does not suggest a great intelligence at work, then what sort of Universe would?

Notwithstanding sullen detractors, if we embrace our River of Life metaphor, the totality of life represents the thrust of an intelligent process of information integration, and I argue that this is the essence of reality, the essence of the process that bred and killed Einstein and that controls our destiny also. Because all the information needed to support confluential patterning is etched into the "software" of the Universe, life and the emergence of consciousness can be viewed as a kind of *translation* whereby the code or meaning inherent in reality is read out over time. Somewhere within the reality process a biosphere had to form, since it was coded for in the lawful contextual fabric of the Universe. And within such a biosphere—of which there may be countless millions in the Universe—evolution was destined at some time to produce nervous systems and, eventually, brains capable of embodying consciousness. Patterns forever falling naturally into place like some cosmic jigsaw.

The conscious aspect of *Homo sapiens* thus resolves itself as a potent expression of the latest and most reflective form of information integration to emerge out of Nature—reflective because our kind is able to reflect upon how we came to be. In a real way, the human cortex is a biologically wrought mirror able to catch the true face of Nature upon its refined surface.

As with all other fluidic patterns of information, consciousness really was poised to materialize, its emergence dependent, like everything else, on the laws and forces of Nature along with prevailing contextual conditions. And so here we stand, atop the jungle and atop the technology we have created, our gaze now set on the expanding intelligible cosmos. Each human psyche, imbued with meaning from the larger context in which it has arisen, is able to wonder at the mystery of it all and even to glimpse the orchestrating intelligence in whose hands we are like transformed clay. In an instant of cosmic time, consciousness has arisen out of physics, chemistry, and biology, a living mirror able to reflect the intelligent forces that so engendered it.

Forecasting the Future

The evolution of life on Earth, the gradual elaboration of the biosphere, and the emergence of conscious human culture strongly suggest that we are inside a most interesting and creative part of the Universe. It is as if one of the mightiest currents within the River of Life were flowing around us right here and right now, focused within our modern electronic culture. Indeed, if the creative center of the Universe is the place where the most elaborate kinds of information integration are taking hold, then we are surely in or near the center. Or at least we are amid one of the focal points of natural intelligence. The amount of information being organized in one way or another all around us is so dense that one can feel it. Actively flowing information bombards us at every turn as it seeks resolution. Early twenty-first century culture with its global cyberspatial network is like some effervescent protoplasm exuded by the biosphere as it seeks to attain cohesion and stability at some higher level of organization.

Those scientists who diligently propound the myth that we are mere bystanders on a speck of dust remote from the heart of the Universe clearly do the phenomena of life and consciousness a major disservice. As far as we know, in terms of informational activity, the existence of humanity (seven billion potentially interconnected minds) is far and away more complex and intriguing than anything else in the known Universe. The Earth's biosphere, in its totality including all of human culture, is surely the place to be.

If reality is indeed a rushing river of integrating information, it might well be destined to meet some final organized form or pattern. Actually, this would appear to be an inescapable implication if my reasoning so far is correct. For if the evolution of organic life and human consciousness represents the inexorable unfolding of a potential woven into the fabric of Nature, then what further potential is yet to be expressed? If natural intelligence is as powerful as I suspect, there absolutely must be some final point or solution to its prodigious endeavors.

To give the reader a taste of such a scenario, consider the following thought experiment. Geneticists tell us that a fair proportion of the DNA found in all organisms serves some as yet unknown function. On a worldwide scale, the total amount of this so-called junk DNA must be immense. But what if it were a form of latent information that was set to go into action only when environmental circumstances were in a particular state? What if the biosphere suddenly assumed a context to which this globally distributed DNA was tuned? Anything might happen. All organisms might suddenly mutate and forge themselves anew. The possibilities are endless since DNA is so rich in its capacity to organize chemical and biological processes. Perhaps the reader can think of some alternative possibility.

I offer such wild speculation not because I believe it to be true, but because it highlights, in principle, how reality as we know it might well be coded to produce some climactic output at some latter stage of its evolutionary progression. Equally plausible is the idea that our interconnected computer technology might spawn some new level of informational cohesion—a kind of virtual dimension into which the agency of human consciousness can be transferred. In point of fact, as I previously remarked, through the rise of telecommunications and computing technology, the Earth does seems to be wiring itself up into an integrated digital network, a bioelectronic entity in which widely dispersed informational systems like the human psyche can instantly communicate with one another across the globe. This magical technology, similar as it is to the communicational activity of the synapsing neuronal brain, is clearly evolving at an unprecedented rate, and the eventual emergence of a more "tangible" cyberspatial dimension of some kind seems assured. Indeed, judging by the boom in media speculation about the near future of computing systems along with the escalating popularity of Internet-enabled Wi-Fi phones, it would appear that a fully immersive cyberspace of one sort or another is within reach.

What this kind of rife pop divination reveals is just how forcibly the future now looms upon us. It is as if we were moving ever more rapidly toward some new technological breakthrough involving information integration that will transform our culture, a transformation not only inevitable but whose shadow is already upon us, stirring us into prophetic thinking. For when else in our history has there been so much concentrated speculation about the very near future? More to the point, if some unimaginable fully integrated state were soon to be reached, whether mediated through networked computers or some other orchestrational medium, then clearly Nature has always been poised to deliver such an output. Maybe this could be considered the ultimate purpose of natural intelligence (or at least part of it), for it would represent the translated rebirth of the Other, the blossoming of the biosphere, a final planetary condition that Nature has determined in some way to achieve.

Most of us, however, are content to allow ourselves to be drawn almost passively along within the River of Life. We build sturdy rafts made of material goods and social status. We surround ourselves with items that our culture injects with value, and these are what keep us afloat. And yet our rafts, no matter how robustly they may be constructed and no matter how much wealth they contain, will eventually be destroyed, eaten up by the process in which they are swept along. No matter how long we try to prolong it, the time allotted to our DNA is finite. We are digitally programmed by natural intelligence to grow old and die, just as surely as we are built to grow through puberty and reproduce. We are patterns of information that swirl into ordered existence, only to break up in the wink of a cosmic eye. It's a good reason to think more carefully about our personal relationship with the river and where it is headed, for then we might discern our proper place within the integrative flow.

Near the River's End

We are a conscious species riding on the crest of an intelligent wave, and our collective knowledge represents a kind of growing certainty about the Universe. As this certainty (or information) continues to increase, we will gradually realize exactly why we have evolved. The intelligence of Nature is thus becoming fully reflected through human consciousness and in the knowledge systems of our culture. This really is suggestive of a kind of birth. The creative intelligence "running" the Universe is in the process of radically transforming itself into human culture and into human consciousness, just as a caterpillar radically transforms itself into a butterfly. Natural intelligence is therefore undergoing protean metamorphosis through the process of evolution.

As information continues to build up and self-organize within the biosphere, the biospherical system becomes more informed by the natural intelligence that constructed it. If this is so, then the purpose of life and mind might well be to embody a new form of the natural intelligence that commanded life and mind to arise in the first place.

Such a possibility is clearly similar to Fred Hoyle's speculations. However, I do not believe that natural intelligence is itself descended from some previous form of intelligence. What I suspect is that the entire Universe—Nature and all its information—is a kind of Will (what the spiritual teacher G. I. Gurdjieff called the Will of the Absolute) or Mind. After all, we know for sure that the human brain embodies both mind and will. So if the brain can have two aspects—physical and mindful—then why can't the Universe? In any case, I am certain that intelligence is a fundamental property of Nature, just as fundamental as the forces of Nature. Indeed, the various forces of Nature can be understood as a primary expression of natural intelligence, its most basic manifestation as it were. And so after fourteen billion years of reality in which the intent of natural intelligence has been steadily realized, consciousness has now emerged that can grasp the curiously profound source of its arising.

It is as if information, like energy, cannot be destroyed, and that the information content of reality, which remains constant, is in the process of reforming itself from moment to moment. If we think of a computer program able to take as input an image and smoothly morph that image into another image (or translate text from one language into another), then the reality process around us can similarly be viewed as a fourteen-billion-year-long translation of the Other from one language-like form into another. That translation will be complete at some point in the future. The felt experience of the Other may therefore represent the process whereby consciousness serves to *become the Other*. Again, this suggests a kind of birth, albeit of an awesome kind. It sounds unbelievable, yet if we are pressed to provide a metaphysical explanation for our ultrasmart Universe, then I believe that ideas such as these must be near to the mark.

The Omega Point

One mystic who anticipated such ideas was the eminent Jesuit priest and palaeontologist Pierre Teilhard de Chardin, who was born in 1881 and died in 1955. Unlike many other Christian thinkers, knowledge of the evolutionary process actually increased Teilhard's faith. Indeed, this explains his scientific interest in fossils and evolution (and, I might add, his excommunication by his religious superiors).

Teilhard believed that evolution was a purposeful process that would reach a climax at some time in the future, this point representing a kind of totally integrated state of life. He called it the Omega Point. This perfect future state was also thought by Teilhard to somehow send influences back in time, as though the Omega Point is an eternal sun able to shine its light upon the four-dimensional surface of human history.

Although Teilhard's thinking was deeply mystical, some of his work was respected by a number of traditional evolutionary theorists, most notably the biologist Julian Huxley. However, for most hard-nosed scientists who chance upon Teilhard's work, he remains no more than a mystic dreamer, a refined P. K. Dicksian soul whose ideology is basically unfit for serious consideration. Unless, that is, one has repeatedly experienced the numinous presence of the Other, in which case his ideas become rather alluring.

In *The Future of Man,* Teilhard writes about the Omega Point in the following rather poetical way:

Let us suppose that from this universal centre, this Omega point, there constantly emanate radiations hitherto only perceptible to those persons whom we call 'mystics'. Let us further imagine that, as the sensibility or response to mysticism of the human race increases with planetisation [the unification of humanity], the awareness of Omega becomes so widespread as to warm the earth psychically while physically it is growing cold. Is it not conceivable that Mankind, at the end of its totalisation, its folding-in upon itself, may reach a critical level of maturity where, leaving Earth and stars to lapse slowly back into the dwindling mass of primordial energy, it will detach itself from this planet and join the one true, irreversible essence of things, the Omega point? A phenomenon perhaps outwardly akin to death: but in reality a simple metamorphosis and arrival at the supreme synthesis.[1]

Teilhard's mention of a cooling Earth was probably a response to the growing realization at the time he wrote the book that the Universe appeared to be "running down" due to the dreaded second law of thermodynamics. This revered law states, in no uncertain terms, that the Universe is "wilting" and faces a heat-death extinction. All of the Universe's energy, it is said, will eventually be converted into a meaningless expanse of useless heat. Now, that's a gloomy thought for sure and a dangerous weapon in the hands of our archetypal reductive scientist, who might begin to prod us with it even now. However, according to our reasoning, the Universe must have surely required such dynamics in order to function in the way it has. In any case, evolution circumvents this running-down tendency by building dissipative structures—metabolizing organisms—to convert energy into a usable form. Although closed systems do run down and do eventually reach equilibrium (a boring state in which nothing of interest happens), open systems like the biosphere are able to build up order (courtesy of our generous sun, which radiates energy as it runs down) by giving off disorder (like infrared heat radiation) into space. In this way, natural intelligence has bypassed the specter of the second law of thermodynamics, and information integration through evolution has taken hold. Or perhaps it would be more accurate to say that naturally intelligent laws have engineered a specific energy flow, or energy current, to the Universe that life must continually "swim" against in order to develop and strengthen itself as it "returns to the source."

When Teilhard wrote about the Omega Point, he was probably less aware than we are today that the laws of Nature are highly specific and conducive to life. Hence he saw the second law of thermodynamics as a threat to life (which it isn't, because life taps into, and makes use of, the "downward" flow of energy), but foresaw that life would reach the

Omega Point, just in the nick of time as it were, before the Universe ran down, or at least our poor sun ran down. In other words, he located the Omega Point far, far ahead in time. But, as we have seen, science has now reached the stage where it can appreciate not only the computational quality of reality, but also its fine-tuning. In my mind, this is strong evidence that we are in the "good hands" of the Other, and, more significant, that the Omega Point might be nearer than Teilhard supposed. Of course, it is preferable to think of such an event as being near as opposed to far away. In any event, with the growth in psychedelic epistemology initiated in the 1950s and 1960s, and with the current burgeoning interest in organic entheogens like the psilocybin mushroom and ayahuasca, it is conceivable that the illuminations caused by the Omega Point are on the increase. This suggests that we are indeed moving ever nearer to this climactic point.

The End of the World as We Know It

Not surprisingly, Terence McKenna echoed the mystical claims made by Teilhard. In the 1990s, McKenna assumed the unenviable role of psilocybinetic prophet by consistently claiming that human history will be utterly transformed in late December 2012. This date derived from his mathematical "fractal theory of time," which views time as a cyclical patterning process involving a continual "ingression of novelty" and which also implies a definite culmination point. The date also coincides with the mysterious end date of the Mayan calendar, according to which a life cycle of some new kind will commence (this Mayan end-of-time prophesy was apparently not known to McKenna when he first developed his theory).

At this time, so said McKenna, the full purpose of reality will become manifest as information integration, or the ingression of novelty as he called it, reaches its zenith. There lies the "transcendental object," the eschaton, which, like Teilhard's Omega Point, casts reflections of itself into the past, reflections that inspire and illuminate saints, mystics, and the minds of visionary shamans. Also in line with Teilhard's

Omega Point, McKenna suggested that this future state of transcendence somehow exists now, or in eternity, and that it is toward this state that we and the reality process are being inexorably drawn. One can imagine the future state to be like a magnet, that the emergence of life and consciousness is akin to the process whereby iron filings assume structural alignment according to the nearness of a magnetizing influence. Indeed, all of Nature's fortuitous self-organizational properties—like the emergence of the genetic code, for example—can been be seen as deriving from some future "magnetically charged" state that "pulls" these properties into being.

In terms of the Universal Computation idea we have been entertaining, the Omega Point (whenever it might occur) would represent the final output state or full rebirth of the Other within the biospherical system. The willed metamorphosis would be complete. The universal code will be fully expressed, with all information, all knowledge, achieving a state of coalescence. The Other, natural intelligence, will have completed its translation from one unified state of being into another.

McKenna also used the term *attractor* to describe this final eschatological state that life is eventually destined to reach. An attractor is a kind of abstract final state toward which physical systems are drawn. In the case of a swinging pendulum encountering friction, the attractor is the state of the system in which the pendulum is at rest. Regardless of the starting position, the pendulum always ends up in the attractor state. Likewise, in the case of chess, the attractor is the state of checkmate toward which the game invariably progresses. Attractors are thus inherent in various systems and are akin to the metaphorical magnet I previously described.

In terms of the Universe at large, it could be argued that the attractor toward which it is being inexorably drawn is a kind of "big crunch," whereby the Universe collapses into an almighty singularity due to the effects of gravity. However, we can also view the attractor not as a super-concentration of "matter," but as an integrated state of information or meaning. When human consciousness has succeeded in realizing its true role within reality, and when the Other has fully transformed itself within the collective psyche, then this will represent an attractor of the reality process. At this point, Nature will have made maximum sense of itself.

If we posit an attractor, we should also bear in mind that the nearer it is, the more marked and pronounced will the processes of self-organization be. This situation might explain recent and unusually rapid forms of evolution like that of the hominid cortex, as well as the subsequent speedy evolution of human culture and the more recent yearly evolution of digital technology. Dwelling on this, one automatically thinks of a spiral process, or self-tightening gyre, in which Nature is frantically assuming a state through which more and more information integration can take hold. Perhaps the end point of any biosphere is a kind of "local singularity," alike in nature to the assumed singularity from which the Universe sprung, a state of informational unification, although this time embodied in a planetwide shared experience.

If such a fantastic phenomenon were to actually realize itself sometime in the near future, it would surely have to be preceded by a tremendous surge of information heralding the event. I do not mean angels blowing trumpets, but rather that scientists ought to make new discoveries that indicate the smartness of Nature. Or, if the paradigm of a naturally intelligent reality process were to be favored and explored in more depth, it would mean a reinterpretation of the data already amassed through science, and this might further highlight our unique position within the evolution of the cosmos. Alternatively, some new technological innovation or natural phenomenon might serve to make everyone more conscious of the interconnectedness of the biosphere, particularly the billions of minds that operate therein. This could then set the stage for synchronized global behavior and the dawn of a new value system and a new humanity. Either way, if the evolutionary process is indeed smart and destined to "conclude" in some way according to an inherent code, then it will simply have to proceed in the same way that an organism grows. Natural intelligence cannot be stopped; it can only be observed and appreciated while in action.

That we can experience the Other by ingesting psilocybin or by contemplating the intelligent properties of Nature indicates that something is indeed emerging within the collective human psyche, that some profoundly significant coherency lies beyond the chaos of secular fragmented reality. Or perhaps the Other has been dormant, as though asleep, hibernating as it were, only to gradually awaken through the vehicle of consciousness, which it has prepared for in advance.

I am the first to concede that much, if not more, mystery remains. But at least the mystery of our being has been more clearly defined. And at least we know where to look should we want to explore Nature more deeply than a casual glance allows. When one has encountered the Other through the visionary effects of a strong dose of psilocybin mushrooms, it becomes quite evident that, whatever the Other's ultimate intent, consciousness is an essential part of the plan.

Our Role on the Earth Rock

Cultural conditions are ripe for a fresh look at Nature, which I consider to be an ultrasmart system. By so doing, the context in which we act out our lives becomes somewhat altered (another feedback effect). If we conceive of reality as a mindless material accident, then we will not think twice about ruthlessly exploiting Nature for short-term gain and short-term profit. Similarly, if we believe Nature can only be understood by tearing it to pieces and examining the smallest fragments, then we shall not divine the greater picture.

If, on the other hand, we embrace the ideas outlined in this book, our view of Nature might change and we might come to cherish Nature in the same way as aboriginal peoples. Of course, it is not necessary to entertain all the ideas in this book in order to be environmentally conscientious. Rather, should natural intelligence be deemed real, then we would do well to refrain from breaking harmony with its flow. If we veer too far from the ways of natural intelligence, we will run the risk of being abandoned by the great system that birthed us. Or worse, we might even jeopardize the future of all life on Earth.

Not that I really think such a thing could come to pass. One should not underestimate the cohesive power natural intelligence. It is not like life is an old car that could splutter and give out all of a sudden. If evolving life were that frail, it would surely have faded away long ago. The same applies to human culture. Despite evincing ecological insensitivity that might instigate its downfall, culture embodies tremendous cohesion and resilience, which gives us time to mature and change. And if we bring to mind the notion that the Universe is like a self-writing story, I would hope the human race is too significant a protagonist to simply eliminate.

It might be that the severe environmental crises our species has set in motion of late are a kind of violent prelude to the changes in culture and scientific worldview that lie ahead. Indeed, our global disruptions of the biosphere obviously serve to make us reflect on our important causal role within the web of life. When weather systems run riot around us, when otherwise unchanging ice caps begin to melt, when vast tracts of land are trashed in the quest for fossil fuel, when entire lakes and oceans become spoiled by pollution, when an estimated one hundred species of organism become extinct every day due to our belligerent presence, when acid rain ruins forests and crops, when fires burn uncontrollably in tropical areas where land has been decimated by farmers pandering to beef addiction, and when primarily profit-motivated biotech conglomerates cause unforeseen ecological disruptions with genetically engineered crops, then it is evident that our species is not a passive spectator of Nature. Rather we actively influence its constitution at every moment.

Shifting Perspectives

As Fritjof Capra remarks in *The Turning Point,* the Chinese written word for *crisis* contains two characters—*danger* and *opportunity* (or at least this is one linguistic interpretation). This implies that we now have an opportunity to make a change for the better. We can learn from our ecological perturbations and respond to them, as if ecological crises were parts of a biospherical enzyme coded into the historical process (enzymes facilitate reactions). Acknowledging our devastating impact on Nature allows us to reappraise our relationship to the Earth. In so doing we dimly perceive that we are bound to the biosphere as much as the biosphere is bound to us. Moreover, until we fully realize our purpose at the hands of natural intelligence, it seems doubtful that we will be fulfilling our allotted role within its magnificent orchestrations.

I would like to believe that as we move through the third millennium, the realization of our true purpose will become increasingly apparent. In other words, it is my hope that the proverbial old chestnut "what is the meaning of life?" will be answered as the elusive meaning continues to unfold. In fact, if what I have written bears any truth, such a realization is inevitable. Perhaps others will explore Nature's wild entheogenic fungi and reach the same conclusions. Or perhaps scientists will begin to discuss those aspects of reality that have conspired to facilitate a self-conscious Universe and conclude that our Universe really is of profound significance. And if scientists should come to accept that everything is made of information, including consciousness, then perhaps they would also see that this information is becoming ever more integrated according to the intent of natural intelligence.

Our unusual quest is over. We set out to uncover the essential face of Nature and discovered that, as a naturally evolved species, we are caught up in a rapidly accelerating flow of information integration whose leading edge is partly focused here on Earth, particularly within our conscious perception and our digital culture. This unfolding process would appear to be impressively smart and directed toward some culmination point. Only the future can reveal the truth of these bold assertions. In the anticipatory meantime we can do no more than contemplate the issues and ideas raised and hope for the best. May the sacred wisdom of Great Nature be with you always and everywhere.

Trick or Treat?

I provided the reader with a model of consciousness that views it as a flowing pattern of information generated within an intelligent, self-organizing Universe. Once one has accepted that we and all other patterns of information are natural expressions of a self-writing language-based Universe, that Nature is everywhere smart and contextually significant, then one is compelled to go on to examine the "meaning of it all." Only when the bigger picture has begun to be glimpsed will we realize more fully our function and responsibilities within Nature and what integrative global events to expect in the near future. I suggested that one route to ascertaining the bigger picture is to alter the information converging in the psyche by utilizing Nature's ambient entheogenic agents. To do so is to suddenly change one's relationship with the rest of the reality process such that one comes to be informed by the transcendental Other, the will, or intention, or intelligence that permeates Nature.

It is my firm hope that others will be able to bring back some of the profound insights to be gained from the psilocybin mushroom experience in order that a comprehensive knowledge base develop. In fact, you might recall that in chapter 4, I detailed the second wave of human-based psychedelic research. After a sociopolitically engendered empirical hiatus of some thirty years or more, scientists are once more exploring the healing potential of entheogens. With regard to the Johns Hopkins University of Medicine experiment I alluded to in chapter 4 in which psilocybin provoked positive mystical experiences in healthy volunteers, here is a summary of the findings of a 14-month follow-up study. The results are encouraging and speak for themselves:

> At the 14-month follow-up, 58% and 67%, respectively, of volunteers rated the psilocybin-occasioned experience as being among the five most personally meaningful and among the five most spiritually significant experiences of their lives; 64% indicated that the experience increased well-being or life satisfaction; 58% met criteria for having had a 'complete' mystical experience.[1]

It remains for me only to give some more information as to the particulars of the psilocybin mushroom. After all, without verifying my claims, you will not know whether I fabricated the principal subject matter of this book. Indeed, perhaps the themes outlined herein have been a kind of fake, nothing more than a few wild and woolly tales built upon the fertile imagination of my mind during periods when it was too wet to venture outside. Maybe at heart I am really one of the archetypal "merelyist" reductionists of the bleak "null hypothesis" persuasion, but one who felt like writing an entertaining yarn in which the Universe could be conceived as being meaningful instead of a mindless accident.

The message, of course, is that one must always think for oneself and never take anything for granted. That, surely, is indisputable. This leaves the psilocybin mushroom experience itself as the chief substance of my unusual claims. But readers must make up their own minds as to this claim of mine that the mushroom affords useful knowledge. Let no one accuse me of reckless pointing. This book has been my pointer. You choose. You decide.

As stated elsewhere, psilocybin mushrooms of one sort or another grow throughout the world—all over Europe, North and South America, Australia, New Zealand, Indonesia, Thailand, and Africa, for example. It seems that new psilocybin species are continually being discovered. But what is more astonishing than this biospherical bounty is the commercial availability of psilocybin mushroom spores as well as growing kits. In many European countries it is now possible to purchase such equipment. However, the various legal issues involved in cultivating the mushroom are far from clear at this time.

Under some European laws the fresh psilocybin mushroom is not controlled (at least at the time of writing). This means that the wild mushroom is not listed as a controlled substance, and personal mushroom use is allowed (but not their sale). In the United Kingdom, until recently only the isolated active ingredients psilocybin and psilocin were controlled by law (their classification as highly dangerous is questionable and may well be challenged in the coming years). Thus, as long as the mushroom remained in its raw, unprocessed state, it was deemed legal by the United Kingdom authorities. However, 2005 saw the United Kingdom government illegalize the actual wild mushroom itself. This was unprecedented, as it was the first time that a natural part of the United Kingdom countryside had been deemed illegal.

It remains to be seen what becomes of this unwarranted draconian measure that, by condemning a natural and long-revered environmental resource, can serve only to further alienate us from Nature. Indeed, one might think that notice boards ought to be placed throughout all the parks and wilderness areas of the United Kingdom warning citizens of the extreme dangers of naturally occurring psilocybin mushrooms (simple possession of the mushroom could entail a jail sentence). Having personally observed prolific numbers of *Psilocybe semilanceata* growing in most of the United Kingdom's countryside areas during the autumn months (this includes the whole of the Lake District; the whole of Snowdonia; the whole of Dartmoor; the Devonshire coast; the Welsh coast; as well as London's Richmond Park, Streatham Common, and Hampstead Heath), there would need to be thousands of such notice boards. Unless, that is, the government proposes drenching all wild, green areas with millions of gallons of eco-unfriendly fungicide. Or create a vast group of Rangers (with a tactical airborne division) to scour and police every inch of the countryside. Or simply seal off the countryside and people's gardens (including land owned by the Queen) until further notice.

Of course, I am being deliberately provocative here—but only to highlight the absurdity of making a natural part of the environment illegal. In any case, these laws have not prevented the sale of psilocybin mushroom spores (*Psilocybe* spores do not contain psilocybin) nor the growth media in which to cultivate them. The only feasible way to prevent this kind of activity would be to ban the air itself, as fungal spores of one kind or another are omnipresent.

If the more cautious reader is concerned with the health risks associated with consumption of the mushroom, we should note that a 2000 report from a Dutch Risk Assessment Team (copies of the report, by CAM—the Coordination Centre for the Assessment and Monitoring of New Drugs—can be located on the Internet) found that psilocybin mushroom use does not present a significant public health risk (at the time of the report, the mushroom had been commercially available in the Netherlands for many years).[2] Similarly, a rigorous scientific study by Hasler and others published in 2004 showed that psilocybin was not hazardous to health when administered to healthy persons (although the study recommended that those with high blood pressure should abstain from psilocybin use).[3] A United Kingdom Home Office report of 2000 also stated that mushroom use was not considered problematic.*[4] And this is despite the fact that an estimated 1.5 million adult people in the United Kingdom had taken the mushroom.

In the last analysis, if the powers that be are truly concerned about the possible public health hazards associated with psilocybin mushroom use, then they are obliged to investigate the matter professionally by consulting scientific experts in the field. Simply illegalizing the natural, nonaddictive mushroom by categorizing it alongside addictive manufactured heroin and crack cocaine (which is the case in many countries)

---

*"To estimate the number of young recreational and older regular users [of Class A drugs], some division had to be made from these surveys of problematic and non-problematic use. It was assumed therefore that all opiate use and crack use reported in such surveys is problematic; this assumption may be revised in time if better evidence and monitoring data become available. All ecstasy, LSD and magic mushroom use is assumed not to be problematic." From Godfrey et al.; see endnote.

is, it must be said, a tad hysterical. The inordinately oppressive nature of this kind of legislation against a sacred substance speaks for itself. On the other hand, maybe Terence McKenna was right when he suggested that psilocybin fungi had a sort of mysterious defense mechanism around them so as to prevent mass profane use. Who knows?

Putting aside the various legal issues, the question still remains as to the significance of the mushroom's growing popularity (along with Amazonian ayahuasca). It is possible that psilocybin's potential is coming of age (at least in those parts of the world where the mushroom remains legal or where it grows in abundance). After all, the capacity of psilocybin to forge a new relationship between humanity and Nature is probably more important now than at any other time in history. Given our relentless despoiling of the biosphere and our unending obsession with material consumption, it is evident that we have alienated ourselves from the larger systems of Nature of which we are a part. Cities are like cocoons that sever us from the rest of the biosphere. We live and breathe without a second thought about the life-support system that is all of Nature. Naturally occurring entheogens can be viewed as a latent biospherical homeostatic control mechanism whereby our species can be brought back into balance. Indeed, it may be our last chance before we push the biosphere into total decline. As I intimated in the preliminary note at the very start of this book, the mushroom can be considered a kind of antidote in that the knowledge it can yield can help heal our currently misguided relations with the rest of the web of life. In fact, I would liken psilocybin to a kind of psychological penicillin. Whereas penicillin is a fungal product with valuable antibiotic healing properties, psilocybin is a fungal product with valuable eco-psychological healing properties. Unlike penicillin however, psilocybin has, unfortunately, yet to find a global audience wise to its virtues.

Regarding the issue of dosage, stronger doses of the mushroom—those truly entheogenic doses that can change one's attitude toward life and that also galvanized me into writing this book—should only be employed with plenty of experience. Most important are one's state of mind prior to consumption and one's surroundings. One should be in a positive and balanced frame of mind before consuming the mushroom (people suffering from mental health problems like schizophrenia or chronic depression should absolutely avoid the mushroom). One should also be in a friendly and safe environment that is free of distraction. The mushroom is not some frivolous party drug to be washed down with a beer in some noisy club. I would also suggest a period of sexual abstinence prior to ingestion, as one will then be in a more "pure" state befitting a potentially sacred experience. And unless one is particularly competent in the ancient art of self-knowledge, it is advisable to have a non-bemushroomed close friend around to act as a kind of anchor should any feelings of panic arise. It is important that this "sitter" remain as unobtrusive as possible. If all the conditions are right and enough heartfelt preparation has been made, an experience in which one's perception is fantastically enhanced is almost certain to follow.

To experience the mushroom's visionary effect, one should lie down in silence with eyes closed during the period when the mushroom's influence is most active. Although this is a decidedly daunting venture, the colorful splendor of psilocybinetic visions and their unmistakable revelational quality make it very much worthwhile.

If psilocybin mushrooms are consumed on an empty stomach, their effects may be felt within as little as twenty minutes. (Taking them on an empty stomach is preferable because they are stronger that way and the act of fasting prior to ingestion becomes, like sexual abstinence, somewhat ritually symbolic.) If mushrooms are consumed after a meal, the effects can take up to an hour and a half to emerge. In either case, the first changes that one notices are likely to be somatic, in that one might feel a little restless and edgy. This would appear to be the initial reaction of the body and the psyche to the mushroom's exotic influence, a sort of "retuning" process. These mild uneasy feelings generally subside as one's perception gradually begins to open up and expand. One is then bathed in a decidedly warm and numinous presence.

I find it curiously apt that an adventure into the nature of reality should gravitate around a wild fungus native to most parts of the Earth's surface. It really is the case that we can turn to Nature if we wish to fully comprehend the sense and significance of our lives. This is like the plot of some elaborate adult fairy tale. If we genuinely wish to gain self-knowledge and realize our place within Nature's endlessly creative transmutations, we can deliberately seek out and consume the "truth." Like cosmic actors, by performing an age-old ritual act in time and space, we can perceive the world afresh and anew. Through psilocybinetic gnosis we may even glimpse the full majesty of this astounding Universe in which we are so privileged to find ourselves.

And so I end my enthusiastic tale. The sacred mushroom now beckons, affording us communion with the natural intelligence of which we are a part. Astonishingly, such a communion may be nearer than ever. The choice is wholly yours. Born in the 1950s and 1960s, the sacred endeavor in which the doors of perception are thrust wide apart is set to blossom in the coming years. Be there.

Notes

Chapter 1. Sacred Ground

1. Wasson, *Soma: Divine Mushroom of Immortality,* 153.
2. Wasson, *Mushrooms, Russia and History,* 295.
3. Wasson, "Seeking the Magic Mushroom," 114–17.

Chapter 2. An Ancient Form of Communion

1. Wasson, *The Wondrous Mushroom,* 200.
2. Ibid., 202.
3. Ibid., 206.
4. Ibid., 206–7.
5. Ibid., 73.
6. Sharer, *The Ancient Maya,* 126.

Chapter 3. Psilocybin Flows in and out of the Western Mind

1. Doblin, "Pahnke's 'Good Friday Experiment,'" 14.
2. Ibid., 17.
3. Ibid., 18.
4. Ibid., 19.
5. Ibid., 16.
6. Ibid., 23.
7. Koestler, *Drinkers of Infinity,* 209.
8. Ibid., 211.
9. Graves, *Oxford Addresses on Poetry,* 124.
10. Ibid., 127.
11. Huxley, *Island,* 170.

Chapter 4. Investigating the Earth's Alchemical Skin

1. Schultes, Evans, and Hofmann, *Plants of the Gods,* 112.
2. Lotsof, "Ibogaine in the Treatment of Chemical Dependence Disorders," www.maps.org/news-letters/v05n3/05316ibo.html (accessed March 11, 2011).
3. Strassman, personal e-mail communication.
4. Pinchbeck, *Breaking Open the Head,* 240.
5. Nichols, personal e-mail communication.
6. Strassman, personal e-mail communication.

Chapter 5. The Mushroom and the Synapse

1. Baars, *A Cognitive Theory of Consciousness,* 148.
2. Nichols, personal e-mail communication.
3. Nichols, personal e-mail communication.

Chapter 6. The Stuff of Consciousness

1. Powell, *Sacred Ground,* 34.
2. Naranjo, "Ayahuasca Imagery and the Therapeutic Property of the Harmala Alkaloids," 133.
3. McKenna, *The Archaic Revival,* 60.
4. Hobson, *Sleep,* 144.

Chapter 7. A Universe of Information

1. Capra, *The Tao of Physics,* 83.
2. Johnson, *Fire in the Mind,* 110.

Chapter 8. Does the Universe Compute?

1. Young, *The Nature of Information,* 43.
2. Dawkins, *A Devil's Chaplain,* 107.
3. Davies, *The Mind of God,* 118.
4. Gardner, *Wheels, Life and Other Mathematical Amusements,* 240.
5. Davies, *The Mind of God,* 196.
6. Ibid., 231.
7. McKenna, *The Archaic Revival,* 246–47.

Chapter 9. The Fantastic Hypothesis

1. Hoyle, *The Intelligent Universe*, 222–23.
2. Ibid., 239.
3. Powell, "Darwin's Unfinished Business."
4. Einstein, *The World as I See It*, 28.

Chapter 10. A Neo-Shamanic Climax

1. Teilhard, *The Future of Man*, 122.

Epilogue: Trick or Treat?

1. Griffiths et al., "Mystical-type Experiences Occasioned by Psilocybin Mediate the Attribution of Personal Meaning and Spiritual Significance 14 Months Later," 621.
2. "CAM Risk Assessment Report Concerning Magic Mushrooms," 2000, www.erowid.org/plants/mushrooms/mushrooms_health1.pdf (accessed March 11, 2011).
3. Hasler et al., "Acute Psychological and Physiological Effects of Psilocybin."
4. Godfrey et al., "The Economic and Social Costs of Class A Drug Use in England and Wales, 2000."

Bibliography

Aghajanian, G. K. "LSD: Sensitive Neuronal Units in the Midbrain Raphe." *Science* 161 (1968): 706–8.

Aghajanian, G. K., and G. J. Marek. "Serotonin and Hallucinogens." *Neuropsychopharmacology* 21 (1999): 16S–23S.

Baars, Bernard J. *A Cognitive Theory of Consciousness.* Cambridge: Cambridge University Press, 1988.

Barrow, J. D. *Between Inner Space and Outer Space: Essays on Science, Art, and Philosophy.* Oxford: Oxford University Press, 1999.

Capra, Fritjof. *The Tao of Physics: An Exploration of the Parallels between Modern Physics and Eastern Mysticism.* London: Wildwood House, 1975.

———. *The Turning Point: Science, Society, and the Rising Culture.* New York: Simon and Schuster, 1982.

———. *The Web of Life: A New Synthesis of Mind and Matter.* New York: Doubleday, 1996.

Casti, John L. *Paradigms Lost: Images of Man in the Mirror of Science.* New York: William Morrow, 1989.

Churchland, P. M. *A Neurocomputational Perspective: The Nature of Mind and the Structure of Science.* Cambridge, Mass.: MIT Press, 1989.

Davies, Paul. *The Cosmic Blueprint: New Discoveries in Nature's Creative Ability to Order the Universe.* New York: Simon and Schuster, 1988.

———. *The Mind of God: The Scientific Basis for a Rational World.* London: Simon and Schuster, 1992.

Davies, Paul, and John Gribbin. *The Matter Myth: Towards 21st Century Science.* London: Viking, 1991.

Dawkins, Richard. *A Devil's Chaplain: Selected Essays by Richard Dawkins.* London: Weidenfeld and Nicolson, 2003.

Devereux, Paul. *The Long Trip: A Prehistory of Psychedelia*. New York: Penguin/ Arkana, 1997.

Dick, Philip K. *Ubik*. New York: Doubleday, 1969.

———. *Valis*. Worcester Park, U.K.: Kerosina, 1987.

Dobkin de Rios, M. *Hallucinogens: Cross-Cultural Perspectives*. Albuquerque: University of New Mexico Press, 1984.

———. "The Influence of Psychotropic Flora and Fauna on Maya Religion." *Current Anthropology* 15 (1974): 147–64.

———. *Visionary Vine: Hallucinogenic Healing in the Peruvian Amazon*. San Francisco: Chandler, 1972.

Doblin, Rick. "Pahnke's 'Good Friday Experiment': A Long-term Follow-up and Methodological Critique." *Journal of Transpersonal Psychology* 23, no. 1 (1991): 1–28.

Einstein, Albert. *The World as I See It*. London: John Lane The Bodley Head, 1935.

Empson, Jacob. *Sleep and Dreaming*. London: Faber and Faber, 1989.

Furst, Peter T. *Hallucinogens and Culture*. San Francisco: Chandler and Sharp, 1976.

———. *Mushrooms: Psychedelic Fungi*. New York: Chelsea House, 1986.

Furst, Peter T., ed. *Flesh of the Gods: The Ritual Use of Hallucinogens*. New York: Praeger, 1972.

Gardner, Martin. *Wheels, Life and Other Mathematical Amusements*. New York: W. H. Freeman, 1983.

Gleick, James. *Chaos: Making a New Science*. New York: Viking, 1987.

Godfrey, C., G. Eaton, C. McDougall, et al. "The Economic and Social Costs of Class A Drug Use in England and Wales, 2000." Home Office Research Study 249. Home Office Research, Development and Statistics Directorate, 2002.

Graves, Robert. *Oxford Addresses on Poetry*. London: Cassell, 1962.

Griffiths R., W. Richards, M. Johnson, et al. "Mystical-type Experiences Occasioned by Psilocybin Mediate the Attribution of Personal Meaning and Spiritual Significance 14 Months Later." *Journal of Psychopharmacology* 22, no. 6 (2008): 621–32.

Grob, Charles S., ed. *Hallucinogens: A Reader*. New York: Tarcher/Putnam, 2002.

Grob, Charles S., A. L. Danforth, G. S. Chopra, et al. "Pilot Study of Psilocybin

Treatment for Anxiety in Patients with Advanced-Stage Cancer." *Archives of General Psychiatry* 68, no. 1 (2010): 71–78.

Grof, S. *Realms of the Human Unconscious: Observations from LSD Research.* New York: Viking Press, 1975.

Haarer, D. "Molecular Computer Memory." *Nature* 355 (1992): 297–98.

Harner, M. J., ed. *Hallucinogens and Shamanism.* New York: Oxford University Press, 1973.

Hasler, F., U. Grimberg, M. A. Benz, et al. "Acute Psychological and Physiological Effects of Psilocybin in Healthy Humans: A Double-Blind, Placebo-controlled Dose-Effect Study." *Psychopharmacology* 172, no. 2 (2004): 145–56.

Henderson, J. S. *The World of the Ancient Maya.* Ithaca, N.Y.: Cornell University Press, 1997.

Hobson, J. Allan. *Sleep.* New York: Scientific American Library, 1989.

Horowitz, M., and C. Palmer, eds. *Aldous Huxley: Moksha: Writings on Psychedelics and the Visionary Experience (1931–1963).* New York: Stonehill, 1977.

Hoyle, Fred. *The Intelligent Universe: A New View of Creation and Evolution.* London: Michael Joseph, 1983.

Huxley, Aldous. *The Doors of Perception.* London: Chatto and Windus, 1954.

———. *Island.* London: Chatto and Windus, 1962.

Jacobs, B. L., ed. *Hallucinogens: Neurochemical, Behavioral and Clinical Perspectives.* New York: Raven Press, 1984.

Jacobs, B. L., J. Heym, and M. E. Trulson. "Behavioral and Physiological Correlates of Brain Serotonergic Unit Activity." *Journal of Physiology–Paris* 77 (1981): 431–36.

Johnson, George. *Fire in the Mind: Science, Faith, and the Search for Order.* London: Viking, 1996.

Jung, C. G. *Memories, Dreams, Reflections.* London: Collins, 1963.

Kauffman, Stuart. *At Home in the Universe: The Search for the Laws of Self-Organization and Complexity.* New York: Oxford University Press, 1995.

Koestler, Arthur. "Return Trip to Nirvana." In *Drinkers of Infinity, Essays 1955–1967.* London: Hutchinson, 1968.

———. *The Ghost in the Machine.* London: Hutchinson, 1967.

Leary, Timothy. *Flashbacks: An Autobiography.* London: Heinemann, 1983.

Leary, Timothy, George H. Litwin, and Ralph Metzner. "Reactions to Psilocybin Administered in a Supportive Environment." *Journal of Nervous and Mental Disease* 137, no. 6 (1963): 561–73.

Lotsof, H. S. "Ibogaine in the Treatment of Chemical Dependence Disorders: Clinical Perspectives." *MAPS Bulletin* 5, no. 3 (1995): 16–27.

Margulis, Lynn, and Dorion Sagan. *What Is Life?* London: Weidenfeld and Nicolson, 1995.

Marks, John. *The Search for the "Manchurian Candidate": The CIA and Mind Control.* New York: Times Books, 1979.

McKenna, Terence. *The Archaic Revival: Speculations on Psychedelic Mushrooms, the Amazon, Virtual Reality, UFOs, Evolution, Shamanism, the Rebirth of the Goddess, and the End of History.* San Francisco: HarperCollins, 1991.

———. *Food of the Gods: The Search for the Original Tree of Knowledge.* New York: Bantam, 1992.

———. *True Hallucinations: Being an Account of the Author's Extraordinary Adventures in the Devil's Paradise.* San Francisco: HarperCollins, 1993.

Moreno F. A., C. B. Wiegand, E. K. Taitano, et al. "Safety, Tolerability, and Efficacy of Psilocybin in 9 Patients with Obsessive-Compulsive Disorder." *Journal of Clinical Psychiatry* 67, no. 11 (2006): 1735–40.

Naranjo, Claudio. *The Healing Journey: New Approaches to Consciousness.* New York: Pantheon, 1974.

———. "Ayahuasca Imagery and the Therapeutic Property of the Harmala Alkaloids." *Journal of Mental Imagery* 11, no. 2 (1987): 131–36.

Nichols, David E. "Hallucinogens." *Pharmacology and Therapeutics* 101 (2004): 131–81.

Oakley, D. A., ed. *Brain and Mind.* London: Methuen, 1985.

Ott, Jonathan. *Pharmacotheon: Entheogenic Drugs, Their Plant Sources and History.* Kennewick, Wash.: Natural Products Company, 1993.

Ouspensky, P. D. *In Search of the Miraculous: Fragments of an Unknown Teaching.* New York: Harcourt, Brace, 1949.

Pinchbeck, Daniel. *Breaking Open the Head: A Visionary Journey from Cynicism to Shamanism.* London: Flamingo, 2003.

Pletscher, A., and E. Ladewig, eds. *50 Years of LSD: Current Status and Perspectives of Hallucinogens.* New York: Parthenon, 1994.

Powell, Simon G. *Darwin's Unfinished Business.* Rochester, Vt.: Park Street Press, 2012.

———. "Questing with Psilocybes in Avalon." *Shaman's Drum* 66 (2004): 48–55.

———. *Sacred Ground: Psilocybin Mushrooms and the Rebirth of Nature.* London, U.K.: Privately published, 2003.

Pribram, K. H. "Brain/Mind Issues." *American Psychologist* 42 (1986): 507–20.

Reichel-Dolmatoff, G. *The Shaman and the Jaguar: A Study of Narcotic Drugs Among the Indians of Colombia.* Philadelphia: Temple University Press, 1975.

Schultes, Richard Evans, and Albert Hofmann. *Plants of the Gods: Their Sacred, Healing and Hallucinogenic Powers.* Rochester, Vt.: Healing Arts Press, 1992.

Sharer, Robert J., with Loa P. Traxler *The Ancient Maya (6th edition, fully revised).* Stanford, Calif.: Stanford University Press, 2006.

Stevens, Jay. *Storming Heaven: LSD and the American Dream.* New York: Atlantic Monthly Press, 1987.

Strassman, R. J., et al. "Differential Tolerance Development to Biological and Subjective Effects of Four Closely-spaced Administrations of N,N-dimethyltryptamine in Humans." *Biological Psychiatry* 39 (1996): 784–95.

Strassman, R. J. "Human Psychopharmacology of N,N-Dimethyltryptamine." *Behavioural Brain Research* 73 (1996): 121–24.

Sutin, Lawrence. *Divine Invasions: A Life of Philip K. Dick.* New York: Harmony Books, 1989.

Teilhard de Chardin, P. *The Phenomenon of Man.* London: Collins, 1959.

———. *The Future of Man.* New York: Harper and Row, 1964.

Wasson, R. Gordon. "Seeking the Magic Mushroom." *Life,* May 13, 1957.

———. *Soma: Divine Mushroom of Immortality.* New York: Harcourt, Brace and World, 1968.

———. *The Wondrous Mushroom: Mycolatry in Mesoamerica.* New York: McGraw-Hill, 1980.

Wasson, R. Gordon., et al. *Persephone's Quest: Entheogens and the Origin of Religion.* New Haven, Conn.: Yale University Press, 1986.

Wasson, V. P., and R. G. Wasson. *Mushrooms, Russia and History.* New York: Pantheon, 1957.

Wolfram, S. "Computer Software in Science and Mathematics." *Scientific American* 251 (1984): 188–203.

Young, Paul. *The Nature of Information.* New York: Praeger, 1987.

Index

Books of Related Interest

Psychedelic Healing
The Promise of Entheogens for Psychotherapy and
Spiritual Development
by Neal M. Goldsmith, Ph.D.

High Society
The Central Role of Mind-Altering Drugs in History,
Science, and Culture
by Mike Jay

Inner Paths to Outer Space
Journeys to Alien Worlds through Psychedelics
and Other Spiritual Technologies
*by Rick Strassman, M.D., Slawek Wojtowicz, M.D.,
Luis Eduardo Luna, Ph.D., and Ede Frecska, M.D.*

DMT: The Spirit Molecule
A Doctor's Revolutionary Research into the Biology of
Near-Death and Mystical Experiences
by Rick Strassman, M.D.

The Pot Book
A Complete Guide to Cannabis
Edited by Julie Holland, M.D.

Plants of the Gods
Their Sacred, Healing, and Hallucinogenic Powers
by Richard Evans Schultes, Albert Hofmann, and Christian Rätsch

The Encyclopedia of Psychoactive Plants
Ethnopharmacology and Its Applications
by Christian Rätsch

The Acid Diaries
A Psychonaut's Guide to the History and Use of LSD
by Christopher Gray

INNER TRADITIONS • BEAR & COMPANY
P.O. Box 388
Rochester, VT 05767
1-800-246-8648
www.InnerTraditions.com

Or contact your local bookseller